Silver Wings, Golden Valor:
The USAF Remembers Korea

Edited by
Dr. Richard P. Hallion

With contributions by

Sen. Ben Nighthorse Campbell
The Hon. F. Whitten Peters, SecAF
Gen. Michael E. Ryan, CSAF
Gen. Russell E. Dougherty
Gen. Bryce Poe II
Gen. John A. Shaud
Gen. William Y. Smith
Lt. Gen. William E. Brown, Jr.
Lt. Gen. Charles R. Heflebower
Maj. Gen. Arnold W. Braswell

Maj. Gen. Philip J. Conley, Jr.
Gen. T. Michael Moseley
Brig. Gen. Michael E. DeArmond
AVM William Harbison
Col. Harold Fischer
Col. Jesse Jacobs
Dr. Christopher Bowie
Dr. Daniel Gouré
Dr. Richard P. Hallion
Dr. Wayne W. Thompson

Air Force History and Museums Program
Washington, D.C.
2006

Library of Congress Cataloging-in-Publication Data

Silver Wings, Golden Valor: The USAF Remembers Korea /
  edited by Richard P. Hallion;
  with contributions by Ben Nighthorse Campbell... [et al.].
    p. cm.
  Proceedings of a symposium on the Korean War held at the U.S.
Congress on June 7, 2000.
  Includes bibliographical references and index.
  1. Korean War, 1950-1953—United States—Congresses. 2. United
States. Air Force—History—Korean War, 1950-1953—Congresses.
I. Hallion, Richard.
DS919.R53 2006
951.904'2—dc22

                                                  2006015570

Dedication

This work is dedicated with affection and respect to the airmen of the United States Air Force who flew and fought in the Korean War.

They flew on silver wings, but their valor was golden and remains ever bright, ever fresh.

Foreword

To some people, the Korean War was just a "police action," preferring that euphemism to what it really was—a brutal and bloody war involving hundreds of thousands of air, ground, and naval forces from many nations. It was also termed a "limited war," in that it took place in a small region of the world versus the worldwide conflict that had ended less than five years earlier. But this "police action," this "limited war," cost an estimated 2.4 million military casualties on both sides, while at least another 2 million civilians were also casualties. The United States military alone suffered 36,940 killed and another 92,134 wounded.

The war in the air was as bloody and violent as that on the ground. The United Nations air forces lost 1,986 aircraft, with the USAF sustaining 1,466 of these. Air Force personnel casualties totaled 1,841, including 1,180 dead. These losses were far greater than can be accounted for in the glib terms "police action" and "limited war."

As the years passed following the end of the war, Korea receded in memory. Another war—in Southeast Asia—became lodged in the public's mind, and the Korean War became "forgotten." But to those veterans and historians alike participating in the proceedings recorded in this volume, their reminiscences and perspectives provide the reader with compelling arguments why the Korean War deserves to be remembered.

About the Editor

Dr. Richard P. Hallion is Senior Adviser for Air and Space Issues, Directorate for Security, Counterintelligence and Special Programs Oversight, the Pentagon, Washington, D.C. He is responsible for analysis and insight regarding the conceptualization, evolution and utilization of sensitive national technological programs and related subject areas. He undertakes high-level assignments at the direction of the Air Force senior leadership, following the Secretary's policies, goals and objectives. Previously, at the time of this symposium, he was the Air Force Historian.

Dr. Hallion graduated from the University of Maryland in 1970. He has broad experience in science and technology museum development, research and management analysis, and has served as a consultant to various professional organizations. He has flown as a mission observer in a range of military and civilian fixed and rotary-wing aircraft. Dr. Hallion is the author and editor of numerous books relating to aerospace technology and military operations, as well as articles and essays for a variety of professional journals. He also teaches and lectures widely.

Contents

Foreword		v
About the Editor		vi
1.	Korea: The Forgotten (Air) War	1
	Dr. Richard P. Hallion	
2.	My Memories of the Korean War	5
	Sen. Ben Nighthorse Campbell	
3.	Learning from the Korean War	13
	General Michael E. Ryan, the Chief of Staff, U.S. Air Force	
4.	The Air Force, Korea, and Kosovo: Past as Prologue	17
	Hon. F. Whitten Peters, Secretary of the Air Force	
5.	Air Dominance: The Essential Achievement	27
	Panel Chairman Dr. Richard P. Hallion	
6.	Air Pressure: Air-to-Ground Operations in Korea	63
	Panel Chairman Gen. John A. Shaud	
7.	From Korea to Kosovo: Learning from the Past for the Crises of the Future	95
	Panel Chairman Dr. Wayne W. Thompson	
8.	Closing Remarks	115
	Dr. Richard P. Hallion	
Glossary		119
Index		121

Chapter 1

KOREA: THE FORGOTTEN (AIR) WAR

Dr. Richard P. Hallion
The Air Force Historian

On June 7, 2000, the Air Force held a commemorative symposium at the U.S. Congress on the Korean War.[1] This symposium, organized jointly by the Air Force History and Museums Program (AFHMP), Air Force Legislative Liaison, and the Air Force Association, consisted of a series of panels of Air Force combat veterans who had flown in the Korean War. A comprehensive exhibit on the Air Force in Korea prepared by the AFHMP accompanied the symposium. This book is the edited proceeding of that symposium.

The organizers wish to thank the Air Force leadership, particularly the then Secretary of the Air Force, the Hon. F. Whitten Peters, and the then Chief of Staff of the Air Force, Gen. Michael E. Ryan, for their support of the symposium. But it is to the veterans of the Korean War that the organizers are most grateful. These individuals took the time and made the effort to travel great distances to recall events both pleasant and painful. Their recollections here help illuminate America's Korean experience.

Sadly, of all the aspects of that little-appreciated conflict, perhaps the least appreciated of all is the air war. Indeed, with Korean veterans at last receiving just recognition of their accomplishments, it is remarkable to the degree that the Korean air war is the one aspect of the Korean War that continues to receive far less attention than it should. For example, almost all the publicity surrounding the fiftieth anniversary of the Korean War—and particularly the speeches of national figures on the June 25, 2000 kickoff at the Korean War Memorial—have stressed the struggle on the ground, with air power either escaping mention, or mentioned only as if it were some sort of sideshow. In fact, even in terms of the land struggle, much of the commemoration has been cast in terms of the bitter fighting surrounding the retreats in the face of Chinese intervention in November–December 1950, which was but one campaign in a war of many. Such a narrow focus makes as much sense as commemorating America's role in World War II in terms of only Bataan or Kasserine, without mentioning Normandy or the smashing of Japanese militarism, Italian fascism, or German Nazism.

Much of this ignoring of the air dimension may simply reflect the innate failure by many to appreciate how air power has transformed America's national security over the last century. The transformation has been so rapid that one feels it is often reflected more accurately by the popular perception of the average citizen than it is in official doctrinal thinking with its often-too-traditionalist and established hierarchy of hoary and questionable "truths." Indeed, for over the last fifty years, it has been America's joint service airmen and air power forces that are the "first to fight." It was certainly true in Korea (where airmen entered combat a week before their ground compatriots), and it has been true in most conflicts since that time, from Vietnam through the Gulf, the Balkans, and on to the post–September 11, 2001 war on terrorism of the present day. In Korea, more often than not, it was the airmen of the U.S. Air Force, the U.S. Navy, and the U.S. Marine Corps who carried the war most vigorously and offensively against the enemy: those same airmen who made the survival of their compatriots on the ground possible.

Ironically, even as the United States recognizes the accomplishments and sacrifices of its Korean veterans, the danger exists that significant aspects of the Korean story will remain forgotten or at least unappreciated, particularly in a time when revisionists seek to rewrite the history of the Cold War as a mere struggle between essentially morally equivalent superpowers. In truth, Korea was an absolutely vital victory in the four-decade-long history of the Cold War, and South Korea (and arguably all of the western Pacific) were saved from communism by what America did there. That message must never be forgotten. And neither should it be forgotten that the United States and its coalition partners waged a bitter and costly three-year air war deep over enemy territory and over the frontlines as well.

This symposium was an attempt to help set the record straight on both counts, but particularly on the air war. Bluntly put, air power was a critical factor—indeed, *the* critical factor—to the success of the United Nations in Korea. Quite simply, without it the war would have been lost and, thus, in all likelihood, Asia would have been lost to the communist cause as well. As the Battle of Britain at the beginning of World War II was for the allies, the Korean air war at the beginning of the Cold War was *the* key struggle that the West could not afford to lose. Thanks to the airmen of the UN coalition, particularly those of the United States Air Force, we didn't. No one has summed up the accomplishments of air power in

Korea: The Forgotten (Air) War

the Korean War better than the former commander of all United Nations forces in Korea, retired U.S. Army Gen. Matthew B. Ridgway. Writing in 1967, he stated, "No one who fought on the ground in Korea would ever be tempted to belittle the accomplishments of our Air Force there. *Not only did air power save us from disaster, but without it the mission of the United Nations Forces could not have been accomplished* [emphasis added]."[2]

The recollections presented here are humorous and sad, thoughtful and passionate. The authors and panelists were encouraged to be frank in their views, and their comments and thoughts (and my own) are thus theirs alone and not official viewpoints or expressions of the United States Air Force or the Department of Defense. Above all else, they highlight a heritage of courage and accomplishment that is—and will continue to be—an enduring source of pride to the men and women of today's global Air Force.

Finally, in closing, I wish to acknowledge the assistance of staff members of the Air Force History and Museums Program in the preparation of this work, particularly Mr. Herman Wolk, Chief of the Analysis and Reference Division, and Mr. Jack Neufeld, Chief of the Project and Production Division. Dr. Wayne Thompson, leader of the AFHRA Analysis Team, provided thoughtful advice and insight. Dr. Priscilla Jones arranged for preparation of the transcripts. Mr. Tom Y'Blood furnished the illustrations used in this work. Ms. Anne Johnson-Sachs, Leader of the AFHRA Outreach and Advocacy Team, supervised preparation of a Korean exhibit that accompanied the symposium. Three key individuals offered tremendous support and continuing interest in the symposium: Lt. Gen. (now Gen.) William J. Begert, then the Assistant Vice Chief of Staff and now the Commander of Pacific Air Forces; Maj. Gen. (now Gen.) T. Michael "Buzz" Moseley, then chief of Legislative Liaison and now the Air Force Chief of Staff, and General (Ret.) John Shaud of the Air Force Association. Their advice, help, and insight were crucial and most welcome. Finally, I would be remiss if I did not acknowledge the stellar contributions of two outstanding individuals: my then executive officer, Lt. Col. Brian Murray, and Col. Walter Washabaugh of Air Force Legislative Liaison. Without their conscientious and dedicated work, this endeavor could not have succeeded.

Notes

1. This symposium consisted of three panels: air dominance, air-to-ground operations, and the legacy of the Korean experience. Each panel had a moderator who introduced the individual panelists and acted as a facilitator. The discussions were recorded on both audiotape as well as video, with transcripts of the symposium made by the Neal R. Gross & Co. transcription service of Washington, D.C. The transcripts are on file with the Office of Air Force History, at both Bolling AFB, Washington, D.C. and Maxwell AFB, in Montgomery, Alabama. The original audio- and videotapes are on file at Maxwell. The edited proceedings here are essentially a complete record of the panels and the major addresses, the only deletions being material that was either repetitive or extraneous to the record of the war. Pauses, "false starts," hesitancies, and other awkward transitions have been smoothed in the interest of making a more readable text. The authors and panelists have reviewed this text for their comments and corrections, and the editor is grateful for their invaluable assistance.
2. Matthew B. Ridgway, *The Korean War* (Garden City, N.Y.: Doubleday, 1967), 244.

Chapter 2

MY MEMORIES OF THE KOREAN WAR

Sen. Ben Nighthorse Campbell

It's a pleasure being here, having the chance to talk to you all about the Korean War. I can't think of any event in American history more important for us to remember than Korea, for it exemplified America's young men and women at their very best. I was in Korea, courtesy of having enlisted in the Air Force. I did that without a high school diploma. As you know, you can't do that now, but I was having a little bit of trouble in school and after football season I couldn't imagine why anybody would want to stay in the classroom, so I quit and went in the Air Force. I was not a flyer; I was an Air Policeman, what are called Security Police today. Starting out, I went through boot camp at Lackland Air Force Base, Texas, outside San Antonio. At that time, the Air Force was a new organization, just having been created by the Defense Act of 1947, and I can still remember the hodgepodge of uniforms that greeted me. Some of the people were still wearing Army Air Forces olive-brown uniforms, and some people had gotten their new Air Force blue uniforms. And some people were wearing brown pants and blue jackets! It was just one hell of a mess.

Things have changed considerably since I was an airman in the Air Force. I visit installations a lot; Air Force Space Command is headquartered in my state of Colorado and we have a number of very high-profile installations, including the Air Force Academy. Some of the officers in this audience might have gone through the Academy. As I go around and see the lifestyle that the airmen have now, we've obviously come a long way. In fact, with an all-volunteer military, there's no question that we have to continue to come a long way if we're going to keep bright young people in the military. It's certainly not like the past, for they have a lot of opportunities on the outside, and they don't have to stay in the military to make a living.

I did want to come by here this morning, for my Korean experience meant—and means—a lot to me. It's my understanding that Sen. John Warner of Virginia and I are the only two current members of the Senate now who served in Korea in the war. There were many people in Congress who were there after the war was over, and there were some that were in the military when it was going on, but they weren't assigned to Korea. On the Senate side, I think the late Sen. John Chaffee of Rhode Island, former Sen. John Glenn of Ohio, and Senator Warner and I were the only four who were actually over there. Being in the Air Force, and not being a flyer, of course, I didn't have to be on the front lines. Nevertheless, I did go up a number of times because I had friends I had gone to school with that were in the Army with the 1st Cavalry or with the Marines. Those were the guys who were really taking a beating.

When I got over there, the American forces had already pushed back the Korean regulars with their Chinese counterparts back a little bit north of Seoul. So the front lines were actually about nine miles north of Seoul, but I remember very distinctly some of the images that I got. I was nineteen when I went over there. We took a troop ship to Japan and we then flew to what was called K–16, what is now Seoul International Airport.[1] Korea was a vicious no-quarter conflict, particularly between the North and South Koreans, and it showed. For example, when we went across the Han River Bridge for the first time, I saw bodies hanged with wire, and I asked the guy that was driving us, "Gee, what were those people convicted of?" And he said, "Collaborating with the enemy." It was a pretty graphic way to illustrate not to do that. And the authorities just left them there, didn't take them down, just left them hanging until the bodies eventually rotted, fell apart, and dropped in the river. Pretty brutal times.

Then there were the planes. At that time, the Air Force was still flying some of the World War II–era propeller-driven North American F–51 Mustangs. Eventually, they were phased out and turned over to the Republic of Korea (ROK) forces as we acquired more of the newer F–80 and F–86 jets—the "hot planes" of the day. As all you young pilots know, they're all antiques today. And I have some distinct memories of nighttime. There was a guy we used to call "Bedcheck Charlie."[2] That son-of-a-gun would come over and bomb us every night I think mostly to keep us awake. We could almost guarantee that, sometime during the night, whatever the heck he was flying, he would come over and throw out a couple of things just to kind of wake us up.

After I got back to the states and got a little older and began to look at Korea in the perspective of other wars, it became obvious to me that it really was a forgotten war. Americans put it behind them and got on with other things. But talk to people who were over there: they haven't forgotten, and we shouldn't either. I had an opportunity the other day to talk to a couple of guys who belong to a fraternal

My Memories of the Korean War

band called the "Chosin Few." They take their name from one of Korea's most brutal battles, the retreat from the reservoirs in the winter of 1950. That withdrawal was one of the most desperate and brutal battles in all of military history. Approximately 80 percent of all the Americans that were in that battle were either killed or wounded, and it was fought in bitter, frigid cold and snow. It was a battle where the Chinese literally completely surrounded the valley by the reservoir and our ground forces had to fight their way out, protected and supported by air power. Despite the danger, they wouldn't leave their comrades, and carried out both their wounded and dead. It was really a brutal thing, but characterized by the most extraordinary heroism as well. That happened just before I got there, as did a lot of other notable ground actions. Being in the Air Force, I didn't have to be on any of those, but I knew a number of people who were, including one friend whom I went all through elementary school and all through high school with, who was killed on Heartbreak Ridge. Those of us who were there had all too much experience knowing friends or family members who didn't come back. But, for too many people today, we've even lost sight of the fact that Korea was a war. Remember that it was the first one where we didn't use the word *war*: it was called a *police action*, or the *Korean conflict*.

Indeed, it's been unfashionable to even use the word *war* since World War II—but Korea certainly was. If you talk to families of the 36,940 Americans that died there, or the 92,134 who were wounded, or the 8,176 that are still carried as missing in action, it was a war in every sense of the word.[3]

In many ways, Korea resembles Vietnam. For example, it's interesting that, although we often talk about Vietnam and the problems with soldiers coming back with serious emotional problems. We had that, too, in Korea, but didn't recognize it. (Indeed, we didn't recognize it in World War II, and again veterans of that war had a lot of the same emotional problems their successors suffered in Korea and Vietnam).

Like Vietnam, sorting out the innocent from the enemy was an ongoing problem. (I shot at people, but I was a pretty lousy shot, so I don't know if I hit anybody or not.) Sometimes we were assigned to remote radar stations. These were very important installations with long-range radar, crucial for bringing our fighters and bombers back. The enemy obviously knew their value, too, and so it was not uncommon to have to defend those outposts at nighttime from infiltrators and guerrillas. In that regard, Korea was like Vietnam in that there were procommunist South Korean guerrillas and North Korean infiltrators almost everywhere. In fact, it didn't make a difference where you were. So *caution* was the watchword, both day and night. It's really interesting that, after Vietnam, military people are held much more accountable about what they do—for example, if they confuse an innocent civilian with the enemy. Korea illustrated many of the same problems. I remember when I first got over there, I couldn't tell a North Korean from a South Korean. We didn't know, and they looked alike. This was a particular problem for base security, for many Koreans were working on the bases. We'd have to search them and inspect their lunch boxes. I remember asking my commanding officer when I got there, "Well, what do we do if we get caught in a situation and we end up shooting somebody and they turn out to be a friendly South Korean?" In those days, things were different from today. His answer was simply "We'll take care of it. Don't worry about it." But all that changed after Vietnam.

It is surprising that Korea dropped as quickly as it did from our consciousness, for in its own way it was every bit as tortuous and difficult as Vietnam. For example, Korea lasted only three years, less than a third as long as Vietnam, and yet the casualties—dead, wounded, and missing—are not all that dissimilar. In some cases, Korea was far worse, particular on the issue of prisoners of war and missing in action [POW/MIAs]. There are about two thousand yet-unaccounted-for POW/MIAs from Vietnam. We have more than eight thousand from Korea, and we still don't know where they are. There is a lot of callousness and cynicism in the way the North Koreans work this issue.

For example, about ten years ago, some of us in Congress who had been in Korea were asked to return to Korea and journey to Panmunjom and retrieve some remains of dead Americans that North Korea had decided to give back. So Sonny Montgomery (who is now retired), Bob Stump (who is the chairman of the Veteran Affairs Committee on the House side), Gerry Solomon, and a couple of others of us went back. I was amazed at the contrasts in what I saw. When I had left Korea, the war was still going on, not to end until about eight months after I came back to the United States. (My last assignment was Nellis Air Force Base outside Las Vegas, and I was an Air Policeman assigned to downtown casino town patrol—and that was much better than Korea, I don't have to tell you!) When I left there, everything was in ruins. The streets of Seoul were just littered with debris, and my most graphic memories were not the battles, not the war, but the kids. I had come from a dysfunctional home, and I was raised in an orphanage. So I guess I've always had a very special feeling for kids that are troubled. Too many of the little kids, many less than six years old, less, had lost their legs or arms, and they had pieces of tire inner tubes tied around whatever limbs worked to help drag themselves along the ground. They would have a tin can hanging from their neck with a wire or string, and if you could give them some food, you put it in that can. If you didn't stay right there while they ate it, be assured some stronger kid would beat them up and take it away from them. In short, these kids, who had already suffered and been through so much, were reduced to animal behavior. That is my most lasting memory of the Korean War. But when Sonny Montgomery and the rest of us arrived, Korea was an oasis. If you've been over there in the last years, it's beautiful: there's a thriving economy, young people happily going to the universities, and it's a different world. That was because a lot of Americans paid with their lives to make sure that Koreans understood the difference between communism and democracy.

We proceeded from Seoul to north of the demilitarized zone [DMZ]. We went up to the last outpost on the DMZ. It's our farthest northern post, and a lot of young people were manning it. We looked through binoculars and could see openings on the other side that the Chinese and North Koreans had made to dig tunnels. That whole area of the DMZ is just riddled with underground tunnels that the North Koreans plan to use to break through into the southern part at any time. In fact, the ongoing search for tunnels is a major part of our defensive activities along the DMZ.

At Panmunjom, the North Koreans turned over the remains of Americans. There were five complete skeletons in caskets, and we inspected them, looking at the dog tags. Satisfied, we signed for them, and we escorted them with honor, care, and respect back to Hickam Air Force Base at Honolulu, where we arranged to have DNA testing to confirm their identities. I said earlier the North Koreans treat the whole POW/MIA issue with callousness and cynicism, and this proved the case. We found we didn't have the remains of just five people. Instead, the skeletons had been pieced together from a bunch of remains. As near as we can tell, a group of Americans had been rounded up, killed out of hand, and stuffed in a hole. Then, decades later, when North Korea wanted some better, favorable trade treatment (in short, they wanted something from the United States), they decided to dig up some remains and give them back. So they dug them up, and they assembled them to make five complete skeletons. Not one dog tag matched any of the remains. That's the kind of regime we are dealing with up in Pyongyang. It really brought home to me the real commitment and sacrifices we Americans made, so many of whom are still missing from the Korean War.

Korea was one of those tragic times that Americans have paid the ultimate sacrifice to stop communist aggression. In my view, as little as I know about military history, I think that Korea was the turning point in the Cold War. It didn't end the Cold War, but it stopped communism there, and then subsequent events, years and decades later, changed the tide completely. In the 1980s, communism began to retreat and finally collapsed entirely with the demise of the Soviet empire in 1989 and the Soviet Union itself in 1991, as you all know.

But, anyway, that was my experience as a youngster over there. My son didn't have to go into the service, and I'm glad he didn't need to. But I still believe that the military offers some great advantages to youngsters, particularly kids like me that were on the loose end, because it gives them some discipline, gives them some direction, some goals and, now, particularly in the Air Force, it gives them skills that they can take home and use. They can become a computer expert, an electrician, a carpenter; they can do something that they can use back in civilian life. That builds a stronger America for all of us. So I've always been a great supporter of all the services, particularly the Air Force.

Before I leave, is there anything I can answer?

AUDIENCE MEMBER: I've got a question, sir. What do you think of the "Sunshine Policy" of South Korea, the summit efforts going on between North and South Korea?

Silver Wings Golden Valor: The USAF Remembers Korea

SENATOR CAMPBELL: My view, when we went back to North Korea, is that the difference between South Korea and North Korea is like flipping a coin, from a bright, sunny, warm, energetic, economically successful community to one right out of the Dark Ages. Everything was gray and dark. Nobody was smiling that we saw. You could see that country was in deep trouble. A few years later, after I came back, Sen. Ted Stevens and some other folks went over to North Korea, and, when he came back, I asked him, "Ted, what do you think the future is over there?" He said, "I think they only have two choices—starve to death or start a war. It's that bad." And so I support this new program of interaction between South and North Korea. North Korea is probably the last of the last completely closed societies, where they don't have any significant interaction with anybody. When our people have gone over there, they have seen what it has cost the North Koreans being an island unto themselves: mass starvation and some really difficult times. When you have a society that is totally depressed, things are totally going wrong, it leads to suspicion and accusations, and sooner or later it leads to some kind of assault. To take the pressure off of their own leaders, they've got to throw something at somebody. I commend the leaders of South Korea that are trying to work with the North Korean leadership and trying to help them improve their economy and society.

We should remember that the Korean people are very, very tough and resourceful. God, they're tough! I'll tell you I wouldn't want to be in their army. During the war, I was on duty one night guarding a girls' university on the outskirts of Seoul, because on one of the top floors of one of the buildings we had a radar station. They used to assign an ROK soldier and an American together on the perimeter and, when we were out there, this ROK guy fell asleep. I didn't think too much about it. I was just musing about home or something, and just about then the two officers of the day came by, an American and a Korean. If the sleeper had been an American, they might have raised hell with him or relieved him of duty or something. But this ROK officer of the day meted out justice on the spot, and he gave that guy a beating with a rifle butt—one of his own soldiers. I just couldn't believe that anybody would be that tough. Certainly in this country, if an officer did that, he'd go to prison for abusing somebody under your command. Maybe it's changed now, but maybe that's what made Koreans so tough.

One more Korean story and then I'll go. I've never had anything against the officer corps, but I did have one memorable encounter with a new lieutenant in my unit when I was in Taegu. Everything off-base was "off limits" because there was so much guerrilla activity, but, as you know, young American boy soldiers being what they are, they'd slip out at night and go get some booze or find a girl, so we had to have regular roundups. We'd go to the local bars, and we'd run them all in and make them march back to Taegu. I didn't care much about it, but this new lieutenant was determined to make an impression. So he made us get up in the middle of the night, take a couple of Jeeps into downtown Taegu, round up a bunch of guys, and march them back to base. I was in a Jeep in the front and there was another guy in a Jeep behind, and the lieutenant had all these guys that we picked up marching along the road.

When you're marching in front of headlights, you can't see your feet very well. Now, at that time, beside all the roads in Korea were trenches holding the accumulated residue of the "honey buckets" the Koreans used for personal waste. In short, you can't see those very well when you can't see where you're walking, and I can still remember him counting "Hut, hut"—and then he fell in one of those trenches. I looked in there, and all I could see ... [were] two eyeballs looking out. Boy! I mean all those guys that we captured scattered instantly—and I scattered too, because I wasn't going to dig him out! We finally got back to base. He was going to court martial us for leaving, but my excuse was my first duty was to gather up those prisoners, right? Needless to say, I didn't catch a one!

Well, in closing I want to tell you the Air Force is a great institution. It's a great organization, and it has kept up with the times and anticipated the future. For those of you who are pilots or want to be pilots, my own view is that you're on the last wave of flying yourself. I don't know for sure, but I have a hunch that, in another thirty years, you'll be operating a computer board just like we have for drones now, except you'll be operating a computer controlling the fighters and the bombers and a lot of other things. In short, the wars for the Air Force will be done at an even greater distance than what we saw in Korea or, more recently, with the Gulf and the Balkans. We are moving toward a time when Americans will not tolerate war if anybody gets killed on our side, and, because of that, we will move more and more toward sophisticated machines that carry the war to the enemy such as uninhabited combat air vehicles [UCAVs]. So, if you're an honest-to-God pilot, it may be primarily flying transports or general aviation airplanes. As I said at the beginning, I didn't fly in Korea, but I did learn to fly private aircraft after I came home. In fact, for a while I had a sporty Mooney that I used to have great fun with. I don't fly it much now, but I know that, having flown for a number of years, it sets you free. That's for sure. And it's probably as close to God as a lot of us are going to get! Thanks a lot and good luck.

Notes

1. Called Seoul City Air Base during the war.
2. Denied the ability to operate by day over the south, North Korean pilots would often fly at low level over UN air bases at night in light-training and utility airplanes, particularly the Polikarpov Po–2 utility biplane. They would drop hand grenades or small bombs as an annoyance tactic; although casualties and damage from these raids were small, they did cause the UN command to devote considerable resources trying to shoot them down. GIs and allied airmen called these intruders Bedcheck Charlies; during World War II, the Japanese had tried similar tactics in the South Pacific, the discordant sound of their engines earning them the nickname of Washing Machine Charlie. As time went on, night fighters claimed an increasing proportion of these nocturnal attackers.
3. These figures, released by the Department of Defense in January 2000, represent the results of a rigorous analysis of military records and are considered as official and unlikely to change significantly. Previous statistics counted 54,246 combat dead, but analysis revealed that this number included all military deaths that had occurred to American forces around the world during the time of the Korean conflict. Thus, the officially accepted number of dead was revised downward to 36,940.

Chapter 3

LEARNING FROM THE KOREAN WAR

Gen. Michael E. Ryan
Chief of Staff of the United States Air Force

MAJ. GEN. T. MICHAEL "BUZZ" MOSELEY: Good morning! I'm Buzz Moseley, the Director of Legislative Liaison, and it is my privilege to introduce the Chief of Staff of the United States Air Force, Gen. Michael "Mike" Ryan. For all of us here in our blue uniforms, this is a bit of an add-on because we already know him and he already knows us. But, for those in the audience who do not know General Ryan, he is the chief of the world's only global air force. He is the son of another great Air Force leader, former Chief of Staff Gen. John Ryan. Mike Ryan is a fighter pilot's fighter pilot. After graduation from the Air Force Academy, he went to pilot training and then to Southeast Asia in F–4s, cutting his air combat teeth in a war a lot like Korea. Since then, he has commanded at all levels of the Air Force, and he was the architect of Operation Deliberate Force in 1995, the highly successful NATO air campaign over Bosnia. He spends most of his day trying to take care of all of us, whether it's over here at the Congress across the river or whether it's in the Pentagon. Sir, we owe you a great debt; we love you, and you've got the mike.

GENERAL RYAN: Thanks, Buzz. I was looking around my office the other day, and I saw a great big hole in the wall where Harley Copic's superb picture *Sabre Dance* used to be and, now, seeing it here on the wall behind me, I know where it went! Buzz and Dr. Dick Hallion's people stole it when I wasn't looking. It's one of the really outstanding paintings in the Air Force art collection, and I cannot think of a more fitting painting to be hanging here, at this symposium.

Silver Wings Golden Valor: The USAF Remembers Korea

I think it's an important time for us to reflect on the Korean War, and I thank Dr. Hallion and Buzz for honchoing this group and bringing lots of people together—those who made the history, and those who can learn from it. History teaches us a lot of lessons if we'll just listen. There are some circumstances about Korea that are reflective of today, and I'd like to just go through a few thoughts on that at the strategic, operational, and tactical level.

First, Korea was fought at the beginning of the nuclear age. Indeed, just the year before Korea began, the Soviet Union had exploded its first atomic bomb. That radically transformed the strategic picture. So, in the first days of the bipolar atomic confrontation, at the very beginning of the Cold War, we fought Korea, and the implications of that early stage of nuclear standoff had to do a lot with the strategy that went into that war.

Second, when Korea broke out, it was in the period of the second-lowest percentage of gross domestic product (GDP) put against defense since Pearl Harbor. It should give all Americans pause when we note that the *lowest* percentage in national defense since Pearl Harbor is what percentage of GDP we invest *today*: it's about 3 percent of GDP. That should be a clear warning, particularly in today's uncertain world.

Third, we fought Korea at a time when the apparent strategic intent and interests of the United States were unthinkingly signaled in a very clear and unfortunate way.[1] Even before the war broke out, the question of our willingness to defend Korea from outside attack was left in question, not only within the United States, but outside the nation as well. Today, we find ourselves in a similar debate, about whether we ought to structure ourselves to be capable of fighting and winning two major simultaneous regional contingencies or not. We obviously need to be very careful in the signals that we send forth to potential adversaries, particularly as we debate sensitive defense issues having far-reaching implications.

So the strategic lessons of Korea—and these are just a sampling—are very, very important for us to reflect on today.

At the operational level, we had just been through one of the largest drawdowns that this country had ever known, coming out of World War II. We had reduced the forces in the U.S. military from twelve million during World War II down to 1.5 million at the beginning of the Korean War. But again this resonates with the present day. Indeed, today we have just gone through and finished the largest drawdown we have had in the second half of this century since the Korean War as we drew our forces down to almost similar levels.

When the Korean War broke out, the United States Air Force as an independent service was only three years old. But, if it was a new air force, it was nevertheless an air force whose predecessor—the Army Air Forces of World War II fame—had invested heavily into technologies that came to fruition during that earlier war and that had residual effects as we went into the Korean War. For example, it was a force that remembered how to be expeditionary. Very, very rapidly, the Air Force was able at that time to project power into the Pacific, bedding down the Thirteenth Air Force, the Fifth Air Force, and the Twentieth Air Force, scattered from Guam to the Philippines, a force of more than one thousand aircraft by the end of the buildup. Today, expeditionary aerospace power is a key aspect of our modern global Air Force operations.

At a tactical level, things have changed substantially since Korea. Then, combat operations were a matter of answering how many sorties it would take to take out a particular target. Today, we talk about how many targets we can take out with *one* sortie. In Kosovo, for example, we had B–2 stealth bombers flying nonstop from the United States and then striking up to sixteen different targets on a single mission.

Korea was a time that air superiority proved crucial. Fortunately, the technology of the jet engine and high-speed flight that came out of World War II and the continued investment in the late 1940s in the whole high-speed revolution led us to aircraft that were very, very capable in the Korean War. This investment, typified by aircraft such as the North American F–86 Sabre, allowed us to dominate in the skies. It wasn't painless or risk free, and it certainly involved some hard fights. Korea was the last war in which any American forces on the ground were attacked by hostile aircraft. Since that time, the Air Force has given its sister services essentially a half-century of unprecedented air dominance.

Finally, we must never forget the people, for they were truly the key of our Korean success. At the tactical level, they made the difference in this war between victory and defeat. Some of those people are here in this room—those who fought, those who suffered, those who helped save a nation. In the end, we have to remember that the outcome of the Korean War was saving the nation of Korea and stopping communism for the first time in the second half of this century, this last century. It was a seminal event on the road to expunging what was one of the most pernicious and exploitive forms of political domination and twisted social philosophy ever to rule captive peoples.

People were important then, and they are critical now. It's America's young people that make—and will continue to make—our Air Force the best air force this world has ever seen. I look forward to hearing some of the comments that are brought forward here and the outcome of this symposium. It's a great pleasure to be with you, and it's an honor to be the head of this great Air Force of ours with these great people in it. Thank you.

Notes

1. Speaking at the National Press Club in January 1950, Secretary of State Dean Acheson stated that the Philippine Islands, the Ryukyu Islands, Japan, and the Aleutian Islands constituted America's defensive interests in the western Pacific. Because he pointedly excluded the Korean peninsula, and because his remarks coincided with the withdrawal of occupation forces back to America, historians have considered this a vital diplomatic misstep, a signal that encouraged Stalin, Mao Tse-tung, and Kim Il-Sung to undertake their subsequent aggression against the south in the belief that the United States would not intervene.

Chapter 4

THE AIR FORCE, KOREA, AND KOSOVO: PAST AS PROLOGUE

The Hon. F. Whitten Peters
Secretary of the Air Force

MAJOR GENERAL MOSELEY: It's now my privilege to introduce the Secretary of the Air Force, the Hon. F. Whitten Peters, who has a lot of Navy experience, which is to our benefit. In the spirit of jointness, we take the good things from the Navy, and he's been one of them. Between Secretary Peters's undergraduate and law degrees at Harvard, he served as a naval officer at the Fleet Intelligence Center in Norfolk. While at Harvard, he was the president of the *Harvard Law Review*. Among other things, it is good to have a Secretary of the Air Force with a legal background. It's also good to have a Secretary of the Air Force that is as aggressive as he is on taking care of our folks, talking care of our modernization planning, our readiness, our parts and pieces, and working with us to ensure we enter the twenty-first century with the required air dominance we need to do our business. So, Mr. Secretary, without any further ado, sir, you've got it.

SECRETARY PETERS: Well, thank you, Buzz. It is certainly great to be here. I am a "recovering lawyer," and, because of that, I feel compelled to make a disclaimer. I was seven years old when the Korean War broke out, and so my first-hand knowledge is somewhat limited. I was about ten I guess when it ended, and the most modern history course I've taken recently, I think, was about nineteenth-century England. So I'm not much on the history of this either, but happily I've had Dick Hallion and his people trying to educate me all week.

Silver Wings Golden Valor: The USAF Remembers Korea

What I'd like to do today is not talk about the fine points of Korea, but talk a bit about what I think is the application of what we learned in Korea to what we we're trying to do today. What I think has been clear to many of us in the Air Force when we look back on the Korean War is the parallel between the Korean War and how air power functioned there and the recent conflict in Kosovo, even though obviously the technologies today are very different.

I think Korea is very instructive, and its anniversary gives us a chance really to reflect a bit about what are the key aspects to air power and air dominance. There's just no question that the Korean War was the pivotal point in the development of today's Air Force. It was our first jet war, and it also marked the beginning of an unbroken record of U.S. air superiority. Lest we underestimate the importance of that record, we need to consider that the very initial stages of the Korean conflict marked the very last time an American commander on the ground ever had to worry about his troops being attacked from the air. In short, for American forces, for almost fifty years now, there has been no realistic threat of our troops on the ground being attacked from the air, thanks to our Air Force. In fact, that is so well understood, is such a part of what we do, and is a such critical enabler of all our joint forces, that I think many take it for granted today.

I also think that it's important to think a little bit about what else Korea was. It was truly the first of the "limited wars" that have become such a part of what we do today. By the standards of the World War II victories in Europe and Japan, the negotiated settlement in Korea seemed to many to be a defeat or at best a draw. Gen. Douglas MacArthur, for example, dismissed the armistice as no substitute for victory. More recent commentators have often referred to Korea as the "forgotten war," but I'm sure among the loved ones of the 36,940 Americans killed it is not forgotten and certainly among the next of kin of those POWs and MIAs that we're still looking for, it is not a forgotten war either. I think military historians also are beginning to awake to the importance of the Korean War and the overall impact of those operations on the way we think about warfare today and the way that our systems have evolved over the last fifty years.

The Korean War really defined the start of the Cold War and led to the rapid expansion of the North Atlantic Treaty Organization [NATO], which is now the backbone of U.S. defense alliances. It fueled the formation of large standing forces in the United States, and, of course, it set the stage for America's involvement in Vietnam. Korea was also the first major action of the United Nations and the first embodiment of the proposition that the United Nations should intervene militarily to suppress armed aggression. With the Cold War now over, we are tempted to believe that the debate over when and how to use military force in a more limited capacity is new, but, in fact, it is not. Korea raised many of the same arguments about the value of participating on a more limited basis in a coalition in a far-off land.

A half century after the Korean War, *Time* magazine recently reported that in a rare example of interservice cooperation—which I would say, by the way, is not

The Air Force, Korea, and Kosovo: Past as Prologue

so rare these days—a Pentagon memo notes that all services are in agreement that the number of Americans killed in Korea should be adjusted from 54,246 to 36,940. I think the very size of that number, whether it's 36,000 or 54,000, shows you that this was not a limited war, but indeed a very significant conflict, certainly the equivalent of a major theater war in today's vernacular.

During Korea, the Air Force dropped 476,000 tons of explosives, and the conflict really exposed us to the reality of post–World War II warfare in which the conventional air power would be used as much to influence an outcome and to change the way that enemy leaders thought as they would be to destroy an enemy's fielded forces on occupied territory.

At the start of the war, the newly independent Air Force found itself sorely tested. This conflict was without American precedent—a war of limited aims. Like the rest of America's armed forces, the Air Force had drawn down rapidly after the victory in World War II and as a result was unprepared in many ways for this conflict. If ever there was a lesson learned in the cost of letting everything just slide, Korea is it.

Yet, with almost no warning, the Air Force effectively injected itself into the war in its first week, providing transportation, evacuation, intelligence, but most importantly the means to delay the rapid advance of North Korean forces. Our unparalleled ability to deliver crushing bomb loads on target—time after time—allowed allied forces time to construct the Pusan defensive perimeter and to prepare for MacArthur's masterful counterattack at Inchon.

Of all its many accomplishments, the Air Force's most critical contribution to the Korean victory was air dominance. During the Korean War, American pilots flew the North American F–86 Sabre jet fighter. In some ways, it was inferior to its Soviet-built rival, the Mikoyan-Gurevich MiG–15. For example, a MiG could fly above fifty thousand feet whereas the F–86 was limited to about forty-two thousand feet, and the MiG was lighter and could climb faster. Maintenance was a headache, and it sounds reminiscent actually of some of our fleets today in that too-often a large fraction of our Sabres were in the depot or in the shop.

The Sabre first saw action in Korea with the 4th Fighter Group in December 1950. The basic Sabre design spawned multiple variants for wide-ranging roles including all-weather intercept, ground attack, and reconnaissance. Despite the deficiencies, the Sabre was a remarkable airplane for its time, and it had better high-speed qualities and a better flight control system than the MiG–15. The Sabre jet came to be considered one of the greatest fighter aircraft of all times, building up an impressive combat record that made a clear difference in the course of the war. Flown by skilled and aggressive pilots and serviced by dedicated young airmen, it dominated the MiG and set a standard for air control that is a hallmark of the Air Force today. It proved beyond a doubt the importance of superior technology, and I think the example of the Sabre in Korea is one of the reasons that General Ryan and I insist that we can never settle for parity as we look for our future technological needs. If we're going to send young men and women into harm's way, we need to make sure that we have a decisive advantage. Certainly, the advantage was decisive in Korea: F–86s shot down 792 MiG fighters while losing just 78 Sabres, a victory ratio of 10 to 1.

Constant air superiority established and maintained in the skies over North Korea also enabled tactical and strategic bombing forces to operate with near impunity behind communist lines, destroying enemy supplies while decimating reinforcements. The intensive continuous bombing enabled United Nations command to twice stave off disaster and twice launch successive offensive drives, the second of which compelled the communist forces to negotiate an armistice.

A fast-forward to Kosovo shows that, today, air power—thanks to modern technology—is even more significant and decisive. Fifty years later in Kosovo, dominance from the sky was never in doubt. So overwhelming was our advantage that most Serbian planes never got off the ground into the fight. As in the Gulf War, far more enemy planes were destroyed on the ground than in the air. No allied planes were lost in air-to-air combat, and, as I've already said, not a single NATO soldier on the ground was ever threatened by an aircraft. The two planes that we did lose fell victim to the evolving highly capable surface-to-air missile threat, which is one we're grappling with around the world, a threat that is increasing and must be met as we think about the threats of the twenty-first century.

Just as attack aircraft went after targets in Kosovo in 1999 without fear of attack from the air, air superiority in Korea a half-century ago allowed constant attacks from B–26s and B–29s to destroy Korean supply lines. Meanwhile, attacks by F–80s, F–84s, F–51s and B–26s decimated enemy frontline troops. Air interdiction and battlefield air attacks inflicted such extensive damage to roads and bridges that it stopped advancing communist forces in 1950 and, after the Chinese intervention, in 1951. And no discussion about Korea would be complete without talking about the airlifters that dropped bridge sections and supplies to withdrawing Marine forces in 1950, and then enabled our paratroopers to jump into combat during the period of the great UN offensives once the conflict had been stabilized.

Gen. Walton H. Walker, the Eighth Army commander, had a keen appreciation for what air had accomplished. During the war, he remarked, "I'll be glad to lay my cards right on the table and state that, if it had not been for the air support that we received from the Fifth Air Force, we would not have been able to stay in Korea." In fact, a significant percentage of all UN sorties were close to air assault attacks in direct support of troops, crucial to the halt-phase air campaign we waged against the North Koreans in the summer of 1950 and against the Chinese in the winter of 1950–51. We'll never know for sure if General Walker could imagine a time in the future when air power alone could turn the tide as it did in Kosovo. But, looking back with 20/20 hindsight, we see that many of the fruits of what we were able to do in Kosovo really had their seeds and roots in Korea with the way that our air power was used first to provide air superiority and then to furnish critical supply and attack operations.

The Air Force, Korea, and Kosovo: Past as Prologue

I think there is also one enduring truth that comes from World War II through Korea, Vietnam, to today, and that is all of this technology does not matter a great deal if you do not have courageous, dedicated warriors to use it. The men who piloted the warbirds of the Korean War, men like Joe McConnell, Pete Fernandez, Jim Jabara, Boots Blesse, Hal Fischer, Robbie Risner, Gabby Gabreski, John Glenn, and Bryce Poe have come to symbolize the skill, courage, and heroism demonstrated during some of that war's most heated battles, and I must tell you that their legacy of heroism and professionalism certainly lives on today in the men and women who make up today's Air Force.

Without air dominance gained by the Air Force's F–86 Sabres against a numerically larger foe[1], all other air operations by the Air Force, Navy, and Marine Corps, and our coalition partners would have been constrained. As a consequence, our ground and sea forces would have been left vulnerable to enemy air attacks with disastrous consequences. Air mobility forces could not have operated as well, and without the enormous exertions of the C–46s, C–47s, C–54s and C–119s, supplying and sustaining the ground forces would have been virtually impossible. Korea would have ended in a communist victory, and the whole political future of Asia and the western Pacific would have been drastically different.

Today, of course, the technologies are vastly different. We have evolved from air superiority to aerospace dominance, superiority, and control. We now consider space with its intrinsic ability to enable information dominance to be a vital part of the realm we must control in both peace and war, but, although the science is advanced and the operating theater greatly expanded, we continue to focus on some of these same concerns that dominated Korea and led to victory there.

The name of the game is still highly trained and dedicated people, operational superiority, agile logistics, superior information, and effective weapons. As recently as a year ago, we applied many of these lessons in the Balkans. It is interesting to note that we today have half the people in the Air Force that we had at the end of the Korean War. The Korean War certainly has taught us that we must leverage our technology to make sure that each and every one of those members of the Air Force can do what they need to do within these vastly smaller forces. We also have learned that we must upgrade our aging "legacy systems" and that we must build a new "systems of systems" infrastructure that can support integrated combat operations ranging from air dominance, to attack, to information operations, and to others as well.

The lessons that guide our modernization programs today are not just "boys must have their toys" as our critics say, but the lesson that, without the high technology, without the ability to draw on the modern assets, we are at a disadvantage even great people cannot offset. In short, we need to make sure that we stay on the technologically correct course. Today, first and foremost, that means the F–22 Raptor. Just as the F–86 played the decisive role in the skies over Korea, securing the air dominance upon which all else depended, the F–22 will provide the air dominance in future conflicts that our whole joint team—the Navy, the Army, the

Silver Wings Golden Valor: The USAF Remembers Korea

Marine Corps, as well as the Air Force—need to fight and win the wars of the twenty-first century. The Raptor is the indispensable tool we need to gain for America's future expeditionary forces the capability to be free from attack from the air.

In addition, we need to understand that today as we did in Korea, we will fight that air war more often over enemy territory, but there's a big difference today, and that is the more modern surface-to-air missiles [SAMs] that make it increasingly difficult for our existing air-to-air assets to fly over contested territory. In Korea, our pilots had to worry about guns—guns on the ground, guns on MiGs. Today we have to worry about very sophisticated missiles, particularly surface-to-air missiles fired by integrated air defense networks. The futuristic F–22 is designed to confront and survive that very dangerous and constantly evolving threat. The Raptor, with its revolutionary combination of stealth, supersonic cruise, maneuverability, and integrated avionics will evade SAMs, destroy its aerial opponents, and thus dominate the vertical battle space of the twenty-first century. It will provide our joint and coalition war fighters in the air and on the ground the same technological advantage and leverage over opponents that the F–86 did for our joint and coalition forces in Korea.

It is essential that the Air Force always provide freedom from attack, freedom to maneuver, and freedom to attack at any time and place of our choosing. That has been an essential understanding of joint concept of operations (CONOPS) for many years. It certainly was something we enjoyed in the Gulf and over Kosovo, and it's something we need to enjoy in the future. This means that we must not only have the F–22 Raptor, but a broad, highly capable and thoroughly integrated system of systems that will allow the Air Force to fulfill its vision of global vigilance, global reach, and global power. That is why our modernization program spans the range from modern food delivery systems, where a very few people can feed five hundred people a hot meal, to better tents, better environmental control units, deployable local area networks, and including the C–17 or other airlifter that brings it all into theater. We need to make sure as we expand and modernize our Air Force that we bring these capabilities forward, that we modernize them in a balanced way across the board to make sure that we can use all of our assets in a most effective way.

We also need to take a lesson from Korea in that we need effective weapons when it comes to fighting air wars. Obviously, we are looking very hard over the next years in bringing on more effective weapons, more precise weapons that are ideally suited to defeat the threats that we now face. Just to list a few, consider the conventional air-launched cruise missile (CALCM), which proved so important in the early days of Kosovo; the joint air-to-surface standoff missile (JASSM), which gives us a standoff capability, particularly important in the early days of a war when the surface-to-air threat is at its peak; the joint standoff weapon (JSOW), which is now being fielded; the joint direct attack munition (JDAM), the latter the satellite-guided bomb that proved so effective in Kosovo; and, finally, the wind-corrected munitions dispenser (WCMD), which allows us to drop cluster and similar area-effect munitions with great precision. All of these are very high priorities and are the end of the "kill chain" that must go along with the space superiority and the air dominance that we need to fight the next war.

Reconnaissance has always been crucially important in warfare, particularly air warfare, where there is a direct connection between reconnaissance and targeting. Although the methods were less sophisticated during Korea, the bombing success in Korea also was directly attributable to the reconnaissance that was then being done with pilots who flew RF–51s, RF–80s, RF–86s, RB–26s, RB–29s, and RB–45s. Today, in the era of laser- and satellite-guided munitions, we have even greater need for precise intelligence, for, the more precise the weapons, the more precise the intelligence you need to establish the aim point. One of the undying lessons I think of Kosovo is going to be that, if you want to drop a satellite-guided bomb, you need to know the latitude, longitude, and altitude of the target. You can no longer look out of most of our aircraft, see a target, maybe circle a couple of times, and then drop one of these bombs accurately on the target. You need to have satellite assets, tactical air, and other kinds of reconnaissance fleets. Now, during Kosovo, our atmospheric reconnaissance effort was primarily the Lockheed U–2 and Boeing RC–135 Rivet Joint, but it also involved the unmanned aerial vehicle [UAV], typified by the General Atomics Predator. Soon we will enter the era of the world-ranging Global Hawk UAV.

One critical aspect of Kosovo operations was our ability to fuse data from all of these and other sources to bring precision intelligence to bear on the battlefield. One of the best examples was Predator, which has a video-feed system. As originally conceived, Predator was never to use that video feed for targeting. That was not in anybody's idea when the aircraft was built, but we have some very smart people working with computers who understand the data streams coming down from space, and these folks were able to put together a Predator targeting system in really no time flat that took that video and registered it against very precise terrain data coming from satellites. This gave us the ability to look at what the Predator was looking at, to put a mouse cursor on the target and get the precise coordinates, then send it right out to orbiting aircraft that could hit those coordinates. That kind of responsive reconnaissance and targeting is where we need to be in the future, and it's that kind of aerospace integration that General Ryan and I continue to stress as vital to the future success of our joint forces.

The other thing that is very, very important is logistics. During the Korean War, our airlifters battled some of the worst weather and maintenance issues in air war history and yet they managed to fly two hundred thousand sorties carrying 2.6 million passengers and four hundred thousand tons of cargo. They participated in two combat operations dropping more than six thousand paratroopers and five hundred and twenty tons of cargo. They dropped the bridge sections that enabled our Marines to withdraw safely in the face of the Chinese onslaught in 1950. Maj. Gen. William H. Tunner expressed the need for advanced cargo aircraft that com-

Silver Wings Golden Valor: The USAF Remembers Korea

bined faster speed, longer range, increased cargo capacity, and short-field capability. Out of that came the now-legendary Lockheed C–130 Hercules. But, only today, with the superlative C–17 Globemaster III have we finally arrived at an airplane that can do all of those things superbly well.

But another thing that I think started with General Tunner's vision was the understanding that you cannot adopt a business-as-usual approach to airlift everything forward. You've got to be lighter, leaner, and more capable and agile in the way you operate, particularly when you have to rely on air supply. We're continuing to work on that today, as well. Just to give you an example: during Korea, a Chinese division required forty-five tons of supplies a day but an American division required six hundred and ten tons per day. It is easy to see which force is more agile. It is easy to see which force was easier to resupply. I think it's also easy to understand why we are committed to reduce the scale of what we have to bring forward.

One of the important lessons of all of the wars we've fought since World War II is that, if you're doing your job from home, you're much less likely to get shot at. We now have robust communications that we used extensively during Kosovo that enabled us to leave a lot of our forces back at home, particularly our intelligence forces. For example, we actually ran the sensors on U–2s flying over Serbia from a distributed common ground station sitting at Beale Air Force Base in California. It wasn't just a one-time experiment. Rather, we did it routinely, we did it well, and the result was that we never brought folks from the field into harm's way. We never separated them from their families. It was a "win" in every dimension, and, it too is the wave of the future.

We also showed in Kosovo that we have really begun to figure out yet again how to do the kind of routine expeditionary operations that we did during Korea but that languished for a number of years after that. During Kosovo, we opened twenty-one new bases in a matter of a very few weeks. It was so easy that I don't think you'll find a single reference to this in any of the Kosovo lessons learned. We now have folks who are more used to living in sleeping bags, setting up tents, and eating meals, ready-to-eat (MREs) probably than any other service, particularly given how many foreign operating locations we've opened just in the last three years since I've been part of the Air Force.

So, in summing up, I think there are enduring and important lessons from Korea. The really significant ones are three. First is that light, lean, and agile wins the day, and we need to get more that way. Second is that vigilance, reach, and power is absolutely critical. The third—and most important—is that we've got to have air dominance. It's just indispensable, just absolutely necessary. The Air Force has been so successful in controlling enemy skies that our joint forces don't know today what it's like to fight without air dominance—and we sure don't want them to find out. All of our war plans assume it as an asymmetric advantage that we have in favor of the United States, but we must remember it is always earned, and never a God-ordained right.

The Air Force, Korea, and Kosovo: Past as Prologue

So, even as we continue to work technical miracles and continue to work the hard issues of recruiting, retention, and deployment, I think we need to understand that we are well within the lessons learned from Korea. I hope through this conference that we'll reinvigorate our appreciation of the lessons from Korea by bringing our veterans here today to share their recollections with us, and to talk to us about the lessons they learned a half-century ago.

With that, I want to thank you all for coming. It's a pleasure having had this opportunity to speak with you.

Notes

1. For example, in June 1951, intelligence indicated that communist forces had three hundred MiG–15s. In contrast, Far East Air Forces (FEAF) had only 89 Sabres at the same time. Despite this, FEAF never lost air superiority over the Soviet, Chinese communist, and North Korean forces confronting us.

Chapter 5

AIR DOMINANCE:
THE ESSENTIAL ACHIEVEMENT

Dr. Richard P. Hallion
Panel Chairman

MAJOR GENERAL MOSELEY: One of the great pleasures of putting this symposium together has been the opportunity to work ever closer with our Air Force historian, Dr. Dick Hallion. Many of you know him as a prolific author with more than a dozen books to his credit, but you may not know that he has also done the definitive history of naval aviation in the Korean War.[1] Dick writes and lectures widely on air power topics and has flying time as a mission observer in a wide range of fighter aircraft as well. So when Dick talks Korean air power, whether about the Navy or about the Air Force, he's got it right. Today he's here to chair the first panel, *Air Dominance: The Essential Achievement*. Dr. Hallion, the floor is yours.

DR. HALLION: Thanks, Buzz, for those generous opening remarks. I'd like to invite the members of the panel to please come forward. And, General Ryan, thank you very much for opening the session. We appreciate it.

On behalf of the men and women of both the Air Force History and Museums Program and Air Force Legislative Liaison, I wish to welcome all of you to this symposium. It's fitting that we have built this symposium around the veterans of the Korean War. They're a cross section of individuals who came from many walks of life and backgrounds, and from across America. Thanks to what they and their colleagues in other services and other nations did, South Korea remained free and remains free to this day.

Our first panel today is on air dominance. Now, since the appearance of the military airplane, control of the air has always proven the first and most important mission of an air force. It was certainly true in Korea, and it remains true today in the post–Persian Gulf and post-Kosovo world. Many commonly think of control of the air as just so-called air superiority. In truth, air dominance should always be the desired goal: to so absolutely dominate your opponent that he is at the same time essentially incapable of projecting his own air power and helpless to prevent air attacks upon his own forces.

Thanks to the veterans on our first panel and their many colleagues, the United States Air Force was able to seize control of Korean skies, not merely exerting air superiority, but air supremacy, indeed air domination, as well.[2] What, may we ask, did that level of air control achieve? First, in the early summer and early fall of 1950, it denied North Korea the ability to use its own attack aviation forces against UN troops and targets. Second, at the same time, it enabled all joint and coalition partners to operate essentially with impunity in conducting their own air attacks against North Korean targets. We interdicted supply lines. We destroyed lines of communication. We directly attacked fielded forces as those forces were maneuvering south and trying to seize South Korea. How significant was that air control? Without air power, Lt. Gen. Walton H. "Bulldog" Walker's Eighth Army could not have withstood the communist assault upon the Pusan perimeter and Korea would have fallen. Walker stated at the time, "I will gladly lay my cards right on the table and state that if it had not been for the air support that we received from the Fifth Air Force we would not have been able to stay in Korea."[3]

But this success proved transitory. When Chairman Mao sent his forces southward across the Yalu in November 1950, the stakes of the Korean War again changed dramatically. Once more, air power had to engage an enemy on the move, but this time there was a profoundly serious danger: the Soviet-built and Soviet-flown MiG–15 fighter. It was a swept-wing jet airplane completely outperforming any straight-wing American jet fighter in the Korean theater at that time. Fortunately, thanks to our acquisition strategy in the late 1940s at a time of military drawdown, we had an answer. It was the graceful swept-wing F–86 Sabre, an elegant and revolutionary warplane as curvaceous and deadly as its namesake. Sabre pilots prevented Soviet Chinese and North Korean airmen from seizing back control of the air, and UN air dominance continued. In 1951, the communist offensive ground to a halt, and one captured Chinese report stated at the time that, had communist forces been free to employ their own air power, "we could have driven the enemy [that is, the UN] into the sea and the protracted defensive battles ranging from 25 January to 22 April . . . should have been avoided."[4] In short, air power had saved Korea for the second time.

With the UN firmly in control of the air, North Korean and Chinese forces were thoroughly pummeled by air attack. Lt. Gen. Nam Il, the chief North Korean

Air Dominance: The Essential Achievement

negotiator, admitted as much during armistice talks at Panmunjom when he stated that these bombing attacks were the decisive factor allowing UN ground forces to hold their positions in the face of massive communist forces. Until the armistice, UN forces fought under an air umbrella that shielded them from the kind of punishing attacks inflicted upon their communist adversaries.

In his history of the Korean War, UN commanding General Matthew Ridgway stated bluntly, "No one who fought on the ground in Korea would ever be tempted to belittle the accomplishments of our Air Force there. Not only did air power save us from disaster, but without it the mission of the United Nations forces could not have been accomplished."[5] This was perhaps the greatest tribute that could be accorded to the airmen who took control of Korean skies.

Now it's my pleasure to introduce the members of the air dominance panel. Each will speak for a few minutes, and, at the end of their presentation, we will take a short break, then reconvene for a panel discussion and a session of questions and answers from the floor.

The first panelist we have is Lt. Gen. William E. Brown, Jr. Earl Brown graduated from Penn State in 1949 and was a distinguished graduate of his pilot training class at Craig Air Force Base, Alabama. As a Sabre pilot, he flew one hundred twenty-five combat missions with the 4th Fighter-Interceptor Wing. He remained in the Air Force after Korea and flew an additional one hundred missions over Southeast Asia in F–4 Phantoms. He's been a numbered Air Force commander and commander of Allied Air Forces in southern Europe. He retired from the Air Force in 1984. He's a ski instructor (and indeed a fanatic about skiing, both water and snow), active as a museum docent at the National Air and Space Museum (where he presented the Charles A. Lindbergh Memorial Lecture for 1992),[6] and a good friend. General Brown, the floor is yours.

LIEUTENANT GENERAL BROWN: Thank you very much, Dr. Hallion.

Perhaps it's fitting that I start because, you see, when I got to Korea, I was a twenty-four-year-old second lieutenant. I had the extreme good fortune to be assigned to A Flight in the 334th Fighter-Interceptor Squadron of the 4th Fighter-Interceptor Wing in Korea. My flight commander was a role model who I was very careful to observe and try to emulate. He had been First Captain at West Point. So all I had to do was watch Capt. Arnold Braswell and try to do as much as I could to be like him, and I find him sitting next to me here today, my flight commander from Korea, Maj. Gen. Arnold Braswell.

There are great strategic themes about Korea and diplomatic decisions and national authority decisions, but, in every war, it finally gets down to a group of young people trying to kill another group of young people. This came home to me very early in Korea. I was assigned as a wingman. So what I want to talk to you about is what a wingman did, because I know very well what that was.

We flew in flights of four aircraft, in "fingertip" formation, in two elements of two aircraft. The two fellows on the outside are the wingmen. The guy sticking out, whose head is up—who takes responsibility, blame, and credit for everything the flight does—is the leader. The guy next to him is the element leader. This formation takes off and flies as a flight of four. When we entered combat and engaged enemy fighters, the flight frequently broke apart but never to less than two aircraft. If the element ever broke apart, they left the combat theater. Now, in the element, you have a leader and you have a wingman. The wingman and the leader's jobs are to find the enemy, seek them out, engage them, maneuver, and kill them. The wingman's job is to help the leader find them, because usually there's an age difference. Some of our leaders were old guys in their thirties, and I was a young twenty-four-year-old. So the difference in eyesight was significant.

After we found the enemy though, then the wingman's job was to maintain surveillance and situational awareness in the big air bubble that surrounds the maneuvering aircraft. Your job, essentially, was never to lose the leader. You always stayed slightly to the rear and on one side or the other, and as long as the leader was maneuvering, you kept the rear clear. You would call him and tell him, "you're clear, you're clear," or, if someone entered that bubble and posed a threat, you would advise him of that. This meant your head was always on a swivel. Early in our training, we were taken out to a Sabre sitting on the ground. You sat in the Sabre and your instructor pilot asked you to look over your left shoulder until you could see your right wingtip. So the wingmen flew with our leaders. We confirmed their kills, and, when we got back, we did other errands for them. This picture exhibited behind me, *Sabre Dance* by Harley Copic, really tells the story, for it depicts an actual event. Col. James K. Johnson, who was our wing commander at the 4th, flies the airplane. He's in an airplane from the 335th Squadron, and he's killing one of the ten MiGs that he got.

Now the Sabre was a great airplane. But what *made* the Sabre a great airplane? There were, I think, five major reasons:

First, it was the world's first operational fighter with genuinely swept-back wings, swept aft at an angle of thirty-five degrees. Earlier, the Germans had very slightly swept wings at the end of World War II on their Messerschmitt Me 262 jet fighter. Their wind tunnel data, and American data slightly later, proved that, by sweeping the wings back, you could approach closer to the speed of sound[7] before the characteristic drag rise would occur. Actually, the Sabre was designed initially as the "P–86" with a straight wing. It never met the performance requirements.[8]

By sweeping the wings back, the speed went from 534 miles per hour to 635 miles per hour, a 100-mile-an-hour gain. The swept wing had poor slow-speed performance, for, at even moderate angles of attack, the airflow over the top of the wing could separate and detach from the surface, thus causing a loss of lift and possible loss of control. So, borrowing from the British, an idea first conceived by Sir Frederick Handley Page, the Sabre had leading-edge slats. Each leading edge of the Sabre's wing could detach at slow speeds and extend forward, creating a little gap or slot between the detached slat and the main wing through which air could flow to remain attached to the upper wing surface. And, of course, it had landing flaps to increase lift on final approach. It's just like you see on the airlin-

Air Dominance: The Essential Achievement

ers you fly on today: look out the window as you come in to land, and the wing seems to explode. The front—the slats—goes forward, the back—the flaps—goes back. Now you can fly slower with control. So the first big advantage was the swept wing.

Second, the Sabre had irreversible hydraulic controls. The flight controls were controlled by hydraulics to withstand the high airloads encountered at transonic speeds, but the force on the flight controls was not relayed back to the pilot's stick. So, with two fingers you could do magnificent maneuvers right up to—and through—the speed of sound.

The third advantage was the tail. The horizontal stabilizer on the F–86 was movable. This was a feature that came out of the test flights by Chuck Yeager on the X–1. By moving the horizontal stabilizer, we could maintain control closer to the speed of sound than the MiG could.[9]

Fourth, the Sabre had truly magnificent visibility with its high-perched clear bubble canopy. You could look three hundred and sixty degrees. The MiG pilot, when he turned around, looked at the rear of his headrest or the back of his cockpit. There was a big canopy brace running fore and aft directly over his head, and the optical quality of the glass itself wasn't great. Also, the MiG had a very poor air-conditioning system at high altitude, so the canopy would frequently freeze up behind the pilot and reduce his visibility to the rear—the most dangerous section of the sky—even further.

Fifth and finally, the F–86 had excellent speed brakes located aft of the wing on the sides of the lower fuselage. The airplane was so slick that it was hard to slow down, but you need to slow down when you maneuver in combat, for combat is fought at all the edges of an airplane's envelope, as fast as you can go and as slow as you can go. These brakes caused very little pitch change, deployed and retracted quickly, and gave us a tremendous advantage in trying to hold position and track a hard-maneuvering MiG.

So, with all of these features, the Sabre just gave us wingmen and our leaders a distinct edge over the MiG: we killed 792 MiGs, and we lost only 78 Sabres. And it helped this wingman get home to tell his stories! Thank you.

DR. HALLION: I think you can all see why Earl Brown is such a great docent at the Smithsonian. That was a concise explanation of the swept-wing, low-speed handling qualities and the flying tail. He obviously hasn't lost the touch. Our next speaker is Lt. Gen. Arnold Braswell, a 1948 graduate of West Point. After undergraduate pilot training, he flew the F–86, but he went to war in Korea first in the straight-wing Republic F–84 Thunderjet with the 49th Fighter-Bomber Wing, before flying F–86s with the 4th Wing. Later in his career, although officially assigned to staff duties, he flew forty missions over Southeast Asia in 1967 in F–4s. He retired in 1983 after a career that included being the J–5, the Director for Plans and Policy on the Joint Staff; a numbered Air Force commander; and commander of Pacific Air Forces. If you get the June 2000 issue of *Air Force*

Silver Wings Golden Valor: The USAF Remembers Korea

Magazine, you can see him in a very dapper pose on the cover by his F–84. General, welcome to the podium; you've got the stick.

MAJOR GENERAL BRASWELL: All right. I won't tell you all how much I paid to have that cover put on there! Actually, I was a bit shocked; that picture was taken with my little Argus camera that I bought in a base exchange in Japan, and through a circuitous route it somehow got on the cover. I will say that it's great to be on a panel with Earl Brown, my old friend from our flight days in Korea, and I must also say that I never had a more reliable and accomplished wingman than Earl Brown. I remember those days often.

I'd like to talk a little bit about air dominance and give you some of my thoughts on that subject. I certainly agree that the term *air dominance* is a better term and more descriptive of what we want than just *air superiority*. We want to dominate the air, and, as it has been in the past, it is an essential achievement if we're going to achieve our objectives in any future conflict.

I think that the value of air dominance is underappreciated today by too many people because there are only a few old veterans kicking around who experienced enemy air superiority and its consequences back in World War II—and then only in the beginning stages of World War II. In Korea, our air dominance was initially threatened by the numbers and by the performance of the MiG–15s. They were a surprise, but we finally (and actually very quickly) were able to gain air dominance over the peninsula because we were able to deny the communists the use of North Korean bases by near-continuous day and with night bombing by the B–29s. The MiG–15 had a fairly short range, so they couldn't go as far south as they really needed to establish control over the air over the peninsula. Our pilots were more skilled and aggressive, and, of course, when we got the F–86s into the act, we had an aircraft that would compete very well with the MiG–15s.

Today and in the future, I think that we have to pay attention to many factors if we are going to continue to have air dominance. I'd like to mention a few of those just briefly.

High-technology aircraft and weapons for air-to-air engagement? Yes, of course. The F–22 will be as critical for future air dominance as the F–15 and the F–16 (especially the F–15) have been to achieving air dominance in our two most recent conflicts. So the F–22 and its weapons will be important in the future, but that's not the only thing we have to have.

We have to have realistic and continuous training. I can well remember the days when I was growing up as a fighter pilot being frustrated by the fact that we were not able to engage in either realistic air-to-air or air-to-ground combat training. We were finally able to achieve what I would call the apex of realistic training with Red Flag, but that didn't come until the mid-1970s. Red Flag, of course, is the realistic combat exercise that we routinely conduct out at Nellis Air Force Base in Nevada.

We have to have long-range, ground-attack capability. This requires a mix of aircraft, missiles, and other precision weapons because, in order to achieve air

Air Dominance: The Essential Achievement

dominance, you must deny the enemy the use of his bases, his command and control systems, his warning and control systems, and his communication systems. That is just as important as having air-to-air capability. You must be able to attack him in his ground installations.

We need effective support forces. We're talking about electronic combat aircraft and forces, tankers, airlift, and effective basing arrangements. We have to have high-technology intelligence and surveillance, via control platforms such as the AWACS and J–STARS,[10] satellite-based systems, the RC–135 Rivet Joint, et cetera. All of these contribute very importantly to our ability to achieve air dominance, for they enable effective air battle management and integration of all our forces. These are extremely important aspects in achieving air dominance.

We have to have adequate forces and sortie generation capability. We're talking numbers here. You have to be able to put up enough sorties to do what you want to do, whether it's air-to-ground or air-to-air. Numbers are important. You can have the best aircraft in the world with the best missiles and weapons systems, but if you don't have enough of them, then you may not achieve the air dominance that you need.

Finally, we must assume that in the future it will not always be as easy as our most recent conflicts. Air dominance is not something that you can take for granted. We have to work at it. All of these factors that I mentioned are important and must be kept in mind. Thanks.

DR. HALLION: Our next panelist is Brig. Gen. Michael DeArmond. He graduated from West Point in 1950, completed undergraduate pilot training at Williams Air Force Base in 1951, and went to Korea as a Shooting Star pilot with the 8th Fighter-Bomber Group but flew combat as a Sabre pilot with the 4th Wing. He completed forty-six missions over there but was then shot down on his forty-seventh, spending the next seventeen months as a prisoner in a Chinese POW camp. Now there's another story here about the airplane that he was shot down in, but I'll let one of our other panelists tell it! He subsequently flew well more than two hundred missions in Southeast Asia in the F–100, went on to other command assignments in the logistics field, and retired from the Air Force in 1977. So, General, welcome to the podium.

BRIGADIER GENERAL DeARMOND: Ladies and gentlemen, I was going to talk about being a wingman, but Earl Brown covered me very well on that. I'll talk a little about the environment at that time, some of the shortfalls of the Air Force because it was a new service, and just what it was like being a new second lieutenant in the 4th Fighter Group. I feel right at home, frankly. The painting behind me shows the 335th Fighter Squadron. I was in the 335th, and I spent a large number of my missions hanging on the wing of my fellow panelist Paddy Harbison over there when we flew combat in a number of dogfights.

I went to Korea as a new F–80 pilot, reporting out of flying school to the 8th Fighter-Bomber Group down at Suwon. But, when I arrived on Christmas Day in 1951, I received orders sending me to the 4th Fighter Wing. I thought I had died and gone to heaven! That was swept-wing time! That was scarf-in-the-breeze time! I knew I was going to be the first second lieutenant ace up there, and I was invulnerable, and it was going to be a great life. I needed only six more kills to become an ace. One was to make up for my airplane, and then the five you need to become an ace! When we got there, the wing had a checkout program for new F–86 pilots. I had never flown the F–86; in fact, I had never seen one. Our captain stood on the wing of a Sabre, told me how to start it, and off I went. We got three or four rides, and I went into combat. We had to test our guns as we flew over sea en route to MiG Alley. The first mission in combat, I was so "clanked up" and so tight I couldn't remember where the gun switch was when we crossed the bomb line. Did you ever try to whisper over your radio with fifteen other pilots listening, "Green 4, where's the gun switch?"

Somehow I survived through my forty-sixth mission as a wingman. But I had reported into the 4th with five other second lieutenants, and only one of us completed his tour. When we talk about that kill ratio up there, there were a lot of very fine guys who never came home from that war, and a lot of them were out of E Flight in the 335th. At times it was pretty grim. I was there when one pilot came back shot up, and he couldn't get the canopy to jettison. The last I saw him was near K–14,[11] squatting in his seat trying to shove the canopy off the F–86, when his airplane went straight into the ground. Another went in, and his last words were, "It's burning like a son-of-a-bitch." So I don't want you to think that we stood back there and knocked the MiGs down out of the sky without losing a lot of very, very good people.

I was shot down on my forty-seventh mission flying off my leader's wing. Unfortunately, in that day and age, there was a lot of World War II–type behavior, and the 335th was not a particularly disciplined organization. My leader, Maj. Zane S. Amell,[12] who I thought was a hell of a fine officer, had won the squadron commander's martini-drinking contest the night before (I think he had had fourteen martinis in something like twenty minutes)—and we had the "dawn patrol"! We got into a dogfight that day, he called a break, and I don't think he could hold the g's in as we turned. Consequently, the MiG pilot pulled his nose back enough to get lead on us (and you notice I'm talking into my hands like fighter pilots do). He hit me with his 23-mm or 37-mm cannon, my controls went out, I was on fire at twenty-five thousand feet going down, and bam!—I punched out. I've talked to a man who saw me go—the airplane blew up just as my ejection seat cleared the tail. Now I'm hanging in my chute at about eighteen thousand feet floating down saying, "This can't happen to me." First, I prayed like I've never prayed in my life. Second, I closed my eyes and said, "You're going to wake up and you're going to be back in bed at K–14. This isn't happening to you."

I'll go into a little bit of the prison stuff. When down, I'm captured and I'm sent to Sinuiju. Then Bud Mahurin,[13] who was commander of the 4th, decided that he ought to do a little fighter-bomber work, and suddenly I'm being bombed by F–86s up hitting Sinuiju! I'm in a cave, with a sixteen-year-old kid as a guard and about three hundred women there. They wanted to emasculate me and everything else, and I'm behind this kid holding him up, and he's swinging a bayonet to keep them away. I wound up spending about seventeen months in captivity, all but two weeks of which was in solitary confinement in a room four feet by six feet. There was an F–80 pilot languishing under the same conditions. For four months, there was ice all around the walls, and it never got above freezing in that hooch. The only reason I can figure I was up there is that the communists were after "germ warfare" confessions, and I would not confess.[14] The Russians had held the other pilot for a time, even though the Chinese story was that there were no Russians up there. I spent a long time as an MIA, and when I returned home my fiancée had already married somebody else, had already had two children, and had named both of them after me "posthumously"—very nice, but strange!

I would say one thing I noticed from being a squadron commander and later a wing assistant deputy commander for operations in Vietnam was the greater professionalism and training of the pilots that we had over there, the younger pilots in particular. One thing that I noticed lacking in Vietnam (mainly because I was forty-something in Vietnam and I was only twenty-three when I went into combat in Korea) was there seemed to be a little less spirit there than there had been in the old 4th Fighter Group. I mean, in Korea we drank. We raised hell. We'd get a few drinks and then jump on the table and recite *Gunga Din*.[15] It was a great life until it ended.

However, the airplanes weren't all that good. I remember flying at thirty-four thousand feet, iced over inside, rubbing my hand, trying to clear the ice off the canopy and trying to hang in position on Paddy Harbison's wing. Paddy told me my job was to clear him and make sure he didn't get shot down, even if that meant my going up in a great ball of fire to alert him that MiGs were around—and I'll never forget that!

I envy you youngsters your age right now; I still feel like I'm seventeen, and I still peek at girls occasionally. The Air Force was a great life, a hell of a fine life, and I miss it badly. Thank you very much.

DR. HALLION: Our next panelist is Col. Harold Fischer. Hal Fischer is unique in having served as a member of the U.S. Navy in World War II, the U.S. Army before Korea, and the U.S. Air Force in Korea and afterward. He received his silver wings in December 1950 and reported to the 8th Fighter-Bomber Group flying F–80s. After flying one hundred five ground-attack missions, he was assigned to a desk. He requested a transfer to a Sabre outfit and received orders to the 51st Fighter Interceptor Group. Six months later, he was a double jet ace, a captain, and had seventy missions under his belt. On April 7, 1953, he claimed two MiGs shot down. Unfortunately, they remained claims because the debris from the second MiG damaged his Sabre, and he had to eject, coming down in China. Hal wasn't released from Chinese prison until the end of May 1955. So, Hal, welcome.[16]

Silver Wings Golden Valor: The USAF Remembers Korea

COLONEL FISCHER: It's a pleasure to be with such a distinguished panel. I walk with heroes and ghosts. Two of the ghosts are my parents, who would be proud of me, because they never thought that I could ever amount to anything because I couldn't drive horses!

I'll give you my personal experience with air dominance. After six hours and forty-five minutes of checkout flying in the F–86, I began flying combat missions. After a few of these, I was assigned to a flight commanded by a Royal Canadian Air Force exchange officer, Sqd Ldr Douglas Lindsay.[17] He was an ace and, being a Canadian, he just wanted to do the job. He was one of those rare individuals who is truly dedicated to getting the job done and believes that results are more important than methods. Without a doubt, he was the best fighter pilot I had ever seen or flown with. As my mission total increased, so did my desire to get a kill. Soon the moment came that I had been dreaming about. I was number two in another flight with Lindsay when the sky was suddenly filled with MiGs. They were everywhere. I called that I was going to make a "bounce," turned to the left, and surveyed the scene for a moment. From the south, about fifteen hundred feet below me, two MiGs were heading north. I eased down and fell behind them, about a mile in trail. I don't think they saw me, and I pulled up the nose of my aircraft, moved the radar gunsight to manual (I felt I couldn't trust it in the automatic mode), and fired several long bursts. Just as I was going to break off the attack, the MiG wingman began a slow descent. I called to the flight lead and said I had one going down. I followed the MiG, and, when I caught up, I rolled around it and got one of the biggest surprises of my life. The canopy was missing, and the pilot was gone! I knew that there was no positive verification on the gun camera film, so when the MiG crashed, I strafed the wreckage for confirmation purposes. That evening, Lindsay told me that it would probably be impossible to sleep; after his first kill as a Spitfire pilot during World War II in England, he said he couldn't sleep a wink. He was right!

In another engagement that saw my second kill, I was flying as element leader and made my attack on a MiG by positioning myself about six hundred feet directly behind him at forty thousand feet altitude. Before I could fire, the MiG entered and completed a perfect loop! My F–86 floundered over the top, and the MiG proceeded into a series of loops. With each successive loop, my advantage increased slightly because of the "flop" at the top. This way, I was squaring a corner of our circle, and the Sabre's flying tail helped out at the bottom. I had the presence of mind to fire only short bursts, so as not to dissipate airspeed at that altitude. Over the Yalu River, the MiG straightened out for a moment, and I prepared to fire a long burst when I observed an object going by my canopy. It was the MiG's canopy, and it was followed shortly by the pilot in his ejection seat! When the gun camera film was processed, the seat could be seen going by.

Numbers three and four followed over the next thirty days. Number four had "341" painted on its nose. When I commenced my attack on him, the rate of closure was so rapid that I had to execute a displacement roll around him to maintain

Air Dominance: The Essential Achievement

nose-to-tail separation. As I rolled, I hit the MiG's jet wash. The jolt was so great that my binoculars hit the stick grip and broke. In addition to all the activity trying to recover the aircraft and myself, the gunsight quit while I was firing, and the guns also stopped. For a heartbeat, I thought of ramming, striking the MiG's fragile high-mounted horizontal tail, which was just inboard of my left wing. I missed by about six inches. Rolling over the MiG (which was rapidly losing airspeed), I recycled the gun switch to "guns, sight, and camera" (the sight came back on), opened my speed brakes, squeezed the trigger, and literally blasted that MiG out of the sky.

The fifth kill was one of both anguish and jubilation. I ended up in a tail chase about four thousand feet behind a MiG. Again, I turned off the radar and computing gunsight, elevated the nose, and fired. The tracers made a small halo around the plane, and gradually a fire began to grow in the rear of the MiG. About the time I had closed to an ideal firing range, there was no need to expend any more ammunition: it was a dying aircraft, with the entire fuselage serving as a flameholder. I pulled up alongside and saw the pilot was beating on the canopy, trying to escape. Seeing my Sabre, he tried to turn and ram me. I thought the only humane thing to do was to put the pilot out of his misery, so I slid my Sabre back onto his tail. Molten metal from the MiG rained on my aircraft as I fired a few short bursts. Then the sounds suddenly changed; three of my guns quit firing, my left rudder pedal went to the firewall, and I thought for sure that I had been hit. I immediately disengaged and cautiously returned home, to find after landing that the intense heat from the burning MiG had caused a misfire of a .50-cal machine gun round. That one exploding cartridge had shut down the guns, severed a rudder cable, and subsequently dumped my cabin pressurization.

The next two kills were in the best fighter tradition of Mannock, Udet, Nungesser, and other heroes of the first dogfights in World War I.[18] I found myself and a MiG at the same airspeed, altitude, and going in the same direction. Immediately we got into a flat scissors maneuver trying to get on the other's tail. Dropping my speed brakes and using aerodynamic braking, I fell in behind the MiG at a range of about six hundred feet. This time, the radar gunsight was working marvelously, and the first burst of a few seconds caused my opponent's aircraft to light up almost from wingtip to wingtip. Before I could fire again, the canopy went by, followed by the pilot. As we were leaving MiG Alley, my flight had to break to avoid an attack. I fell in trail behind my wingman and told him to take us home. As we climbed out, I spotted a MiG closing behind my wingman at a range of about three thousand feet. I dropped in behind the MiG at about the same range, and he seemed to have seen me. He turned left, and I zoomed into a yo-yo. He continued, and I ended up behind him at about three hundred feet, almost in a full stall. I fired a burst that struck right behind the canopy, and the MiG immediately snapped into a spin. There was nothing else to do but spin with him! Both of us entered the spin at about thirty thousand feet altitude, and I would take short bursts when my F–86 pointed at him. He spun all the way into the ground.

Silver Wings Golden Valor: The USAF Remembers Korea

My next victory held the most danger and was fraught with the most mistakes. It began with a new wingman who had been a professional musician and could play a mean clarinet. Our flight was late getting into the area, and battles had already begun; the fight was taking place about fifty miles northeast of the mouth of the Yalu River. As we came into the area, climbing through forty thousand feet, we dropped our tanks and spotted four MiGs in a standard fingertip formation. There were four F–86s behind them at a great distance. As we jockeyed for position, we almost collided with the other Sabres, since neither formation wanted to give way and lose the advantage. No one was firing because the range was so great, but the MiGs appeared to be aware of us. We were now over China, above a solid layer of clouds, and the MiGs were letting down into it. Guessing where they were going, I continued down with my element and occasionally could see the MiGs going in and out of cloud layers.

Then we all broke out: the MiGs were to our left and in a turn. It was almost easy to join up with them. In fact, my join-up with the number two MiG was *too* good, as I was too close to open fire effectively. My wingman called me clear, and just as I got into position to fire, a volley of cannon tracers went by my right wing and canopy. Immediately thereafter, my wingman called me clear again, and I thought he had negated whoever was shooting at me. I continued my attack, but once again a burst of fireworks passed my right wing and canopy before I could fire. Still, I didn't look back, and once more my wingman called me clear. I was very nervous by now, but not once did I look around to my six o'clock.[19] I suspect the reason I wasn't nailed was I was so close to the MiG in front of me that his buddy couldn't get a good shot without hitting his friend. Finally, I was clear to fire, and it was no problem to dispatch the aircraft in front of me once I could get my mind settled down. A few good bursts and the battle was over: the MiG was on fire, and the pilot bailed out.

My next kill was a relatively easy one. I saw a MiG firing on an F–86 and dived down on him. I fired and got his attention. He disengaged and headed north. I fell in behind him and easily got him burning. The pilot bailed out. Shortly thereafter, my tenth kill was official. Then came the last day of my war. I fired on four MiGs. The first I missed because I accepted an aircraft that hadn't been boresighted accurately on the ground. I went in and fired, and one hundred feet to the left at one thousand feet, that's where my bullet pattern was. So I aborted and, seeing three MiGs below, I made a high-speed pass. I rolled around the last MiG, fired, rolled over, hit the element leader, and then hit the lead. I found out later that one aircraft, piloted by Sr Lt Konstantin Ugryumov, touched down on one landing gear leg after being hit twenty-three times behind the fuselage and wing root. (He demonstrated this to me years later at the Kiev War Museum on a MiG–17.) Another MiG I fired at, flown by a Chinese pilot, landed on two legs, and, of the third I fired on, the Chinese pilot ejected. That was air domination. Then, as I pulled over the top, the throttle came back of its own accord and, as I smelled smoke, I ejected. Aerial domination was lost!

Air Dominance: The Essential Achievement

DR. HALLION: Our final panelist is AVM William "Paddy" Harbison of the Royal Air Force. Paddy joined the RAF in 1941, shortly after the epochal Battle of Britain, but still at a time when air dominance was very much a big issue in European skies. He subsequently flew Spitfires and Mustangs with Fighter Command through the war, and then, afterward, the fastest piston-engine fighter ever to enter service, the superb twin-engine DeHavilland Hornet. A consummate fighter pilot and tactician, he was posted to the United States in 1948 to fly the F–86 with the 4th Fighter-Interceptor Group. He was assigned to the Central Fighter Establishment (CFE) in England in 1950 but then was reassigned to Korea with the 4th to assess lessons learned with the F–86 versus the MiG–15. There he again flew combat, shot down a MiG, and wrote a classified report for the Central Fighter Establishment on the F–86 versus the MiG–15.[20]

Now, for years it was very difficult to get hold of this report, because it was classified and in the records of the Public Record Office outside London. I managed to find one, and we're revealing it to you here today. It's a handout that's contained in a computer game called *MiG Alley!*[21] The producers never sent him a copy of it, so, Paddy, we're going to rectify that today. Paddy went on to a very distinguished career in the Royal Air Force before his retirement in 1977. He served as air attaché for the British embassy here in Washington and as commander of No. 11 Group, Royal Air Force Strike Command, the successor to Fighter Command in World War II, responsible for the air defense of Great Britain. So Paddy, the floor is yours.

AIR VICE MARSHAL HARBISON: First, it's a great privilege to be invited here to join this panel of my peers and to talk about the air war in Korea. As you know, the United Kingdom was heavily involved in the Korean War, but more so by our Army, the Royal Marines, and the Royal Navy, than the Royal Air Force. The RAF as such was really out of the fighting over the Yalu, although we provided two Short Sunderland flying boats squadrons to the theater, and, of course, our RAF Transport Command logistically supported our troops in Korea.

However, interest within the Royal Air Force was intense on how the air war in Korea was going and how we were doing in the fighting over the Yalu.[22] In 1951, as Dick said, I was on the staff of the Central Fighter Establishment at West Raynham. In those days, the CFE was the center of all fighter excellence in the RAF and responsible for the development of tactics. CFE people were eager to get someone to Korea to observe the air war. After some persuasion, the U.S. Air Force agreed to accept a team of four people from CFE to go to Korea to observe this war. I was commanding the All-Weather Development Squadron at the time, and the commandant of CFE came around, seeking three volunteers. After he got the volunteers, I said, "What about the fourth?" And he said, "Oh, well, Paddy, *you're* the fourth!" (The reason being was that I had been an exchange pilot at Riverside, California, with the 1st Fighter Group for over two years and was fairly experienced on the F–86. In fact, we were the first group to get the F–86. I made my first flight in the airplane in February 1949, which is early on).[23]

Silver Wings Golden Valor: The USAF Remembers Korea

Anyway, CFE selected the four-man team. A very experienced World War II ace, Wg Cdr John Baldwin, led us. I was the squadron leader, and we had two flight lieutenants.[24] We duly arrived in theater, where we ran into a bureaucratic obstacle straightaway: the medical staff wouldn't accept the fact that we had received all the necessary inoculations, because they were recorded on the wrong form. Accordingly, we had to have them all over again!

Two of us were assigned to the 4th Group at Kimpo, myself and a chap called Brian Spragg. Wing Commander Baldwin and Flight Lieutenant Knight went to Suwon and the 51st Fighter Group under Col. Frances S. "Gabby" Gabreski. My wing commander was Col. Harrison R. Thyng. Our arrival at Kimpo was really very sad, for the flags were flying at half-mast because Maj. George A. Davis, Jr., the then-leading fighter pilot at the time and later a posthumous recipient of the Medal of Honor, had just been shot down. George was an old friend of mine, for we served together at March AFB for a year, and I knew him very well indeed.

Mike DeArmond mentioned the unit that he went through and a little bit of the flying training experience of fighter pilots; I thought it was fascinating. The 4th had established a program called Clobber College, where you flew training sorties accompanied by an experienced instructor. I must say that I thought I was experienced on the F–86—and indeed I was—but they really flew the airplane to its limits, exploring corners of the envelope that I hadn't seen. After being cleared at Clobber College, we started flying missions. I was then able to start to fulfill my role, which was to observe the operations from the cockpit of an F–86, arguably the "best seat in the house."

During my time in Korea, we had difficulty enticing the MiGs to engage. It was very frustrating to fly to the Yalu, some two hundred thirty miles north, see these enormous formations tracking back and forward in contrails above us, and not being able to engage them. They indeed had the initiative, and, when they decided to engage, they came down to attack us in numbers. Once they did that, we could mix it with them, but, if they wanted to, they could stay out of trouble. It was a very long haul up to the Yalu, and at that time we had no ground control radar support of the sort that was furnished by Dentist, a radar station on Cho-do, an island in the Yellow Sea, later in the war. We had Y-Service information before takeoff; for example, people would say MiGs were reported in the Antung[25] area or in the Suiho area, "Heads up!," et cetera, and other aircraft who could sight them visually coming across would track them and pass the information over the air. But the main warning for us was the Mark I eyeball, suitably bloodshot.

I was very impressed by the very intelligent use of the contrails.[26] Each morning, both Sabre wings did a weather record to check the base of the clouds to see if the fighter-bombers could work below it. They also had to check the contrail level, noting where it started, because contrails were used tactically. You could fly just below the contrail, watching the MiGs. It was a very useful thing to do. The MiGs had all the advantages. They had a safe haven at Antung, the complex of several airfields just north of the Yalu, in Manchuria. You could do a count in the

Air Dominance: The Essential Achievement

morning: something approaching four hundred airplanes lined up, quite safe (thanks to the restrictive rules of engagement) from our bombers. You're well aware, I suppose, of the parameters under which the F–86s operated, and we were very much inferior numerically.

How then was superiority gained? Well, first of all, by the caliber, the determination, and the tenacity of the 4th and 51st Wing pilots, and, conversely, by the timidity of the MiG pilots who were not very aggressive. Had they been more aggressive, things could have been very different. Not all of them were timid, and, when you met an aggressive MiG pilot, he could be very good indeed, and it would be a mistake to hold them all in contempt. I was very nearly shot down once, but I got away with it. I was pursued from some thirty-five thousand feet down to the deck level with a MiG on my tail firing all the way, and the only time he left was when he had run out of ammunition, but he couldn't pull enough g^{27} to get deflection enough to hit.

When you think of it, one only needs to reverse the scenario to appreciate the difference in ground rules. Had F–86s been able to operate from a place such as Antung, with the straight ground-controlled intercept (GCI) control, radar control, operating over friendly territory, and have the MiGs operating out of Kimpo as we were, the loss rate of the MiGs would have been absolutely astronomical. As we now know, Russian and Chinese pilots were the main opposition, and they were operating, of course, to their own agenda. They didn't wish to reveal their identity, and this to some degree hamstrung them.

Conditions at Kimpo Air Base were very, very crowded. During my time there, we were limited to using only half the runway. The other half was under repair, and, when you think of seventy-five airplanes lined up, taking off and landing regularly, aircraft coming back short of fuel, people crash-landing because they had been hit, fighter-bombers coming in, it really was amazing. All of the peacetime regulations that one learns to prevent accidents went by the board, and we just had to accept the risk.

Korea being the first jet war, and thus highly publicized, pilots such as Hal Fischer became household names. But it wasn't a young man's war; rather, most of the people were World War II veterans. Young pilots who came along—like Mike DeArmond, who said he arrived with no experience—were definitely experiencing "on-the-job training." Very soon they caught the fever. The competition was fierce to get on a mission. The principal fighting unit, as Earl Brown said, was a two-ship element, and thus a good wingman was worth his weight in gold. I was particularly fortunate in getting one of the very best with Mike DeArmond. During a BBC interview, he told the interviewer that his contribution to Anglo-American solidarity was to permit himself to be shot down instead of me. This went down very well in the United Kingdom, I suppose, though I stress that I was not his leader on his last mission!

I must pay tribute to the maintenance and servicing personnel and the individual crew chiefs who serviced our airplanes at Kimpo. They operated under the very worst circumstances, in the open, and they worked minor miracles to keep the aircraft in the air. In fact, they would plead with you, "Don't write the airplane up. I'll have it ready in the morning for you." And indeed they did.

Unfortunately, the senior RAF officer, Wing Commander Baldwin, perished on his thirteenth mission, a weather reconnaissance sortie. He was last seen upside-down at seven thousand feet in clouds where the hills were up to five thousand feet. We never found his wreckage. For some time, it was suspected he might have been a prisoner, but I think now that has been ruled out. So I was left at very short notice to write this great enormous report that Dick talks about on the F–86 versus the MiG–15, except that no one had told me what it was they wanted me to write about! This was a real blow, for up to then, I had been enjoying myself.

I look back on my time with the 4th Group and indeed with the 1st Fighter Group before that at March with tremendous nostalgia, particularly for the 355th Squadron. Those people I flew with in both groups were above the average. The Royal Air Force learned about air superiority the hard way and had to fight for it over the Channel in southern England in 1940. Think of the consequences had the battles over MiG Alley a decade later gone the other way and had we not prevailed. Thank you very much.

DR. HALLION: Thanks very much, Paddy, for that rundown. At this point, we're going to engage in a panel discussion up here among the presenters that we've had this morning. I think they've raised a number of issues that are quite interesting. The question I'd like to start with, because various people have mentioned it, is the issue of the appropriateness of training you had before you all found yourselves in Korea. Paddy Harbison touched on an aspect of this that was very, very important, the in-theater training operation called Clobber College. But I'd like to go beyond this to your reflections on other training you might have had—for example, those of you who went through Williams AFB or Nellis AFB before heading to Korea. What sort of introduction did you have to combat in terms of the appropriateness of training and training weaknesses? What lessons do you think are here?

MAJOR GENERAL BRASWELL: Well, I'll be glad to start. In my own experience, when I went to Korea, I had no formal training outside of the training we got in our fighter squadron. I'm talking about combat training, because I went directly from flying school to a fighter wing in Massachusetts, and we did a little air-to-air gunnery there. We didn't have an adequate air-to-ground gunnery range. We didn't really get much combat training. What we did get was sort of self-generated, and one of the things that we tried to do—that I tried to do while I was there—was try to engage some Navy or Marine Corps units that were in that area. Occasionally, we got a chance to have just simply air combat training, which was very rare, but there was no real organized program to do anything like that. Our training was very rudimentary and very poor, to be frank about it. We went into Korea, and we got a little training there in the F–84, and I did my first dive-bombing in Japan. Nevertheless, we didn't have good training; it was only after the war

Air Dominance: The Essential Achievement

started that we began running these people through the training schools at Nellis and at Luke Air Force Base to get gunnery, bombing, and other training to prepare them for combat. Our combat training has certainly evolved and has much improved since then. But it was very inadequate in those days.

BRIGADIER GENERAL DeARMOND: I'd like to reinforce what General Braswell just said. When we went through Nellis, I was Class 51–E. We were supposed to get eighty or ninety hours in the F–80. I think I got about forty-five or fifty because of the in-commission rate. The aircraft had very, very poor maintenance at the time. We did get on the range, but it was a formal bombing range, nothing like the dynamic Red Flag operations they have now. Another factor was the general management perspective toward loss of pilots there. I believe the year I went through, Luke lost about fifty pilots, Nellis lost about forty-five or fifty, and nobody gave a damn. The attitude was sort of, "That's the way you weed out the weak pilots." I know one instructor who took two pilots through a thunderstorm at night to see if they could hang on his wing, and both of them wound up dead. Compare that to what I went through at Luke over a decade later in the F–100s for Vietnam. Luke had lost three pilots all year, and two of them were German pilots going through on the F–104. So there was a maturing, a growing of management philosophy in preparation for the Vietnam War compared to the "anything goes" attitude at the time of Korea. Then you could bounce a guy until he turned final in the traffic pattern, and people were going down in midair collisions, and the discipline was really very poor.

LIEUTENANT GENERAL BROWN: I went to Nellis for combat training in 1951, and what General DeArmond said is true. We graduated in December, in propeller-driven F–51 Mustangs. In January, the following year, we went to Williams Air Force Base for jet transition into the T–33 and the F–80.[28] Then my whole class returned to Nellis, where we all flew the F–80. We flew formation training, including close formation, spread formation, and fluid-four combat formation. We dropped weapons, all the weapons the F–80 could drop, and then, after about halfway through, by which time we had thirty or forty hours, the class was split. Half the class continued in the F–80, and I was in the group that went to the F–86. I got forty hours of F–86 training, continuing then with formation flying every day, close formation, fluid four, et cetera, but the concentration then was on air-to-air gunnery. We fired on a rag [on a towed target], and we fired our guns at the ground again. We fought simulated combat, but always F–86s against F–86s. The Air Force has learned that this is not really the best way to do it. Our class, 51–H, had gone through flying school at Craig Air Force Base, Alabama, without losing any students to accidents. Our first loss was at Nellis. The feeling among the pilots then was, if you could make it through Nellis, combat would be a piece of cake. Just as General DeArmond said, the rule was "Devil take the hindmost," and the tradition was "Every man a tiger." Competition was vigorously encouraged. There was a saying among the guys in the bar that "A fighter pilot has to beat somebody every day, and, if you can't beat an enemy, you might as well beat a friend." So there was definitely an encouragement to be aggressive, encouragement to be competitive, but that climate made training very dangerous.

After I got to the 4th Wing, with my class, we were all young fellows. We graduated with our wings in December 1951, and, in May 1952, we're at combat, and we went through Clobber College. There were ten missions. I was fortunate because one of my instructors in Clobber College was 1st Lt. Charles G. "Chick" Cleveland, who later retired as a lieutenant general commanding the Air University at Maxwell Air Force Base. We called Chick Cleveland the "Ivory Ace": 99.99 percent pure. He had four kills, four probables, and four damaged. I understand recently that the American Fighter Aces Association has awarded him his honorary ace.

One final comment, on aces. What's so big about aces? We have an ace sitting here with ten kills, Hal Fischer. Here are some statistics. I estimate that about five hundred pilots flew Sabres in Korea. With 792 MiGs destroyed, 78 Sabres lost, a kill ratio of ten to one results. Of the 792 MiGs that were confirmed destroyed, the thirty-nine MiG-killing aces shot down 305 of them. Less than 8 percent of the pilots shot down 38 percent of the aircraft destroyed.

So it's the same thing you see in any great physical activity. One Michael Jordan is worth a whole lot of ordinary basketball players. One ace is worth a whole lot of journeyman fighter pilots. There's something distinctly different about those individuals who first can see the airplane before anyone else can, but the overwhelmingly significant difference is that they want to get into the fight. They fly to the sound of the guns. There are guys who pick up weapons and go to war and never shoot them, and, if they shoot them, they never hit anything. Then there are guys who are just aching to get in a fight. Whenever there's a fight, that's where they want to be. They have a great sense of situational awareness. They can keep track of diverse things happening around them without any argument. They can fly the airplane to the very limits of the flying envelope, as slow as the airplane can possibly go, as fast as the airplane can possibly go, and turn as hard as the airplane can possibly turn.

I know all these things, because as a wingman, I flew with three of the leading aces. I flew with Jim Jabara,[29] and I flew with Pete Fernandez.[30] (Joe McConnell[31] was the number one Korean War ace, then Jim Jabara, and then Pete Fernandez.) I flew with "Boots" Blesse,[32] who had ten kills, and I watched these fellows as young lieutenants observe everyone around them to try to figure out "What is it that they're doing that I can't do?" And those perceptions I just enumerated were my conclusions. So we're sitting in the company of the Air Force equivalent of Michael Jordan when we're sitting here with Hal Fischer.

DR. HALLION: With that in mind, Hal, would you like to comment yourself on training because, when you were over there, going from the air-to-mud side of things, you certainly became very dominant air-to-air.

COLONEL FISCHER: General Brown, thank you very much for that compliment. I wish I could have recorded it. The desire to be a fighter pilot is inherent.

Air Dominance: The Essential Achievement

One of the greatest aces was Erich Hartmann, the "blond knight of Germany," and he said, "Perhaps the greatest fighter pilot in the world was killed on his first mission."[33] So there are fighter pilots right in this room who could have been or maybe will be aces.

My training was going through Nellis in F–80s. I didn't want them! I volunteered for F–51s because I thought that it was the last of the true fighters, but they just changed. They dropped the –51s, and then I was flying this airplane that scared me. It ran out of fuel, went too fast. I got used to it when I went into combat, flying the F–80. The F–80 was a good airplane, but they did a lot of things to it. They wanted to have it be, or replace, the F–51, and so this is what I ended up with, in this part of the training that we had to go through. The F–80s would be loaded down with a huge volume of fuel, over 930 gallons. It didn't mean they could carry that much, they were never designed for it, but they had tanks that were specially designed, and, when you flew formation with those big tanks,[34] the wings would flex up and down. We had six .50-cal machine guns, could carry five-hundred or one-thousand-pound bombs, rockets, or napalm. Then they would take off and fly from 200 to 250 miles and have about ten minutes in the target area. This was all training, how to fly at that time. We could get up to twenty-three to twenty-four thousand feet. Coming back, we could ease up to thirty to thirty-four thousand. This was the training that I had when I did some tap-dancing and got myself assigned back to FEAF [Far East Air Forces] combat crew assignments. There I met some of the aces coming through and managed to get myself assigned back to the 51st—because the 4th was full of prima donnas!

And I wasn't one of the chosen few. I think I had six hours and forty-five minutes in the F–86 before I went on my first combat mission. The thing that really scared me was when I turned final, and I couldn't see the wing straight out there, because it was swept back, and I lost my reference. As far as training is concerned, I was trained not by the Air Force but by a Canadian, Doug Lindsay. On about my third combat mission, he attacked a MiG but didn't fire. I said, "You're clear, clear." And then he fired nine rounds and shot that MiG down. Then we went back, and, as we landed, I didn't have enough fuel to get to the revetment. I didn't worry about anything after that!

Now there's another thing about flying. In a different frame of mind, it's something like knowing without knowing, and doing without doing. When you're in a combat situation, you'll do things you never even thought you would do, and you'll know something: you'll know somebody's at your six o'clock, and you will really be afraid, but you won't see them. So part of that is training; I can't tell you how to do it. The last thing I'd like to say is from Gen. Adolf Galland: "We are *Jagdfliegers*. We are hunters and not killers. Be very kind to your enemy because he may be your friend tomorrow."[35]

DR. HALLION: Hal, thanks for those comments. You've raised an issue other people have as well, and that is there were some people flying with you folks that were already pretty legendary in the fighter business, really great leaders. You think of Harry Thyng, Vermont Garrison, Royal Baker, Francis Gabreski, and Bud Mahurin.[36] I gather these individuals did something that really placed them in the top ranks of the "fighter-teacher"—they seem to have been far less concerned about their own high scores than they were about bringing new guys along and making certain that the unit as a whole functioned well. Is that perception correct? Do you have anything to add on that, any of you?

COLONEL FISCHER: That is correct. One of the finest leaders happened to be Col. Jimmy K. Johnson. He started out in Panama, went to Europe in World War II, and then got himself assigned as the wing commander of the 4th. He probably was one of the greatest wing commanders—besides Gabreski, of course—and then there are squadron leaders like Mahurin and, of course, there's George Davis.[37]

DR. HALLION: Do any of you have any recollections or thoughts you'd like to offer on the impacts by the leaders? Yes, General DeArmond?

BRIGADIER GENERAL DeARMOND: Yes, I would like to address the fact that, although they were very interested in the overall efficiencies of their wings, at the time there was a lot of political pressure because of people going across the Yalu River and shooting down MiGs. I'm talking about Harry Thyng in particular, who was a fine officer. I was at a briefing, and we were going to be in a four-ship flight with Paddy Harbison (and I was on Paddy's wing), and Thyng said, "I'll court martial the next son-of-a-bitch who goes across the Yalu River after a MiG." So we take off, we go up, he sucks it up at Sinuiju at forty-eight thousand feet with the throttle back as far as he can get it, and we hang there and the rest of the 4th goes home. Two MiGs take off from Antung and head for Mukden,[38] which is up in Manchuria. He looks at those, and it's like a bird dog on a prey. Down we go! We catch those MiGs on the outside of Mukden, and he shoots them both down. We head on back, come in landing (as Colonel Fischer said) on fumes, get out of the cockpit, and I'm a second lieutenant and I think he thinks the others were more reliable. So Thyng asks, "Lieutenant, where did I shoot down those two MiGs?" I said, "Sir, I was terribly confused. I think you shot them down in the mouth of the Yalu." He said, "You've got a *bright* future, son!"

DR. HALLION: Now Paddy Harbison touched on a number of issues, and I think Paddy wants to comment on this one as well. Paddy, your thoughts?

AIR VICE MARSHAL HARBISON: I might add that our normal mission was one hour thirty minutes, one hour forty, but that mission that Mike talked about with Colonel Thyng was two hours, and we were *really* short of fuel, I'll tell you! As far as training is concerned, and experience, my view—and I reported this to the RAF—is that a high proportion of the pilots when I was there in early '52, were World War II pilots. The average age was somewhere around twenty-eight to thirty, and people like Mike, second lieutenants in those days, were "on the job training," and they learned the hard way, and they learned very quickly. But my recommendation was that any future Royal Air Force person going to Korea ought

Air Dominance: The Essential Achievement

not to go there directly but ought to go through Nellis and get some grounding before they did. And that, in fact, happened from then on.

DR. HALLION: Paddy, you touched on the caliber of the opposition. We know now what was long suspected at the time, and that was that there was a very heavy Soviet involvement in the air war right from the very beginning.[39] You had MiG regiments going down to Manchuria and flying combat over North Korea. At the time, how did all of you assess the quality of the opposition? Were there times where you could tell when more experienced units had been moved into place as opposed to less experienced ones? Did you have a feeling when you were fighting Soviet pilots who might be World War II vets as opposed to Chinese pilots who were just getting into the airplane and that sort of thing?

AIR VICE MARSHAL HARBISON: Yes, occasionally you could be unfortunate enough to meet what was known as a honcho, and that was a probably very good Russian MiG pilot. As I said, the good ones were quite good. The average ones were quite mediocre, but they had their own agenda, and, had all MiG pilots been as aggressive as our people in the 51st and the 4th, I think the result might have been a little different. We might have had a problem that might have entailed us, sacrosanct or not, taking out the MiGs on our bases at Antung on the complex there. They had all the advantages and we didn't.

MAJOR GENERAL BRASWELL: You never really knew whether you were up against a sharp guy or not until you actually engaged him, and I think most of their pilots were mediocre—but there were some sharp people. One comment I would make about the Soviet training and Soviet pilot is that we didn't know whether we were flying against Chinese, Soviet, or North Koreans. We had no idea at the time who we were engaging, but we now know that many of them were Soviets. The Soviet air force for many years, and maybe the Russian air force today, has had a history of not giving their pilots much authority but of trying to control them basically from the ground. There was sort of a fetish about not allowing individual pilots or flight leaders to have a great deal of freedom, and I think that worked to their disadvantage. I'm certain it did in the Korean War as well as in their later years.[40]

DR. HALLION: What was your feeling from your perspective in your units at the time, all of you, about command and control? Did you think we had very effective command and control procedures for conducting the superiority air war over the North? Did you see any deficiencies? What would be your thoughts on that?

AIR VICE MARSHAL HARBISON: Well, I've addressed this. I don't think we had *any* command and control. It was at a local level at Kimpo itself. The squadron brief would be very good, but, as I said, in our time, we had no radar information. We had some Y-Service information and intelligence, that "there's a MiG airborne in such-and-such an area," and we were told, perhaps, that they're coming over and at what altitude, but we had no discrete control whatsoever. And as I said, the best early warning was the Mark I eyeball target acquisition system.

Silver Wings Golden Valor: The USAF Remembers Korea

MAJOR GENERAL BRASWELL: He's right about that. We had very little effective assistance from the ground in conducting the air warfare, and, of course, we had no such thing as AWACS in those days. So, as far as the war against the MiGs was concerned, it was an air war that was being planned and fought at the squadron level. And, by the way, flights of four were the norm. In World War II, it was very common to have fighter sweeps with an entire squadron taking off and flying in formation until they became engaged. In the Korean War, we learned that that was very inefficient, and a flight of four was really the largest unit that you really wanted to employ. So we flew entirely in flights of four, and very rarely flew in squadrons of eight except for the fighter-bombers, which is a different story.

DR. HALLION: Earl, did you have a comment on that?

LIEUTENANT GENERAL BROWN: Yes. In a typical mission, you took off and flew thirty minutes to get there. You stayed in the area for thirty minutes, and, if you got in a fight, then you would fight. And then you took thirty minutes to come home, so one-and-a-half hours constituted a typical mission. The two-hour mission that Mike and Paddy mentioned is extraordinary. One of the biggest differences I noticed in my career in the fighter game was when we got air refueling.[41] Now, suddenly, the constant concern about running out of fuel was lessened. But, in Korea, once the mission was launched, command and control then went right to the flight commander, because the briefing had been held, and the wing commander had had his say. As General Braswell mentioned, we would launch the flights with some degree of separation between them so that we could keep airplanes in the area over an extended period in case the MiGs came down.

My second point, Dick, is from the conference we attended in Chicago a little over a year ago.[42] Listening to forty scholars, whose main area of study is the Korean War, I was astounded to hear a professor say that frontline Soviet air force pilots flew the majority of the MiGs we flew against. The Soviets rotated entire units from the Eastern bloc countries, from bases in the Soviet Union, rotated them through Korea, and this explained this rise and fall we saw in the number of sorties.[43] It would go up as a new unit became more proficient. Then it would go down as they rotated home and a new unit came in. It also explained this rise and fall in aggressiveness. Once they had completed initial training, they became more aggressive. Then they would rotate and go home, and a new unit would come in. The new pilots would be very tentative, and they would look at us from across the river and then gradually get more and more aggressive. There were relatively few Chinese flying the MiGs, and almost *no* North Koreans.[44] I was absolutely astounded to learn that.

DR. HALLION: One of the interesting things, Earl, that I picked up there (and you'll recall it) was when we had a speaker who detailed Soviet messages down to their forces in Manchuria.[45] They were having a very difficult time bringing the Chinese up to speed in the MiG–15, no end was in sight, and consequently Stalin sent a very curt message to the commander of Soviet training in

Air Dominance: The Essential Achievement

Manchuria that read, in effect, "What are you trying to do? Turn these people into flying professors?"[46] General DeArmond, do you have a comment?

BRIGADIER GENERAL DeARMOND: Basically one of the problems with positive radar control over there was the lack of identification of friend or foe. You get into combat, and, if you're looking into the sun or something, the MiG and the F–86 look quite similar, and friendly fire was not an unusual circumstance. The closest I've ever been to being killed and the only time I've heard bullets go by the canopy—I had the headset and the whole thing on, and he just came by overhead and broke hard—and nothing against Hal Fischer, but it was four guys from the 51st who almost shot me down.

COLONEL FISCHER: Well, there's no excuse for one F–86 pilot mistaking an F–86 for a MiG. I was initially with the 49th Wing flying F–84s, and some of the pilots there were not familiar with the F–86. We were on one of my earlier missions, and MiGs were reported to be in the area; we hadn't seen any yet. Suddenly, an F–86 zoomed by us and pulled up. My own leader pulled his nose up and began shooting at him. I radioed, "No, no, no, that's an F–86!" But it was not uncommon for the F–84 pilots to mistake an F–86 for a MiG.

LIEUTENANT GENERAL BROWN: I had a flight commander in addition to General Braswell named Tom Garvin. Tom was a magnificent cartoonist and artist, and he looked at the MiG, and he looked at the Sabre, and he saw the Sabre as an arrow and the MiG as a boomerang. So, in our flight room in the old Korean hutch we lived in, he painted on the wall various views of both aircraft, and he emphasized this arrow shape on the Sabre and the boomerang shape of the MiG. Now both airplanes have the same degree of wing sweep, thirty-five degrees. This is what we both got from the German wind tunnel research data. But, in the way the airplane looked from afar, this is one of the outstanding differences. He also emphasized the high horizontal tail on the MiG and the way the tail on the Sabre sat lower to the fuselage. And this was very useful to the young jocks looking at airplanes and trying to determine whether they were MiGs or whether they were Sabres.

DR. HALLION: One point several of you have mentioned is the constraints that were imposed by the nature of the air war. You were flying in an area where the enemy could operate aircraft, from a sanctuary against you, and could pick the time, place, and circumstances of the encounter, to a very large degree. You've mentioned the difficulties this imposed. Adding to that, of course, were the problems that you touched on, such as the challenge to get back without running out of fuel. There was controversy at the time among some of the pilots on the effectiveness of the Sabre's gunsight and of the .50-cal machine gun as an air-to-air weapon—particularly the fact that it simply lacked the punch to kill a MiG rapidly compared to the 20-mm cannon. Would any of you care to comment on that?

AIR VICE MARSHAL HARBISON: Before we get on to that, Dick, I'd like to comment on the aggressiveness of the MiG pilots. Mike and I mentioned earlier that we were both very unfortunate in meeting extremely aggressive MiG pilots. I don't quite know how it happened, but at thirty-five thousand feet a MiG got between Mike and myself and started firing at me. The evasive maneuver that the F–86 used was a steep spiral dive, full bore, pulling as much g as you could. We didn't really have a lot of thrust, and gravity helped you to do that; thus we started off downward. I was pulling the maximum g I could with the stabilizer trim run back. My helmet came down over my eyes, and my mask came off, and the only help I got from Mike was that he kept telling me on the air, "Pull tighter, he's out-sucking you!" That really wasn't much of a help, but Mike was trying to fire at the same MiG, and he couldn't get enough deflection to hit him, either. We descended right down to ground level, and then I think he either fired all his ammunition or gave up on it.

Earlier, I did mention radar was tracking the MiGs. In other words, people would broadcast and say there's a MiG flight, and it's coming south, and it's at such-and-such an altitude. We were trailing quite a large formation, and the bulk of the Sabre group were farther north of us. They started turning south, asking us where the MiGs were, and the Sabres were coming head-on. You could see the contrails, and I appreciated that fact, so I made the following statement, "Please remember that the last two MiGs in this formation were built in the U.S.!"

LIEUTENANT GENERAL BROWN: I have a story about telling MiGs from Sabres. I had flown sixteen or twenty missions and had never seen a MiG. I started in May and June 1952, and they were flying at a lower rate. Finally, one day we did get into the MiGs. We were in a flight of four; I was number four. My element leader was a fellow named Gene Rogge, and we were making our big circle up there. I had been told in Clobber College, "look over your left shoulder until you can see your right wing," "always keep looking to the rear." After sixteen or twenty missions, I discovered that this really was not as important as lowering your seat so you get your legs stretched out, for you needed to really be comfortable while you made these circles in the sky. You had to cinch up your shoulder harness so, in case you bailed out, you wouldn't get hurt. In this position, with my seat lowered and my shoulder harness cinched up, we passed a flight of Sabres, and the element leader said, "There're MiGs over there." I though, this guy is a new guy and he doesn't know what he's talking about. They were Sabres. I could look across and—all of a sudden these Sabres turned toward us, and indeed they *were* MiGs! I got separated from my leader. The MiG moved in at my six o'clock and started firing, and I got a big hole in my right wing. I could look through the hole and see the ground, and I knew that something had gone desperately wrong. This guy was actually trying to kill me. In Clobber College, Boots Blesse had said, "If you ever get locked up where the guy is in your six o'clock and he's pulling lead, and you're both hunched over pulling as hard as you can, the 'last ditch maneuver' is to release the g's, let the airplane go in the *opposite* direction from the turn, turn over, and go into a spiral toward the ground." That's what the air vice-marshal just mentioned. And so I did. At the last minute, just as I released the g's, over my head—over the canopy—came this array of 37-mm and 23-mm bullets. I

Air Dominance: The Essential Achievement

turned away and went to the ground. When we got finally got back to the base—and after the "instructional lecture" that I had gotten from my element leader, from my flight leader, and from the squadron commander!—we looked at the gun camera film from Gene Rogge, who was my element leader. Gene Rogge's gun camera film showed me, showed the MiG shooting at me, and showed the 37mm coming out and plinking on my wing. This happened just as he squeezed the trigger, because then his .50-cal bullets were going out into the MiG, and he shot that MiG down. And the reason I'm here today is because of a fellow named Gene Rogge. But that was the last time I *ever* mistook a Sabre for a MiG! It was the last time I *ever* sat low in the seat with my seat belt cinched up. After that I raised the seat *all* the way to the top. I loosened the parachute harness and the shoulder harness so, indeed, I could look over my left shoulder until I could see my right wingtip. I never lost the leader again.

MAJOR GENERAL BRASWELL: I used to resent wearing a hard-hat helmet because in these small canopies you couldn't turn your head and see as well as you could if you had a leather helmet on as in the old days. I used to wish that I had a leather helmet to wear so that I could see much better.

You wanted us to talk a little bit about .50-cal's and the gunsight issue. The gunsights were not ideal, but they were not bad in the F–86E. We had radar gunsights, and the problem with the gunsight was much less than the problem of making sure you could maneuver to attract the enemy. The .50-cal's certainly were not the best weapons to have. We should have had 20mm, and we should have had them much earlier. Other air forces did. I don't know to this day why the Air Force stuck so long with the .50-cal guns. It was a bad mistake. They should have been put in the original F–86s.[47]

LIEUTENANT GENERAL BROWN: I think after General Braswell had left, we got a test program for Gun Val. You were gone when Gun Val happened.[48] Lieutenant Colonel Jones[49] came over, and we had Sabres that mounted four 20mm's on each side. And they got to go on the best missions, most likely kill MiGs. We discovered a problem with the 20-mm guns that we had, and that was when you fired 20mm's, the Sabre lost air speed. So you could fire the guns, the .50-cal's, and maintain air speed. If you fired the 20mm's, it slowed you down. Further, for some reason, the smoke from those 20mm's would go in the intake, and you'd have compressor stalls, and occasionally, every now and then, an airplane would flame out. So we had to go to a different kind of 20mm for the F–86H.

At Nellis, we practiced with a radar gunsight. They put a reflector on the rag, and you could lock onto the rag, and you had to do something to set the wing span of the target. At Nellis, the in-commission rate was very poor, and, when we got to Korea, it was dismal on the F–86A. And the improved radar ranging system that came with the E model was not much better. It was very difficult to maintain. I was the second lieutenant film assessor, and I talked to almost every ace. I would spend hours in intelligence looking at the film and assessing kills, damages, and probables. On almost every occasion that I looked at an ace's film, the wings of the MiG would be out the side of the picture, he was so close. Hal, you know more about shooting them down—did you make many long-range shots?

COLONEL FISCHER: Only if I had to, sir. If they wouldn't come to me, I'd have to chase them.

LIEUTENANT GENERAL BROWN: Most of the shots were made from very close range. So the guys just literally did without the gunsight, and I read an account from Ralph Parr[50] in which he actually shot an airplane down in a Sabre that had no gunsight at all!

AIR VICE MARSHAL HARBISON: The A–1CM was the radar gunsight that we used, and, in fact, the sight was very good if you could keep it serviceable.[51] Our problem was maintaining it, and the vibration. We did a test gun firing every flight. Once you crossed the bomb line, you did a quick burst, and the vibration itself was enough to send it up. When it *was* working, it was quite good, and, in fact, in climbing through the clouds, you could put the radar on the formation ahead of you to maintain your spacing on the climb out. It was quite useful. Some of the airplanes had the Mark 18 gunsight that was not radar ranging, and, apart from having lower range, it was quite good.

DR. HALLION: Thank you, Paddy. At this point, I think we'll go into our question-and-answer session. I think we've had a very fine panel here this morning. After every war the United States has fought and, indeed, after every air war in this last century, we've seen people claim that each was the last great fighter war. They've argued that, in the future, we'll never have a need to go air-to-air or beak-to-beak with somebody, and, of course, that's probably the most pernicious myth of air power in the twentieth century.

Every single war that we've found ourselves in, we've needed to exert control of the air, particularly air dominance. We learned that to our sorrow in Vietnam a little over a decade after the Korean War. Of course, it was the Vietnam experience that completely reshaped the way that the United States across all its services approached the issue of control of the air and the development of high-technology-optimized fighter aircraft. We saw that pay off in the Gulf War. We've seen it over the Balkans more recently. Basically, since the time of the development of the F–15 and F–16, we've enjoyed an unprecedented period of air dominance for the United States. That's why, of course, we're trying to press ahead with the F–22 to ensure we have that same level of air dominance for the conflicts of the twenty-first century. The F–86 represented as great a technological advantage over the F–80 and other early jet aircraft as the F–15 represented over the F–4 generation and as the F–22 represents over the F–15 today. This is something we all need to keep in mind.

I'd like to thank our panelists for taking the time and effort to come here and be with us today. Next, we turn to you, the audience. I know many of you have expressed interest in questioning them on some of the things that you've heard today.

Air Dominance: The Essential Achievement

AUDIENCE MEMBER: I've read some of the accounts of the Soviet side of the story. My question very simply for you is the Soviets' claim that U.S. forces violated the Yalu River line quite frequently and, in fact, achieved most of their MIG kills while their opponents were in their traffic pattern or basically over their bases when they were low and slow. What do you have to say to that?

LIEUTENANT GENERAL BROWN: I'm shocked! I'm shocked! I'm *shocked* that they would say a thing like that![52] [Laughter].

MAJOR GENERAL BRASWELL: A lot of kills did occur beyond the Yalu River.[53] How many, I have no idea, but a lot of them did, but not too many in the traffic pattern, though.

BRIGADIER GENERAL DeARMOND: I'll take one exception to that. I have one damaged in the traffic pattern at Antung when he pitched.[54]

MAJOR GENERAL BRASWELL: I said not *too* many!

BRIGADIER GENERAL DeARMOND: But also there was a very fine pilot—Class of '49 at West Point—D. D. Overton, who found out apparently where their high cone was over across the river and how they were using it. D. D. would sit up over there until they started down or something. But he got in serious difficulties over that.[55]

MAJOR GENERAL BRASWELL: Because he came back and told exactly where he was!

AIR VICE MARSHAL HARBISON: I think the theory of hot pursuit was used. If you were close, you could go across by accident.

DR. HALLION: I have to confess I have relatively little sympathy for the Soviets on this issue. They proved themselves far more expert at shooting down unarmed transports and aircraft over national waters in times of peace. Next question, from Col. Sam Dickens.

COLONEL DICKENS: One of my friends with whom I went through pilot training in Class 52–E was Dick Moroney. He flew wing on Fernandez for some time and thought the world of Fernandez, for he really respected the wingman role. Sometimes Fernandez gave up opportunities to get kills because his wingman was calling "break!", a MiG was about to shoot Moroney down, and Fernandez would pass up a kill lest he endanger his wingman. Then another friend of mine from the same pilot training class, Richard Frailey,[56] was shot down by one of our own—in fact one of our biggest—aces: Jim Jabara. What was memorable about Frailey when he was shot down was that, as he descended, he was asking what to do about a 35-mm camera that he recently had bought in Japan! But is there any comment about the leader and the consideration of the wingman?

COLONEL FISCHER: I'd like to amplify on Jabara shooting down his wingman.[57] Jimmy K. Johnson, commander of the 4th Fighter-Interceptor Wing, had requested Jabara, and Jabara had married Jimmy K.'s secretary. Well, when Jabara got back, he went to Jimmy K. He was crying—which is good—and he said he had shot down his wingman. Jimmy K. had already gotten information from Cho-do that his wingman was okay. I don't know the details of how he got in front of Jabara's guns, but I know those other details.

LIEUTENANT GENERAL BROWN: That's the ultimate case of mistaken identity! I was there when it happened. I knew Dick Frailey, and, of course, Jabara was absolutely crushed, and the story about Frailey's camera is absolutely true. The guy [Jabara] is asking him if he's going to bail out over near Cho-do, when he's going to get out. And he [Frailey] was worried about this brand-new camera that he just bought. His airplane was still going. I can only say that we have friendly fire in ground units, and this was an unfortunate case of friendly fire. And it's another indication of how aggressively Jim Jabara would press the battle. Jabara was the *ultimate* warrior when it came to going to the sound of the guns without orders. He would go wherever the guns where sounding, looking for some; if you're with him in a bar fight, he's just looking for a guy to punch—but if you're not careful, he might, in his excitement, punch *you*.

DR. HALLION: Other questions?

BRIGADIER GENERAL DeARMOND: If I may make a comment in regard to aggressiveness on the part of the flight leads, it was somewhat of a race. William "Skosh" Littlefield is one of the fine lieutenants I shipped into the 4th with, and he was on George Davis's wing when Davis jumped a massive number of MiGs.[58] He said he had never seen so many MiGs in his life. That was the mission on which Davis got shot down.[59] Second item, as far as flight leads shooting down their wingmen, I think of equal concern to wingmen is the number of wingmen that a flight lead has lost to *enemy* fire. I think I was the *fourth* wingman to have been lost off the individual that I was flying with.

DR. HALLION: Thanks, General DeArmond. Hal?

COLONEL FISCHER: The individual who has credit for Davis is Mikhail Averin. A Soviet pilot, then-Captain Leonid Savichen, wrote later "Coming to their aid, I got on the tail of a turning Sabre and from 800 meters began to fire on the leading Sabre. Suddenly I had spent cartridges dropping near me from shells from above. I looked up and saw Mikhail Averin was firing on a Sabre. His fire was more accurate, and from the rudder of the Sabre, parts came off and the aircraft dove into the ground, and the wingman withdrew. In two days, the confirmation about the death of the ace George Davis and his being shot down was acknowledged. All our aircraft returned to the base at Antung."[60]

DR. HALLION: Other comments or questions? Yes, General Clark?[61]

LIEUTENANT GENERAL CLARK: With total respect to the current crew here talking about their experiences, I think one of the things they've missed is the fact that some of these people and others became the educators of the Air Force in a brand-new type of aerial war. I've talked about Boots Blesse, for example. He came back having had significant experience in Korea, both in learning how to shoot down airplanes and being successful at it, but he also put his brain in gear, as you folks have, and decided that the next war wasn't going to be the same. People were going to understand the performance of airplanes better and know how to get

Air Dominance: The Essential Achievement

on that next MiG's tail. He and a young officer, John Boyd,[62] literally built the next generation of aircraft. The contractors who were building airplanes and trying to design better airframes took the brain power of what Boots had put together and what John Boyd had done by going to school. Boyd learned to be an engineer after he had been a fighter pilot, and he developed some of those awful tech orders that were produced afterward that told you how to fly an airplane to its maximum performance. I think—again with due respect to the airplanes that were shot down—the greatest thing that came out of this war was new education and new educators who developed the new combat airplanes and new combat tactics that ultimately became standard in the United States Air Force.

DR. HALLION: To elaborate on that comment, certainly one of Boots Blesse's greatest contributions was when he distilled the lessons of Korea into a widely distributed publication entitled "No Guts No Glory."[63] And that particular document was, if you will, "rediscovered" at the time of the Vietnam War. It formed the basis for a lot of work by a number of people that reshaped fighter training, which had lagged in the intervening years. One of those that I think deserves a great deal of respect and the salute of us all here today is the late Moody Suter.[64] I think there's a little bit of every MiG kill since the creation of the F–15 and F–16 embodied in Moody Suter's work.

MAJOR GENERAL BRASWELL: I'd like to second what General Clark just said, that there was a great deal of learning. Out of World War II, we had a bunch of very effective fighter pilots who were experienced, like J. C. Meyer,[65] and so forth, but it was mostly individual learning, and there was not a scientific approach to trying to translate that into lessons for every fighter pilot. The first person who did that, in fact, was Boots with his paper, "No Guts No Glory." So we did learn from that, and we applied lessons and we learned to take a scientific approach to the issue of how to engage effectively in air-to-air engagements.

But I would like to caution everybody to . . . [remember] now that we are almost light-years ahead away from the type of weapons and the type of aircraft that we were using in Korea. We have today aircraft like the F–15 and F–16, beyond-visual-range missiles. You cannot see whom you're shooting at. So you have to have some way of identifying him at a distance. The dogfight is still with us, but it's far less important as we learned in the Gulf War than the ability to catch the enemy before he catches you, and to catch him out of his range but still in your range, and to fire your missiles at him. Missiles are the weapon of choice now, not guns, even though there is still a role for the guns on fighter aircraft. We have to think in new terms, and we must be careful not to try to apply old lessons to new times and new weapons and new capabilities.

DR. HALLION: I think General Braswell has made a very fine point there that we'll use to bring this session to a close. It echoes an enduring truth in military history, and that is we have always sought to destroy the enemy at a distance before the enemy comes within striking distance of us. It's a principle that goes back to the dawn of time. David didn't close with Goliath; he hit him with an

Silver Wings Golden Valor: The USAF Remembers Korea

"aerospace weapon:" a rock. We're certainly seeing that principle continuing to the present day, and it is why, as I said earlier, we need to ensure that this country gets the F–22.

LIEUTENANT GENERAL BROWN: Dick, before we let these young people go, I would just like to comment on two documents. First, Boots Blesse's "no guts, no glory" phrase has become widely known in the Air Force. I would like you to know that General Blesse also had a corollary to "no guts, no glory" when some of us, the young fellows in the squadron, started to maybe carry things a little too far. I offer it to you for your future years: the corollary is "Guts will do for skill, but not consistently."[66]

And my final pitch is there was a fellow in the 4th Wing named Jim Horowitz, a flight commander and West Point graduate in the 335th Squadron. After the war, Jim Horowitz changed his name to Salter and wrote *the* definitive book about flying Sabres in Korea. I encourage you to read *The Hunters*.[67] James Salter today is one of the most respected authors in America. Occasionally he comes to Washington, D.C., and does readings. If you see an advertisement saying that he's reading at a bookstore, go hear him, because he usually reads from *The Hunters* the passage that describes the mission to MiG Alley and back. I strongly encourage you, if you have any interest in what it was really like, to read that book. He describes it the way it *really* was.

DR. HALLION: Jim Horowitz, now James Salter, also wrote a wonderful memoir entitled *Burning the Days*.[68] I'd strongly recommend you take a look at it. It has an excellent discussion on his training and then his service in Korea. On that note, thanks very much for attending. I think this has been very profitable, and I think it's only an inkling of what we will see this afternoon when we have some equally fascinating panels and presenters. Thank you all very much. General Moseley?

MAJOR GENERAL MOSELEY: This morning's session was a pleasure for a fighter guy who's spent a lot of time at Nellis. I've done a lot of work with some of the folks who were mentioned, such as General Blesse; and, having been Moody Suter's weapons officer, I think it's refreshing to know that a lot of these things remain constant and that the principles are the same whether it's an F–86 or an F–15 or an F–22. So, from a fighter pilot to our panelists this morning, thank you very much for your participation. We look forward to this afternoon.

Notes

1. *The Naval Air War in Korea* (Baltimore: Nautical & Aviation Publishing Company of America, 1986).

2. Shortly after the Inchon landing, Chairman Mao sent a telegram to Stalin that read in part "The enemy dominates the air.... Accordingly, we do not now have any certainty of success in annihilating a single American corps in one blow." Stalin subsequently sent MiG–15s to remedy the situation. See Sergei N. Goncharov, John W. Lewis, and Xue Litai, *Uncertain Partners: Stalin, Mao, and the Korean War* (Stanford, Calif.: Stanford University Press, 1993), 276. In fact, Stalin had been ready to send MiG–15s to cover deployment of Chinese forces on the Korean border as early as July 13, 1950. See ciphered telegram 3305, Stalin to Chou En-Lai and Mao Tse-tung, 13 July 1950, reprinted as Document

Air Dominance: The Essential Achievement

22 in Kathryn Weathersby, "New Russian Documents on the Korean War, Introduction and Translations by Kathryn Weathersby," *Cold War International History Project Bulletin* (Mar. 1999).

3. See USAF Evaluation Group, *An Evaluation of the Effectiveness of the United States Air Force in Korea*, book 2, vol 1 (HQ USAF, Jan. 1951), 227–28. Copy in the collections of the AF Historical Research Agency archives, Maxwell AFB, Alabama; also quoted in Robert F. Futrell, *The United States Air Force in Korea, 1950–1953* (Washington, D.C.: Air Force History & Museums Program, 1996 ed.), 146.

4. Report of the Chinese Special Aviation Group, extract in *USAF, Far East Air Forces Intelligence Round-Up*, n 69 (22–28 Dec. 1951); quoted in Futrell, *USAF in Korea*, 285.

5. Matthew B. Ridgway, *The Korean War* (Garden City, N.Y.: Doubleday, 1967), p. 244.

6. See Lt. Gen. William E. Brown, Jr., USAF (Ret.), *A Fighter Pilot's Story*, Charles A. Lindbergh Memorial Lecture, May 21, 1992, and published as Number 4 in the *National Air and Space Museum Occasional Paper Series* (Washington, D.C.: National Air & Space Museum, 1992).

7. The speed of sound is 760 mph at sea level, but, because it gradually decreases with altitude, pilots and aerodynamicists refer to "Mach number" (after Ernst Mach, a nineteenth-century Austrian scientist and philosopher) rather than miles or kilometers per hour. Mach number is the speed of an airplane divided by the speed of sound at the altitude at which the plane is flying. The speed of sound at any altitude is referred to as Mach 1. Technically, speeds less than Mach 0.75 are *subsonic*, speeds between Mach 0.75 and 1.25 are *transonic*, and speeds greater than Mach 1.25 are *supersonic*—but in practical (and popular) terms, flight below Mach 1 is subsonic and flight above Mach 1 is supersonic.

8. The Army Air Forces' straight-wing P–86 was never placed in production, because it offered no advantages over the existing AAF Lockheed P–80 Shooting Star and the Republic P–84 Thunderjet. But a virtually aerodynamically identical variant (having a strengthened landing gear), the FJ–1 Fury, served briefly with the U.S. Navy. It offered no performance advantages over other straight-wing naval jet fighters such as the Grumman F9F Panther and McDonnell F2H Banshee, and thus failed to win large production orders. It served primarily as a trainer and as a means for the Navy to gain operational experience with jet airplanes. In the early 1950s, the Navy ordered variants of the swept-wing F–86 family modified for carrier service (the FJ–2, –3, and –4 Fury), and these proved much more successful. North American redesigned the original P–86 design with a swept wing based on German wind tunnel data, data from the National Advisory Committee for Aeronautics (NACA, whose engineer Robert T. Jones had independently discovered the benefits of the swept wing in 1944), and the company's own internal design studies undertaken at the end of the war, including studies of forward-swept-wing configurations.

9. This was one of the key discoveries and products of the post–World War II transonic research aircraft program. Some early pioneer aircraft, such as the Wright Flyers, Bleriot monoplanes, and the like, featured all-moving "slab"-like horizontal tails. These required near-constant manipulation to keep an airplane in trim. Then, at the time of World War I, designers made a portion of the horizontal tail nonmoving, calling it the "horizontal stabilizer," because it stabilized a plane in level flight. Attached to this stabilizer were movable trailing-edge control surfaces called elevators (because they controlled whether a plane climbed or descended). Until the jet age, most airplanes employed a horizontal stabilizer with movable elevators. As originally designed, the F–86 was no exception. Experience from high-speed dives showed that conventional elevator effectiveness markedly decreased the closer a plane flew to the speed of sound. Indeed, in some cases, a pilot could quite freely move the control column (the joystick) fore and aft without any noticeable change in pitch attitude. Aerodynamicists and controls engineers theorized that making the fixed horizontal stabilizer movable as well would enable a pilot to regain adequate pitch control authority even at transonic speeds approximately Mach 1. Test flights of the Bell XS-1 (which did have an experimental adjustable horizontal stabilizer) in the late 1940s confirmed that a plane with such a movable horizontal tail could maintain control closer to the speed of sound than a plane lacking such a feature. So the Sabre was redesigned with a completely movable horizontal stabilizer in addition to its elevators. Until the Sabre entered the transonic region, the movable horizontal stabilizer would be left in a neutral position, acting like a fixed surface, and the pilot would rely on his elevators for pitch control. But at high speeds, particularly greater than Mach 0.9, an F–86 pilot could command pitch both by pulling back on the stick to move the traditional elevator, and then use stabilizer trim to control the position of the horizontal tail to dramatically increase pitch control authority. In contrast, the MiG had a fixed stabilizer, so the MiG pilot could rely only on his elevators for pitch control. Thus, the faster a MiG flew, the less controllable it became, whereas the faster a Sabre flew, its pitch control—all important in "pulling lead" on a maneuvering enemy—was still very good. Testing on Okinawa of a MiG–15 flown to South Korea by a defecting North Korean pilot immediately after the Korean War confirmed that the Sabre had far more effective longitudinal control characteristics at transonic speeds. Indeed, the Sabre could marginally exceed the speed of sound in a high-speed dive, whereas the MiG was limited to Mach 0.92; at that velocity, its speed brakes would automatically deploy to prevent the airplane from possibly going out of control at higher Mach numbers. Arguably, the Sabre's tail design was the most important single factor in its dominating the MiG. And, because of that domination, the communist air forces were unable to intervene in the land battle, and prevent UN air-

Silver Wings Golden Valor: The USAF Remembers Korea

men from doing so—and, because of that, UN ground forces were able to withstand the massive communist onslaughts of 1950 and 1951. It is not too much to conclude that without this feature, the air war would have been a far closer-run thing than it was, and that Korea in all likelihood would have fallen under communist control. After Korea, the advent of fully hydraulic flight control systems with various forms of stability augmentation led to the reintroduction of the slab tail. The Sabre's successor, the North American F–100 Super Sabre, was the first to employ a one-piece horizontal tail for transonic and supersonic flight control, and this kind of configuration became standard for all subsequent American jet fighters from the Century series (the F–100, F–101, F–104, F–105, and F–111); through the F–4, F–5, and A–7; and on to the present-day F–15, F–16, and F–22.

10. The Boeing E-3 Sentry Airborne Warning and Control System (AWACS) and the Boeing E–8 Joint Surveillance and Targeting Radar System (J–STARS).

11. Kimpo Air Base. Other examples include: K–8, Kunsan; K–10, Chinhae; and K–13, Suwon.

12. Maj. Zane S. Amell, 335 FIS, 3 kills, subsequently killed in a postwar landing accident in the United States. For more on Amell, see James Salter [James Horowitz, pseud., 335 FIS, 1 kill], *Burning the Days: Recollection* (New York: Random House, 1997), 136–38. Salter writes "he ended up with three victories and a wingman drenched in flame who went down one day near Sinuiju. As I think now of his eyes, they seem to me small but like those of traders or old policeman, wise. In the air you heard his grating voice and assurance, like a man stepping blithely into traffic looking the wrong way. He liked to drink and was given to extravagant gestures."

13. Col. Walker M. "Bud" Mahurin, subsequently shot down and taken prisoner. See his memoir, *Honest John: The Autobiography of Walker M. Mahurin* (New York: Putnam, 1962). The later F–86F could carry two one-thousand-pound bombs and was used increasingly toward the end of the war as a fighter-bomber.

14. Throughout the Korean War, the communists brutalized aircrew POWs as they tried to coerce UN airmen into confessing to false claims of engaging in germ warfare against the Korean people. These allegedly voluntary statements were then published in communist-front publications and by leftist Western "journalists" such as the notorious North Korean propagandist Wilfred Burchett. The methods of coercion—including mock executions and shootings, starvation, beatings, generalized mistreatment, and failure to furnish medical care to wounded and injured prisoners—were not equaled until the North Vietnamese demonstrated their own brutality toward U.S. POWs in the Vietnam War over a decade later. See Kathryn Weathersby, "Deceiving the Deceivers: Moscow, Beijing, Pyongyang, and the Allegations of Bacteriological Weapons Use in Korea," *Cold War International History Project Bulletin* (Winter 1998).

15. For more on DeArmond reciting Rudyard Kipling's epic poem of the Northwest Frontier, see Salter, *Burning the Days*, 192.

16. Colonel Fischer's remarks include more detailed reflections upon his air combat experiences sent to the editor after the symposium. The editor wishes to thank Colonel Fischer for making his contribution available for incorporation.

17. Sqd Ldr James D. Lindsay, Royal Canadian Air Force, 39 FIS, 2 kills. Lindsay was one of five RCAF pilots to shoot down MiGs while on exchange duty with the USAF in Korea.

18. Edward "Mick" Mannock, an Irish-born fighter pilot with the Royal Flying Corps (later the Royal Air Force), scored 73 victories despite being almost blind in one eye. Killed in 1918, Mannock was the finest offensive fighter tactician of World War I. Ernst Udet, one of the most playful and colorful of World War I airmen—he flew a red-and-white candy-striped Fokker D VII—later became a well-known stunt and motion picture pilot between the wars. Far less successful as director of the Luftwaffe Technical Office, Udet committed suicide in 1941. Charles Nungesser, a recklessly impetuous French ace, survived the "Great War" despite an extraordinary accumulation of serious wounds and injuries. Ironically, he is best remembered today for having disappeared in May 1927 with fellow airman François Coli on an ill-fated attempt to cross the Atlantic from east-to-west in the single-engine *L'Oiseau Blanc* (White Bird) biplane. Nungesser and Coli vanished just days before Charles Lindbergh successfully completed a solo crossing from west-to-east in the *Spirit of St. Louis*.

19. In air combat, the sky is divided into a clock: 12 o'clock is dead ahead, 3 o'clock is directly to the right, 9 o'clock is directly to the left, and 6 o'clock is directly astern. The latter position is where an airplane and pilot are most vulnerable and has led to a popular fighter pilot expression, check six.

20. Sqd Ldr W. Harbison and Flt Lt R. Knight, Royal Air Force, *The F.86 v. the MiG-15*, Report AIR 20/7728 (West Raynham, UK: RAF Central Fighter Establishment, 1952).

21. Empire Interactive, *MiG Alley* (San Francisco, Calif.: Empire Interactive, 1999) designed for use on a Windows 95/98 CD-ROM operating system. This game, one of the finest flight simulations created to date, was justly rated as "the best-handling and best-looking flight sim to hit the shelves this year" by *PC Gamer* (Dec. 1999).

22. The western portion of the Yalu River, which marks the boundary between North Korea and Manchuria, was in the very heart of MiG Alley.

23. The XP–86 Sabre prototype first flew in October 1947 and first exceeded the speed of sound in April 1948, during a dive. The USAF accepted the first production model F–86As later that year. The

first British pilot to fly the Sabre was test pilot Roland Beaumont, in the summer of 1948.

24. A word on RAF rank structure: a wing commander is equivalent to a USAF lieutenant colonel, a squadron leader is equivalent to a major, and flight lieutenants are equivalent to captains.

25. Now called Dandong. "Y-Service," a British term, was also adopted by some Americans, although the American term was *radio intelligence* (later SIGINT, for signals intelligence) for intercepting enemy message traffic. The Air Force Security Service (AFSS) monitored communist communications, with often spectacular results. In one case, the Fifth Air Force commander was apparently aware of a planned North Korean attack on a friendly island before the North Korean air commander received his orders to conduct the raid; the result was three enemy airplanes shot down and several others, including two MiGs, damaged. The major listening post was on a small island off the western North Korean coast, Paengnyong-do, commonly called "P-Y-do." See David A. Hatch and Robert Louis Benson, *The Korean War: The SIGINT Background* (Ft. Meade, Md.: Center for Cryptologic History, National Security Agency, 2000).

26. The condensed streamer of exhaust vapor formed at altitude behind a piston-engine or jet-propelled airplane. Contrails immediately signal the numbers, direction, speed, and location of a formation of aircraft.

27. The term g refers to the force of gravity. 1g is standard conditions. 2g is twice standard gravity, and so forth. The F–86 was stressed to a maximum of 7.33g. Pulling back on a control column increases the g loading that a plane experiences. The tighter and more abrupt the maneuver, the higher the g. Today, in the era of fly-by-wire flight control systems, a pilot can immediately command upward of 9g if necessary to help evade a threat such as an air-to-air or surface-to-air missile.

28. Known originally as the TF–80C, the T–33 was a two-seat armed trainer derived from the F–80.

29. Maj. James Jabara, 334 FIS, 15 kills.

30. Capt. Manuel Fernandez, Jr., 334 FIS, 14.5 kills.

31. Capt. Joseph McConnell, Jr., 39 FIS, 16 kills, subsequently killed after the war flight testing the F–86H at Edwards Air Force Base, California.

32. Maj. Frederick Blesse, 334 FIS, 10 kills. Blesse, author of the very influential post-Korean tactics manual discussed subsequently, eventually rose to the rank of major general in the Air Force. See also Maj. Gen. F. C. Blesse, USAF (Ret.), *Check Six: A Fighter Pilot Looks Back* (Mesa, Ariz.: Champlin Fighter Museum Press, 1987).

33. A Nazi fighter pilot who claimed 352 kills, mostly on the Russian front.

34. Called Misawa tanks, these tiptanks were much larger than the standard F–80 tiptank, thanks to having a cylindrical extension inserted between the front and back of a standard tank.

35. *Jagdfliegers*, literally translated, means flying hunters, a statement attributed to Lt. Gen. Adolf Galland, a Nazi fighter commander who was in charge of the Luftwaffe's fighter forces in World War II.

36. Col. Harrison R. Thyng, 335th FIS/4FIW, 5 kills; Lt. Col. Vermont Garrison, 335th FIS, 10 kills; Col. Royal N. Baker, 335/336 FIS, 13 kills; Col. Francis S. Gabreski, 4/51 FIW, 6.5 kills; Col. Walker M. Mahurin, 4 FIW, 3.5 kills.

37. Maj. George A. Davis, Jr., 334 FIS, 14 kills, Medal of Honor (posthumously).

38. Now known as Shenyang, a major Chinese industrial and aircraft-manufacturing site.

39. Despite Soviet disclaimers at the time and afterward, a strong Russian presence existed in North Korea and Manchuria throughout the war—not surprising, given that, even before the war, Soviet advisors had supervised the creation of the North Korean military. Stalin, for his part, viewed Korea as a vital strategic block to a possibly resurgent Japan, as well as a possible means of distracting the United States from his main area of interest, Europe. The first Soviet air division sent to Korea, commanded by Lt. Gen. Ivan Belov, arrived in August 1950, equipped with 122 MiG–15s. Throughout the war, the Soviets went to great lengths to cloak their role. For example, MiG pilots were instructed not to eject over the Yellow Sea lest American search-and-rescue forces pick them up. One MiG pilot who did so was strafed in the water by his own squadron mates as American rescue forces neared him. Another Soviet pilot, Lt. Yevgeny Stelmakh, committed suicide rather than be captured by UN forces after he was shot down attacking a B–29. See Jon Halliday, "Air Operations in Korea: The Soviet Side of the Story," in William J. Williams, ed., *A Revolutionary War: Korea and the Transformation of the Postwar World* (Chicago: Imprint Publications, 1992), 149–70; Michael J. McCarthy, "Uncertain Enemies: Soviet Pilots in the Korean War," *Air Power History* (Spring 1997): 32–45; and Kathryn Weathersby, "Soviet Aims in Korea and the Origins of the Korean War, 1945–1950: New Evidence from Russian Archives," *Cold War International History Project Working Paper No. 8* (Nov. 1993). Stalin's role in the Korean War, as revealed through newly available Soviet documentation, is the subject of a forthcoming detailed analysis by Dr. Weathersby.

40. Soviet fighter thought emphasized rigid ground-controlled intercept tactics, and the Soviets passed this to the Warsaw Pact and other client states as well. This approach was never very good, and its weaknesses were glaringly evident in the Persian Gulf War, when Iraqi fighter pilots were essentially flying blind and with no clear idea of what to do after F–117 attacks had shattered their integrated air defense network.

41. Korea constituted the last air war that the United States fought without the benefit of aerial refu-

eling. Although air refueling at the time of Korea was already employed for the Strategic Air Command's B–47 bomber forces, it was not yet a routine operational technique for fighters, although some significant flight-refueling operational test and evaluation was undertaken under combat conditions over Korea.

42. In March 1999, the Robert R. McCormick Tribune Foundation and the U.S. Naval Institute sponsored a conference on the Korean War at the McCormick Foundation's Cantigny Center in Illinois. Over two days, a distinguished panel of historians, veterans, and commentators analyzed key issues of the war. For an excellent summary of the conference, see Col. Joseph Alexander, USMC (Ret.), "Remembering the Forgotten War," *Naval History* (Apr 2000).

43. There is an interesting comment on this from the former commander of the Soviet Union's 303d Air Division, Maj. Gen. Georgy Lobov: "Rotating Soviet air units (rather than individuals) through the Korean conflict had an inherent flaw. New pilots went into combat without experienced colleagues beside them. Newcomers 'stepped on the same rake,' sometimes smashing their faces in blood. ... There was a decline in MiG activity after each turnaround of pilots, and one consequence was increased losses. The Americans, in contrast, rotated people, not squadrons. 'Elders' coached newcomers as they gained experience.... If F–86s won a battle with MiG–15s, pilots and commanders were to be blamed and replaced [and the] second group of pilots was selected more carefully than the first." Quoted in Robert F. Dorr, Jon Lake, and Warren Thompson, *Korean War Aces* (Botley, U.K.: Osprey Publishing, 1999 ed.), 23–24.

44. According to Chinese sources, Chinese pilots did not first fly combat against American airmen until January 21, 1951. For more on Chinese involvement in the Korean air war, see Xiaoming Zhang, "China and the Air War in Korea, 1950–1953," *The Journal of Military History*, 62 (Apr 1998): 335–70. Zhang concludes, "Chinese leaders and the PLAAF [Peoples' Liberation Army Air Force] could not delude themselves about the capabilities and performance of their pilots and aircraft during the war. America's air superiority not only prevented the Chinese air force from providing ground support, but also inflicted heavy losses on Chinese lives and materiel on the ground; consequently the Chinese did not achieve the total victory that their leaders had so eagerly pursued. In the face of sustained U.S. air bombardment, Chinese pilots' war experience was confined to defense" (p. 369).

45. The speaker was Dr. Kathryn Weathersby, who, together with Chen Jian, presented translations of Stalin and Mao's Korean War papers. Drs. Weathersby and Chen are collaborating on a forthcoming book of Korean War documents from the Soviets and Chinese.

46. On June 13, 1951, Stalin sent a ciphered telegram, number 3557, to the Soviet advisor in Peking that read: "According to our information, our pilots are training the Koreans very slowly and in a slipshod manner. You and General [Ivan] Belov apparently intend to make professors rather than battle pilots out of the Chinese pilots. We consider this to be overcautiousness on the side of our aviation specialists. ... The Chinese troops will not fight without air cover. ... Report the fulfillment. Filippov [Stalin]." Stalin also urged the Chinese to employ the straight-wing MiG–9, an airplane somewhat equivalent to an F–80, against bombers, but without apparent success; the MiG–9 is not even indexed in the official USAF history of the Korean War. See the previously cited Weathersby, "New Russian Documents.," Documents 68 and 69.

47. With its gun package in close proximity to the nose engine inlet, the F–86 was potentially vulnerable to gun gas ingestion, which produced distortion and pollution of the airflow through the engine so that the engine would compressor-stall and flame out. The six .50-cal guns did not induce such problems, but four 20-mm cannon did. Eventually, the F–86 was successfully modified to carry four 20-mm cannon (on the F–86H series), as was the later Navy Fury series. Australian Sabres were modified to carry two fast-firing 30-mm cannon.

48. Gun Val is shortened from Gun Evaluation. In January 1953, the Air Force Air Proving Ground sent eight F–86F Sabres modified with four 20-mm cannon to the 4 FIW. Combat trials from then through May were disappointing; the planes experienced compressor stalls and some flaming out, and one aircraft was lost. Consequently, trials continued using just two cannon. But the two-cannon Sabres lacked any greater punch than the standard six .50-cal Sabres. Four cannon would have been ideal, but, as mentioned earlier, four cannon virtually guaranteed compressor-stalling the J47 engine, causing it to flame out in the midst of a dogfight—clearly an unacceptable risk.

49. Lt. Col. George L. Jones, 335 FIS/4 FIW/51 FIW, 6.5 kills.

50. Capt. Ralph S. Parr, Jr., 335 FIS, 10 kills. On July 27, 1953, roving over North Korea well east of MiG Alley, Parr shot down the last communist aircraft lost in Korea, an Ilyushin Il–12 transport gunned down near Chunggangjin, allegedly with a number of senior Soviet military commanders, advisors, and observers on-board. Not surprisingly, therefore, the shootdown triggered a short-lived diplomatic protest from the USSR.

51. The complex A-1CM electronic sight replaced the earlier Mark 18 "eyes only" optical sight fitted to early Sabres. The A-1CM sight was coupled with a small fire control radar, the AN/APC-30 (and sometimes the AN/APG-5C radar) located in a small radome installed in the center of the upper lip of the Sabre's nose intake. With the short-range radar locked onto a MiG, and the sight slaved to the radar, the pilot had a much greater expectation of scoring a hit if he placed the sight pipper on the enemy air-

plane. Eventually, the simpler A-4 sight replaced the A-1CM in the F-86F.

52. Echoing the aggrieved tone of French inspector "Louis" (Claude Raines) in *Casablanca* when he "discovers" that gambling is taking place in "Rick's" (Humphrey Bogart's) nightclub.

53. For the record, FEAF combat operations policy stipulated that "Every effort was made to avoid violating the Soviet-Manchurian border [and] no bridge on the Yalu River or other targets near the Korean border were to be attacked *when there was a possibility of violating the air space over Manchuria*" [emphasis added]; see FEAF Operations Statistics Division, *USAF Report on Korea: A Summary of Combat Operations, 1 Jul '52-27 Jul '53* (Japan: Directorate of Statistical Services, DCS Comptroller, 10 Dec. 1953), 3. Catalog K134.78-101, Issue #3. Copy in the collections of the Air Force Historical Research Agency, Maxwell Air Force Base, Ala.

54 *Pitched* refers to a break maneuver when a fighter flies past a runway and breaks abruptly into a turn (typically to the left). This turn, if continued, places the fighter onto the downwind leg of its landing approach. Pilots refer to this as pitching out.

55. Capt. Dolphin D. Overton, III, 16 FIS, 5 kills. Overton, who previously flew a Korean tour in F-84s, shot down five MiGs in four days, a Korean record, from January 21-24, 1953. Overton had claimed two others as well, on January 23, although these were never officially confirmed; his squadron commander, Lt. Col. Edwin L. Heller (3.5 kills), was shot down on the same sortie more than one hundred miles north of the Yalu. The Fifth Air Force commander, Lt. Gen. Glenn O. Barcus, subsequently ordered Overton back to the United States, and the Joint Chiefs of Staff cautioned UN Commanding General Mark Clark that there were to be no more violations of the Yalu. Heller endured brutal torture from the Chinese until his release from captivity. See William T. Y'Blood, *MiG Alley: The Fight for Air Superiority* (Washington, D.C.: Air Force History & Museums Program, 2000), 38–39; and the previously cited Futrell, *USAF in Korea*, 611.

56. 1st Lt. Richard Frailey, 334 FIS, 1 kill.

57. Frailey often flew as Maj. James Jabara's wingman, but not on the mission in question. In the closing weeks of the war, on June 15, 1953, Jabara shot down Frailey in a case of mistaken identity, aggravated in part because Frailey's flight leader had taken his four-ship of Sabres, Red Flight, north of the Yalu. Jabara saw the flight's contrails and immediately assumed they were a formation of MiGs. He began his attack on the flight leader, but, as the flight turned away, the angular relationship caused him to switch his fire to Red Four: Frailey. He fired a total of nine bursts, three of which hit and damaged the Sabre's wing, engine, and cockpit (one bullet passed between Frailey's arm and chest), knocking out his instruments. Fortunately, frantic transmissions of "Cease fire! Cease-fire! We've got friendlies firing at Sabres!" caused Jabara to break off his attack. Frailey had taken a camera on the flight in an attempt to be the first Western pilot to secure a still photograph of a MiG–15 in flight. As Frailey nursed his badly damaged F-86 toward the Yellow Sea and an eventual bailout, he radioed, "I don't want to eject, I've got my new camera with me." Jabara, now helping fly cover for Frailey, replied "Screw the camera, I'll buy you a new one." Frailey subsequently ejected just offshore, coming down within range of communist guns, which began to fire at him. Fortunately, despite the shellfire, a Grumman SA–16 Albatross amphibian landed near the pilot, picked him up, and returned him to Kimpo. For further details, see John Lowery, "MiG Fever," *Air & Space* (Apr/May 1999): 16-17. Cho-do was the site of the Dentist radar installation and also served as a forward base for air-sea rescue forces.

58. 1st Lt. William W. Littlefield, Jr., 334 FIS.

59. Maj. George A. Davis, 334 FIS, 14 kills. On February 10, 1953, Davis led his squadron to cover fighter-bombers attacking rail targets near Kunu-ri. A large formation of Soviet-piloted MiGs appeared to the west, and, unhesitatingly, Davis and his wingman left the main body of the Sabres and engaged the MiGs near the Yalu. Davis shot down two MiGs and was closing on a third when a fourth MiG shot him down. The MiGs abandoned any effort to engage the fighter-bombers. The USAF recognized Davis's courage and selflessness by awarding him the Medal of Honor posthumously.

60. Translated by Colonel Fischer from Russian pilot memoirs in his possession.

61. Lt. Gen. Lynwood E. Clark, a distinguished Korean veteran and member of the audience. During his Air Force career, General Clark flew 141 combat missions in Korea in F-80s, F-84s, and F-86s, a further 51 missions in Vietnam in A-1s and O-1s, and held a number of key positions, including commander, Alaskan Air Command.

62. Then-Lieutenant John Boyd, who flew Sabres in Korea. Subsequently, Boyd became a noted fighter tactics instructor, and, eventually, a controversial and tireless member of the 1960s–70s Fighter Mafia, advocating "pure" air superiority fighters before his retirement as a colonel from the Air Force. Boyd's work on energy maneuverability and agility metrics undoubtedly had a profound influence upon the development of the F–15 and F–16. He likewise conceptualized the so-called OODA Loop (Observe, Orient, Decide, and Act), and his later work on grand strategy and military education is credited with reshaping the Marine Corps' operational and strategic thinking. Boyd's influence on aircraft design occurred from the mid-1960s onward, after he had reached higher rank, and logically followed his influence in the 1950s on the training of fighter pilots. Further, Boyd's work complemented that of an unsung hero of fighter reform, Maj. Gen. Arthur C. Agan, the Air Staff's Director of Plans. Agan put together a 1965 Headquarters Air Force study team that generated an influential Air Force position

paper on air superiority that resulted in the F–15. See Robert F. Futrell, *Ideas, Concepts, Doctrine: Basic Thinking in the United States Air Force*, v. 2, *1961-1984* (Maxwell AFB: Air University Press, 1989), 471; and Jacob Neufeld, *The F-15 Eagle: Origins and Development, 1964–1972* (Washington, D.C.: Office of Air Force History, Nov. 1974), 6–19. For one summary view of Boyd's work, see Franklin C. Spinney, "Genghis John," *U.S. Naval Institute Proceedings* (July 1997): 42–47.

63. First issued in March 1955, but reprinted extensively since that time. See, for example, Frederick C. Blesse, "No Guts No Glory," *USAF Fighter Weapons Review* (1977): 26–30, 55.

64. Col. Richard M. "Moody" Suter, a noted fighter tactics instructor and the father of the Red Flag exercise program, which was established, at his suggestion, by Tactical Air Command in 1975.

65. Col. John C. Meyer, 4 FIW, two kills in Korea, had shot down twenty-four German aircraft during World War II as an Army Air Forces Mustang pilot. Meyer had a distinguished Air Force career, finally serving as commanding general of Strategic Air Command.

66. This was Rule 19 of Blesse's rules for offensive fighter operations. The rest of the rule was "Know your job in combat or someone else will be flying in your place."

67. New York: Harper, 1956; reprinted, Washington, D.C.: Counterpoint, 1997. This book was also made into a popular motion picture starring Robert Mitchum and Robert Wagner.

68. New York: Random House, 1997.

Chapter 6

AIR PRESSURE: AIR-TO-GROUND OPERATIONS IN KOREA

Gen. John A. Shaud
Panel Chairman

MAJOR GENERAL MOSELEY: To chair our panel *Air Pressure: Air to Ground Operations in Korea*, we're very fortunate to have Gen. John Shaud here with us today. He's the executive director of the Air Force Association. General Shaud is a graduate from the United States Military Academy at West Point. Following graduation, he entered the Air Force and became a B–47 pilot, then a B–52 pilot. He's flown RF–4s in Southeast Asia. He served as Deputy Chief of Staff for Personnel; as Commander, Air Training Command; and his last assignment was as Chief of Staff, Supreme Headquarters Allied Powers Europe. On a more personal note, he also served as the chief Air Force planner, at which time he was unfortunate enough to have several of us in this room as his employees. He has continued to mentor and take care of us over the years to make up for those shortcomings and our failures to support him. So, sir, we appreciate your mentorship and support. He has been making outstanding and wonderful contributions to the Air Force, and the men and women therein, by his work at the Air Force Association. Sir, you're a national treasure to all of us, and we appreciate your being with us today.

GEN. BRYCE POE: I notice Buzz Moseley didn't call you a piece of Air Force heritage, John, but I will. Thank you for coming.

GENERAL SHAUD: Thank you very much, sir! I'd like to ask my panel to come forward now if you would. It's my great privilege to be associated with these heroes at the table and in the audience. How about a round of applause for

Silver Wings Golden Valor: The USAF Remembers Korea

them, please? Let me also thank another person, Dick Hallion, who really put this together. What I'm trying to do is to fit this particular panel into the array of presentations we're going through today. This morning, Dick chaired the panel on air dominance. That's a great way to start, because without air dominance not much is going to happen. Air dominance makes opportunity for other operations that are dependent upon the effect that you are looking for, that the National Command Authority is after.

Let me define Korea in the following way. I see three phases. The first phase was the attack of the North Korean People's Army across the 38th parallel. It was tremendously successful. Finally, in August, at the Pusan perimeter, we held. It was the halt that was provided by air interdiction that enabled our soldiers to gather and to get their resources together and then to counterattack. That went very well. As you recall, our valiant Eighth Army came out of the Pusan perimeter as Douglas MacArthur led us through the landing at Inchon, and we moved forward. In fact, it went so very well I think they must have paused only momentarily at the 38th parallel and then kept going north. By the month of October, our UN Command forces were very close to the Manchurian border, and advance parties were overlooking the Yalu River. This is Phase 1 of the Korean War, and, certainly at the beginning, our Air Force is very much participating in a halt-phase style air campaign.

Then came the second phase. It began surreptitiously in October, when the Chinese communists began to infiltrate across the Yalu River. Subsequently, the great Chinese push began around Thanksgiving, and again we had forces heading southward. Seoul fell on January 4, 1951, and it wasn't until those middle weeks in January that again there was a successful halt. On January 25, 1951, our UN Command again began to press northward and, around June 1951, established a main line of resistance. (The West Point stuff shows up every once in a while!) Anyway, there we were, north of the 38th parallel, and this marked the end of the second phase. As with the first phase, we had stopped an advancing army, had pushed them back north again, and this time it ended in a stalemate. There we were from July 1951 until July 27, 1953, when, finally, the cease-fire was signed. It was in that two-year period, July '51 through July '53, that the title of our panel, which is *Air Pressure*, really came to bear. What was going on then was pressure against the communist forces to come to the table, to remain at the table, and to sign a cease-fire. At any rate, our United States Air Force—our fledgling United States Air Force—was absolutely invaluable and a participant in all three of these phases. Another reason I went through this drill is that, as I introduce the speakers, one thing you all should note is when were they participating in the Korean War. Their participation was very much defined by which of these three phases they were part.

Now let me describe the "air order of battle" for this afternoon.

I'd like to start with Gen. Russ Dougherty. In June 1950, General Dougherty was a major assigned to Japan. After war broke out, as a pilot, he also found him-

Air Pressure: Air-to-Ground Operations in Korea

self as kind of a utility infielder flying transports for people mainly heading southward. Anyway, General Dougherty will describe that to you. Our next speaker will then be Gen. Bryce Poe, and, as the Secretary of the Air Force said earlier today, he was one of the first jet pilots of our United States Air Force. In fact, he took off out of Itazuke, famous in song and story, on June 28, 1950, on the first combat mission of a RF–80.

Next will be Col. Sam Dickens, a West Pointer, class of '51. Those '50 through '52 classes found themselves in great numbers in Korea, and Sam was a recce[1] pilot over there in 1953. He flew RF–86s. Frankly, before this symposium and panel [were] convened, I didn't even know what an RF–86 was, but allegedly there was one, and Sam will talk to us about it.

Our next speaker is Maj. Gen. Phil Conley. You've got to give Annapolis equal time here, and Phil, out of the Naval Academy Class of '50, freshly minted, both a second lieutenant and pilot, found himself as a forward air controller flying a trainer airplane, the T–6, also termed a Mosquito. So we'll hear from Phil.

Then we go to Col. Jesse Jacobs. Jesse represents a good many Korean War pilots in that he was a B–17 pilot in World War II who suddenly found himself in Korea flying transports and also F–80s! There's a story behind there somewhere, and we'll hear from Jesse about this.

Finally comes our clean-up hitter, Gen. Bill Smith. I've got to be really careful about this introduction. This is a former professor of mine. Sir, I'm delighted always to see you; you're looking well. Nice tie! General Smith was over in Korea, first as a forward air controller with the 25th Infantry Division, then flying out of Taegu (K–2) with the 49th Fighter-Bomber Group, and Bill will wrap up and provide some summary comments for us.

Now I'd like to ask each of the participants again according to the air order of battle to come up here and speak. Our first panelist is Gen. Russ Dougherty, who retired as commander of Strategic Air Command. As I mentioned earlier, he was there at the very beginning of the Korean War, flying transports. General Dougherty?

GENERAL DOUGHERTY: Never let it be said that I should take on the Secretary's comments, but I wanted to tell the Secretary that we lacked some air cover at night in the tent city that was right outside Taegu. Bedcheck Charlie[2] used to come over about three or four times a week and drop five or six little twenty-pound bombs. He created absolute chaos in that tent city, among the staff officers of the Fifth Air Force Advanced who were living there. You can't imagine the chaos when one twenty-pound bomb drops on a tent in the middle of your tent city, but we had it every night. That's where I first heard the phrase, Bedcheck Charlie, and, boy, did we lack air superiority over that tent city on those dark evenings when that two-seat biplane would chuck-chuck-chuck-chuck down from the north, unintercepted, and drop bombs on us in tent city!

In five minutes, let me describe one of the most backward, unprepared garrison-conditioned bunch of "warriors" that I believe I've ever seen, and that goes for the Air Force and the Army both. We were the least prepared for combat of any bunch I've ever seen—completely conditioned by a garrison mentality—and there we were, suddenly, in a war. I was living at the University Club; my wife was up in the mountains at a rest home, and she couldn't come because we didn't have housing. I had a roommate, and he was flying in a troop carrier outfit—C–54s[3]—and I was a judge advocate. But I was also flying out of Haneda[4] in a utility flight, flying Gooney Birds,[5] and I was an instructor pilot.

I had gone over to Korea for a few days with the chaplain from Far East Air Forces, had taken him around and had an IP[6] to fly around with the chaplain. So I took him to several places in Korea including Kimpo, and then I took him across to the western part of Japan, to a base called Miho. We had some troops up there, and the forward echelon of a B–26 outfit[7] was located there, and the chaplain blessed them and did his usual thing, and I hung around the club. Then I got word that my roommate's C–54 had been burned up on the ground at Kimpo,[8] and my roommate was last seen running south with a bunch of people in front of the North Korean forces, heading for Osan on foot! Now this is inconceivable! But they burned up his C–54, and that was the first casualty of the war that I knew about—and it came home to me real fast.

So I got the chaplain back and found out what was going to happen, and our base flight out at Haneda got just as busy as can be. To paraphrase what we were doing over the next two or three weeks, we were taking young company-grade officers and NCOs[9] out of Tokyo in "pinks and greens" with Sam Brown belts[10] and pro-kits[11] and flying them into Korea. We'd take them in on Monday and bring them back out on Wednesday, wounded. The casualty rate on NCOs and company-grade officers in the 24th Infantry Division up there was just incredible. We were flying first into Osan, but that became too hot. Then we went into Taewon, and that soon became too hot as well.

Flying Gooney Birds, we flew the "iron beam,"[12] of course. We didn't have any other way. There was just one railroad, so you couldn't miss it. Flying up that railroad, we flew below the level of hills—hills populated by people in long white robes, a lot of whom were shooting at us. On one flight, I had a bunch of replacement lieutenants and captains in the back, all armed with pistols and rifles. The Gooney Bird has a ventilator hole in each window, and the next thing I knew, the sergeant came up and said, "Major, they're shooting out the windows back there!" And I went running back. Sure enough, boy, they had the rifles in those windows, and they were shooting up in the hills, and one of them had even taken a good piece off the wingtip of that Gooney Bird! So I had to stop my own war. That was the closest to combat that bunch had gotten (and I, too), and I couldn't take that. They could have shot me down in a minute.

But that was the kind of ragtag operation we had. It was desperate, and it was awful. We got back into the Pusan perimeter. I'm going to pass this photo around, so you can take a look at what Pusan looked like the second week of war. Somebody built a shed out in front of a tent and put up a sign, "Base Operations: Air-

Air Pressure: Air-to-Ground Operations in Korea

drome of Hospitality and Beauty." Then some other wag put up, "File Your Clearances Here Before You Take Off." My pilot said, "Boy, the war's over—now we have to file clearances!"

But just to give you some of the little vignettes that you run into when you're flying utility aircraft hauling people around in the opening days of a war, I went into K–3, Pohang, and we had lost that air base. The North Koreans were overrunning it, and we evacuated the tower people. They came running down that tower just like rats off a sinking ship and jumped into the Gooney Bird. We landed over the enemy, turned around, picked them up, and took off back over the enemy. And, when I got stabilized up in the air safely, the sergeant came up and said, "Boy, you got a bunch of guys that are just going to destroy us back there!" I said, "What's going on?" He said, "They've all got rifles, they're all in terror, and they're in shock." I went back, and this one guy was clutching his rifle, shaking, and he said, hysterically, "I'm a tower operator! I'm not a infantryman!" And somebody said, "Get the rifle away from him!" I said, "You get it away from him, boy! I don't think he's going to let it go." But this is the kind of thing we faced. We flew them back to the hospital, and then to rest camps in Japan. It was like that for weeks. It was an incredible demonstration of guts to me that we held on to the Pusan perimeter, just incredible.

For example, we couldn't destroy the West Bridge at Seoul.[13] Because I was an instructor pilot cleared into all bases, I had to take a Japanese lieutenant general (who was in prison in Sugamo and who had been the chief of engineers in Korea) to brief our pilots at Taegu (K–2) on how to knock down that bridge. We had been blowing holes in the span; they'd fix it in a few hours. Then blow more holes in the span, and they'd fix them in a few more hours. The old Japanese general was quite a gentleman: a world-class military scholar. He got in there, and he briefed all of our pilots—including a group of Marine pilots who had Corsairs[14]— over there on how to knock down that bridge. He said, "Quit trying to hit the flooring. You've got to go into the uprights." And he told them exactly how to do it, the angle of the bombs, and the size of the bombs, and how to fuze them. And the guys went out, strapped on their gear, and, boy, they were gonna get that bridge! And when they got to the bridge, they found the Marines had already knocked it down! The Marines had left the briefing early: they all had all they needed to know, and they went in and got that bridge.

In one of these readings, General Partridge[15] said he had a "wild man" for an intelligence officer. This guy had about 600–700 people over in Korea on a bunch of radios, and he was giving the best information that anybody had, but he was an absolute wild man.[16] That wild man was Major Vandover and he needed a utility pilot, and I lived next door to him, and he glommed on to me. So I found myself flying in all sorts of oddball places, riverbeds and things, delivering his radios. This was my first association with what we call the SSO.[17] This guy really had a network. And he ran it with these little radio sets and operators, and he had to plant them around all over the combat zone. And it was my job to plant them. I went in a riverbed one day on a supply mission to the 1st Cavalry Division, had trouble getting out, and I found how important it is for a division to have a radio, a sergeant operator, and an officer as a forward air controller.[18] They had just lost theirs, and they couldn't get in any sorties for close air support. They looked at me like I was manna from heaven! And I knew I had to get out of the riverbed, that I had to get out of there, or I was going to be stuck with the infantry in the 1st Cavalry Division, and I was, for several days.

Now I'll make a last observation as a utility pilot. If you've ever been in the infantry in combat close to the enemy, it's the most God-awful experience in the world. The first two or three days, you know, you think you're going to die. The third day, you think you are dead. And from then on, it doesn't make any difference anymore. I got out of the 1st Cavalry Division with the greatest appreciation for the infantry in combat that anybody will ever have. And that's why I like this aerospace capability we're developing so that we can prevent the enemy from getting in hand-to-hand combat, because, when you get in that situation, he's as big as you are, and, if he's closer with a bigger knife, he's going to get you. This is no way to fight a war. This is attrition war of the type of trench warfare in World War I in France, or like World War II.

So I'm glad that I had that eye-opening experience. It lasted a year for me. We went through Wonsan, evacuating wounded Marines out of Wonsan back into the hospitals at Iwakuni. Utility airplanes didn't have a single hero in Korea, and that's all right, but they did a great job. Finally, we got the troop carriers organized over there with Jock Henebry[19] and a few of his people, and they began to stabilize and organize things. But, if you'll see that picture that's being passed around, that's what Korea in 1950 looked like when it was dressed up. It didn't all look that good.

My last story: we brought General Ridgway[20] in. General MacArthur was leaving, and Ridgway was taking over. I was out from Taegu, at an Army post. They had a pierced-steel plank runway about three thousand feet long. I had gone in there to set up some of these radios that Major Vandover had, and a Constellation[21] came in and flew low over this pierced-steel planking. We said, "What in the world is he doing here?" Then he disappeared. Because he was so low, he went behind a hill that was in the traffic pattern! He came around and landed, and that thing stood on its front feet and just barely stopped at the end of the planking, with smoking brakes—really a mess. They finally got a ladder out there, and out came the general. The pilot said, "Sir, just a minute. We're at the wrong airfield. I'll take care of it! I'll get you right over to the other one in a minute!" He said, "Son, I've flown the last mile I'm going to fly tonight!" Utility airplanes had a hell of a war over there! Thank you.

GENERAL SHAUD: Thank you very much, General Dougherty. Our next speakers will be two recce pilots. The first will be Gen. Bryce Poe. General Poe is a retired four-star general, and he flew recce in two wars, and I was with him in one. He was in the same outfit with me, the 12th Tactical Recce Squadron in Viet-

Air Pressure: Air-to-Ground Operations in Korea

nam. General Poe, it's good to have someone there who had some idea of what it was we were supposed to be doing, and we thank you for that, sir. General Poe, as I mentioned earlier, was also the first to pilot our jet RF–80[22] into combat, on 28 June 1950. General Poe, a few comments if you would, sir?

GENERAL POE: This character wasn't happy because I took all of his back-seaters![23]

GENERAL SHAUD: That's true.

GENERAL POE: And I had to teach them! You've forgiven me?

GENERAL SHAUD: Yes, sir.

GENERAL POE: Before the war, I was very happy to be flying the jets, first in the United States and then in Yokota, Japan. Our 82d Tactical Reconnaissance Squadron—renamed the 8th TRS before the war started—was the first jet unit in the Far East. We were the only jet recon outfit in Japan, and, as early as 1948, some of our people already had a "500 Club" of half a dozen pilots who had over five hundred jet flying hours—extraordinary given how new the jet was. And our maintenance personnel were equally outstanding.

Before the war started, I flew some interesting missions, mostly from Misawa, and I couldn't tell anybody about them except General Stratemeyer.[24] On the flightline, we kept all of those missions quiet, and I didn't even tell my boss. I was cautioned to be careful with the Soviets, but I never had a problem. Then, in June 1950, came the Korean War. For me it was very much a "come as you are" party. That morning, I was playing tennis with two other officers at Yokota, when Lt. Col. Jacob Dixon, our squadron commander, pulled us off the court and sent us straight to the flightline. The four of us headed south to Itazuke, arrived in darkness, and, on the morning of June 28, I flew that first combat recce mission.[25] That was a tremendous mission. I had to find where we could go, and, all of a sudden, in the black dark, I found one little bit of a break in the clouds, and I found the North Koreans. By dark, we had F–80s, F–82s, B–26s, and B–29s attacking their columns. We had serious problems and losses, but we really knocked the hell out of those people. It was something of which I was very, very proud.[26]

We were pushed back, of course, and had the defense of the Pusan perimeter. But we flew long-range recce all the way to the Chinese border, using extra fuel tanks that we would jettison. This always irritated the logistics people, that we just tossed off the tanks.[27] Once I had a problem running the Chinese border because my engine was bad. As I flew south, the Navy cleared me to fly over the *Helena*[28] at a certain place. But when I came over the *Helena*, they started shooting at my airplane! This irritated the Air Force, and some Navy character said, "Well, the fault was the British sloop *Black Swan*." Maybe somebody could tell me what the *Black Swan* did, but it was the *Helena* that fired on me!

I was pulled again into Misawa to look at the Soviet airfields, and things got pretty hot. We'd have two or three missions to look at the Soviets, and then come back to Korea, and then have two or three more missions to look at the Soviets. I dropped fuel tanks there, too, but that was okay—because I had General

Silver Wings Golden Valor: The USAF Remembers Korea

MacArthur's permission to do so! Finally, things got so hot with the Soviets that I would take somebody to cover me, and we'd have the F–80s out. I was sure glad to see them! They never had to fight, but I was sure glad to see them. After this, General MacArthur called me for briefing, just one-on-one, and he knew all the targets and all the places. He really impressed me. He said, "If I have to, I'll have you go in again, but I don't want you to." He took about five minutes for the briefing, and the man was just tremendous. My dad was not impressed with MacArthur in World War I and World War II, but MacArthur changed his mind by the way he treated his boy.

When the Inchon landings came at last, I had about seven times the work.[29] The front split at Seoul, running west and east, and eventually joined together.[30] We had tremendous recce demands, and the Marines and Navy sometimes covered our recce operations.[31] It was a very pleasant thing when you had the Navy looking out for you with their blue airplanes.[32]

Then along came the Chinese intervention in November. We recce'd targets at Anju and Sinuiju, in MiG Alley. One time, we had one RF–80 and two escort F–80s that tangled with three MiGs. I didn't tangle with them, but a classmate of mine did on another mission, to check on the location of enemy fighters. Somebody had said, "Well, you don't need any escort fighters," so my classmate had to fly his aircraft solo. He was jumped, and they tangled for a long time, but he was lucky and got back. We didn't fly any of those airplanes unescorted again.

I recall another episode where we had another outfit with C–119 aircraft[33] that came out to get the wounded Marines out. It was a fantastic thing. There was one airplane like that and one airplane like this, taking off in all directions! It looked horrible, but they got all of those wounded Marines out, well, not all the Marines. The healthy ones walked or rode out, but, still, it was a fantastic thing.

After Korea, I flew as an exchange pilot with the Royal Norwegian Air Force and the Royal Danish Air Force. NATO had very high priorities, and I found out that, as a result, we often didn't get in Korea what we needed. It was really irritating to me, but we certainly made do! I remember a NATO general rationalizing it for me by saying, "You can handle things in Korea, but I don't know how much we can handle things in our base out here." So that's one thing that I've remembered. I also remember a wonderful guy who even told the British queen we could do things others thought simply impossible. In closing, I appreciate very much the opportunity to be here today. Thank you all very much.[34]

GENERAL SHAUD: Bryce, that's impressive. For all the things you've done for the Air Force, sir, we thank you. The next speaker we have is yet another recce pilot, Col. Sam Dickens. Now you have to remember that Sam was there in 1953, and Sam was flying RF–86s. This is a little different situation than what Bryce Poe was involved with in the last half of 1950. Sam?

COLONEL DICKENS: Thank you. I was struck this morning by one of the comments made by Colonel Fischer about fighter pilots. He didn't quite say it this way, but there are fighter pilots, and then there are pilots that fly fighter aircraft.

Air Pressure: Air-to-Ground Operations in Korea

And there's a difference between the two. Of course, that's been a continuum since World War I until today. I feel like you were the first, General Poe, with the 8th Tactical Reconnaissance Squadron; and I'm toward the last, when the 8th Tactical Reconnaissance Squadron became the 15th Tactical Reconnaissance Squadron, which I joined. You can imagine the chaos (as has come across in these discussions), certainly in the beginning of the war with the demand for intelligence information. We heard how human intelligence from the ground was so effective—the radios, et cetera—but we needed to complement this with photographic intelligence, and we started off with virtually one squadron. I think there were strategic RB–29s that were employed as well. Overall, then, there was a tremendous demand for collection of information about targeting, enemy forces, disposition, et cetera.

Finally, to get us all together, early in 1951, the Air Force turned to a genuine reconnaissance hero from World War II, Col. Karl L. "Pop" Polifka.[35] One of the books I've read about the World War II was written by a British author and entitled *Evidence in Camera*; it's about reconnaissance.[36] She talked about Colonel Polifka and how he ended up flying some very dangerous missions in World War II under an assumed name because he was officially prohibited from flying some of the missions. So he logged in under somebody else's name.[37]

So Colonel Polifka was brought in and formed the 67th Tactical Reconnaissance Wing with the 67th Tac Recon Group. It had three squadrons. There was the 12th Tac Recon Squadron, which was an RB–26 night operation, using flares. They had all kinds of problems dropping the flares and getting them to properly illuminate, to take photography at night. Then there was the 45th Tac Recon Squadron, the "Polka Dots" squadron, which flew RF–51s. Then there was the 15th Tac Recon Squadron, which had been the 8th. The 15th was the only recce squadron that was equipped with jet aircraft, the RF–80s. Missions were divided between the RB–26 night photography; the RF–51s for close-in targets (closer to the friendly forces), visual reconnaissance, and photographic reconnaissance; and the RF–80s doing missions that were deeper.

It didn't take too long for people to realize that the RF–80—which had a Mach limitation of 0.8—was not the aircraft to be operating in MiG Alley![38] But targets were up in the northern part of North Korea—so, despite escorts of F–86s or F–84s, RF–80s were flying very hazardous missions into MiG Alley and were being lost. A couple of the pilots in the 15th had flown F–86s in the United States. We were at Kimpo Air Base, K–14, near Seoul, and the 67th Tac Recon Wing was on one side of the base and on the other side was the 4th Fighter Wing. So these former Sabre pilots went over and looked at some of the F–86A aircraft that were in bad shape, that weren't being flown, that you couldn't even have called "hangar queens." They were trying to figure out how to rig some cameras on the F–86, and they came up with some ideas that were given approval. As a result, modifications were made in Japan, and the first RF–86As arrived in December 1951. The first missions were flown in 1952.[39]

Silver Wings Golden Valor: The USAF Remembers Korea

The markings of those first 15th Tac Recce Squadron RF–86As were those of the 4th Fighter Wing. We, of course, wanted the communists to think they were fighters. Each one of these RF–86As with cameras was almost hand built, and some of them still carried two .50-cal. machine guns. They didn't want the RF–86As to be in any scraps because, as they always reminded us recce pilots, "you haven't completed your mission until you bring the photos home." It's not knocking out a bridge and being killed in the process. Unless you get home with the film, you haven't completed your mission.

So we really didn't want these RF–86A pilots to think they could become aces even if they had a couple of guns. So pretty soon there weren't any guns in the RF–86As, but there were all sorts of other modifications. One of the pilots who flew missions in early 1952 was escorted by F–86s up in the Sinuiju area, and his mission (as he reported in a letter that I received) was trying to get photos of POW [prisoner of war] camps. These were what we called "dicing missions."[40] You know—they were really right down on the deck! When he started down, the escort fighters stayed high, and the recce pilot went sweeping across with a forward-oblique camera taking pictures. He had to do that a couple of times—and it's never good to fly over a target area that's heavily defended more than once. One of our RF–80 squadron commanders was killed taking photos of dams. He made a second pass, was going across too slowly, and was shot down. His wingman, who had not gone on the pass with him, felt it was a terrible mistake.

As these missions went on, the RF–86A proved pretty successful, but it had a significant drawback. To mount 36-inch cameras, they had to put them horizontally in the fuselage, with the lens focused on a mirror set at a 45-degree angle to look down. Well, our technicians never could quite get the flutter out of it. You'd have some vibration, and so the photographs were fuzzy. Expert photographic interpreters could figure it out, but it certainly wasn't the finest quality, even if it was the best that we could do with the RF–86A.

Now, I got over there in the early spring of 1953. We'd go across the airfield and see our buddies in the 4th Fighter Wing. We looked at them enviously because they were flying F–86s, this beautiful airplane, and the missions I was flying at that time were all in the old RF–80. Even so, there was an awful lot of excitement. I think most of us who were in recce really wanted to be fighter pilots; but, being recce pilots, we really got to know our aircraft. We learned how to fly instruments well, we knew how to do visual reconnaissance, and we could find any spot in North Korea with a map, which most fighter pilots couldn't do.

In fact, on my way over there, I was in Japan and met a fighter pilot going back to the United States after one hundred combat missions. He said to me, "What are you going to do?" I said, "I'm going to be a recce pilot." He said, "Well, how do you find your targets?" And I said, "Well, visually, you know, you get a map, and you find the target." He exclaimed, "Impossible! The terrain all looks the same!" That was the perspective of someone who was flying high up to MiG Alley and back without worrying about the terrain below him.

Air Pressure: Air-to-Ground Operations in Korea

When I got over there, there was a Major Howell, who had come over as a second lieutenant, a redhead. He had flown some missions with the 4th Fighter Wing and then came to the 15th Tac Recce Squadron. He was a very aggressive pilot and had a couple of spot promotions. He went from second lieutenant to captain in probably about six months. One time, on one of his recce missions, he lacked sufficient fuel to get back, so, unfazed, he landed at Cho-do and brought the RF–86 down on the beach for refueling before recovering back to K–14 later on. That's the kind of guy he was.

Very quickly we had shown that the RF–86As could do productive recce missions, although, admittedly, they were not doing them as well as they ought to have been because of the photographic problems I mentioned earlier. To give one example, on the last day of the war, the 27th of July 1953, we flew three RF–86A missions well north of the Yalu. We were trying to gain all the information possible before the truce went into effect about airfields, aircraft, et cetera. Deep-penetration mission preflight briefings were given by Far East Air Forces intelligence officers, not Fifth Air Force ones, even though the wing was under Fifth Air Force, because the RF–86A flew mostly classified top-secret missions. So, to compare our operations with the regular Sabre operations, the RF–86s—if not on a daily basis, nevertheless quite frequently—flew top-secret missions well north of the Yalu. In contrast, Sabre fighter pilots who strayed either deliberately or accidentally across the Yalu to get MiGs were being chastised for breaking the rules of engagement!

Well, the Korean War ended, all the training and flying continued, and then one day the 15th Tac Recce Squadron got orders to go to Komaki Air Base near Nagoya, Japan. So we deployed with three RF–86As and some RF–80s. We got over there, and we were greeted with eight RF–86Fs! They were beautiful—brand new—and more were coming in every day. These RF–86Fs had all been modified in Japan from later F–86F fighters; they looked a little bit different, as they had bulges on the side that inspired some of us to call them "Mae Wests." The bulges covered twin 40-inch K–22 vertical-mounted telescopic cameras for detail shots. Additionally, the RF–86F had a 6-inch K–17 camera in between the K–22s for general photographic purposes and orientation shots.[41]

We went right to work, immediately familiarizing ourselves and checking with the tech reps.[42] What are the capabilities of this airplane? What's the max range? I have a "Dash One"[43] on the F–86F at home, and, when you look at the information about it, it's talking about flying clean, talking about flying with so many bombs, two drop tanks, et cetera. But you never find out anything that really tells you the maximum range with, say, two 200-gallon drop tanks and two 120-gallon tanks. So we experimented with this. We ran training missions over Japan with different tank configurations, and we obviously settled for the max range capability, simultaneously carrying two 200-gallon tanks and two 120-gallon tanks.

I asked the tech rep, "We want to be climbing at maximum speed. You restrict us to thirty minutes of flying at maximum power. But what happens if you fly for more than thirty minutes? He said, "Well, a drastic reduction in overall engine life, but, on any particular flight, no problem at all." All right. What's the tailpipe temperature for takeoff? Six hundred and ninety degrees centigrade at full military power is going to give you your best takeoff performance. But we weren't interested in that. We could get airborne. Instead, we wanted to know how many titanium "rats and mice" should be welded into the tailpipe to arrange to be able to get 690 degrees centigrade at forty-two to forty-five thousand feet. That's where we wanted our maximum thrust, not sea level.[44]

So, one day in late March 1954—a long time after the Korean War—six of us deployed in these brand new RF–86s to K–55 at Osan. We spent the night there and the next morning took off and flew top-secret missions that were directed by the Joint Chiefs of Staff and approved by President Eisenhower. Some flew over China, and others flew over Vladivostok, with recovery in Misawa. Of course, within the squadron, this was still top secret. The other pilots all suspected something was going on, but no one said anything. The aircraft themselves and the modifications were assumed to be secret as well, and so our own air defenses in Japan weren't notified, leading to occasional scrambles.[45] Our guys told us, "The Soviets don't really have that good radar at altitude." I don't think we really believed this, but we were all young and eager, and we were going to do what was required.[46]

These limited-penetration missions continued through 1954 over China, North Korea, and the Soviet Union, many over communist airfields.[47] We could get two hours and forty minutes endurance comfortably. A mission that I flew with my ops officer (I was his wingman) was 1,240 nautical miles, landing in Misawa. At altitude, we could do Mach 0.92, which was not bad in 1954, and we got great photography. We discovered MiG–17s all over these Russian airfields that no one knew anything about; in fact, we captured an airborne MiG–17 on film. Overall, we didn't feel the F–86 was much of a match for a MiG–17.[48] Up to this point, the MiG–17s had been reported only west of the Urals. On other missions, we flew over Port Arthur, the Darien peninsula, several targets in North Korea, Shanghai, the Sakhalin Islands, Soviskaya Gavon, Vladivostok, and Khabarovsk. These have only recently been declassified, thanks to Cargill Hall, the historian of the National Reconnaissance Office. We hope that all of these missions will be declassified in the future.

In closing, I'd like to reflect on the people in my squadron. Our squadron commander was a lieutenant colonel fighter pilot veteran of World War II. Our operations officer was a major, a reconnaissance pilot. We had a captain who was trained as an RF–80 pilot at March Air Force Base, Lavern H. Griffin, one of my heroes I've maintained contact with. And everyone else was a second lieutenant, from ROTC, aviation cadets, West Point, and the Naval Academy. We flew combat in RF–80s with no ejection seats, at a time when all the planes in the states had ejection seats. We had manual canopies on some of them, which took a crew chief to close and open, and you wondered "How will I get out of this thing?" But I don't know of anyone who turned down any of these missions. Thanks very much.

GENERAL SHAUD: Great, Sam. Thank you. That completes the recce—no play on words!—picture. One thing to think about is that reconnaissance was critical to our overall war effort, and, especially, the strategic bombing campaign. As Rosie O'Donnell[49] and others said, the effectiveness of the bombing campaign had a whole lot to do with the effectiveness of the reconnaissance.

Now we're working our way close to the FEBA—the forward edge of the battle area—and no one knows that, Phil, like a FAC.[50] I'll tell you, I can't wait for you to tell me how you take off in a trainer airplane and fly around looking for the action where there is in fact a lot of action taking place. Maj. Gen. Phil Conley?

MAJOR GENERAL CONLEY: Thanks, John. Well, officially my outfit in Korea was the 6147th Tactical Air Control Squadron, but everyone in Korea called us the Mosquitoes. Our mission was simple. We were to control all the coast air support strikes between the front line and the "bomb line," the front line being what is now called the FEBA, the forward edge of battle area. Essentially, at the time—I was there in 1952—the war had been stabilized and ran pretty much along where the demilitarized zone, the DMZ, is right now. Eight miles north of that was the bomb line. Above the bomb line, fighter-bombers could go after anything that they saw, but, from the bomb line on down to the front, you had to have a Mosquito or a ground forward air controller controlling the attack.

My outfit, the 6147th Tactical Control Group, didn't exist before the war—or as it was called in those days, a "police action." In the whole Air Force, there was only one tactical air control squadron. And, when Fifth Air Force requested it, they were told to form a squadron out of their own resources, which they went ahead and did. They formed what I call a "pick-up team." They had some fighter pilots, they got the behind-the-line pilots, and they asked for volunteers everywhere. And they took anybody they could get their hands on. The aircraft we flew was the T–6.[51] The T–6 was a World War II advanced trainer with two tandem seats, with a student pilot in the front and an instructor pilot in the back. I had flown the T–6 in basic and advanced flying school, and then I graduated in the F–51 Mustang. The T–6 was not intended as a combat aircraft and thus had no armor plating, no self-sealing fuel tanks, and no redundant systems. To turn it into a combat aircraft, we put 2.75-inch-diameter smoke rockets under the wings, using these rockets to mark targets, and we were off to war.

I arrived in Korea a second lieutenant in February 1952 with less than three hundred hours total flying time, all of it in flying training or gunnery school. There was no prior training to be a Mosquito pilot. You were just given a set of orders and sent to Korea. I went to K–6 Air Base at Pyongtaek, about thirty miles south of Seoul, and there I had three-and-a-half days of ground school. The next two days, I flew two local flights—a day checkout and a night checkout. The next day, I went on my first combat mission. The first eight missions were flown with an instructor. For the first four, you sat in the back seat and observed what was going on; for the last four, you were in the front seat, and the instructor was in the back. The next seven missions were flown with an experienced observer. These observers were all Army types, both U.S. and allied, and we were very happy to have them. One thing we talked about earlier today was the F–86 pilot having a wingman. Our observer functioned in the same way, as another pair of eyes that could look for targets. Of course, the most important thing was that these observers all came from artillery forward observation posts and thus knew the area and knew about putting in air strikes. So they knew a lot about Army–Air Force operations. Another thing we did, we taught all these Army guys how to land that T–6. We figured if something happened to us, we wanted that guy in the back seat to bring us home! After our first fifteen missions, we were given a flight check and declared combat ready.

Now here's how a typical mission went: after our usual briefing, we took off and flew to our designated area. My area was I Corps on the western-most sector of the front. I Corps consisted of three divisions: the 1st Marine Division was anchored on the Yellow Sea, next to them was the 1st British Commonwealth Division, and then a U.S. Army division. The Marines had their own tactical air control squadron in Korea. During the course of the war, there were certain times when the Air Force controlled (or sort of semicontrolled!) some of the Marine missions. But, in essence, during World War II, the Marines had really developed their own air–ground team, and, because they were much more comfortable using their own air control and their own tactics, we weren't invited into their area.

Because we flew over the same terrain every day, we obviously got to know this terrain very well. We could quickly pick out any changes to any positions. On arriving in the area, I would check with the ground forward air controller, who was a Mosquito pilot attached to a ground unit. If there were no preplanned strikes, the ground forward air controller would usually ask you to go out and do a recce. He wanted us to look for evidence of enemy activity and check for any possible targets. If we found a target, we'd make a request for the fighter-bombers. When the strike aircraft arrived, I would brief them on the target location, report any aircraft fire, the direction of attack I wanted them to go in, and the location of friendlies and also the location of the nearest emergency landing strip in case they had a problem. After each pass, I talked to the next pilot coming on in and adjusted his aim point. It was a little difficult in that we marked the targets with our smoke rockets, but these were 2.75-inch-diameter rockets, and they weren't very accurate. So ordinarily you probably didn't exactly hit the target. And, as the fighter-bombers would drop their bombs, from one bomb drop to the next, we'd move them, say, up a ridgeline or down into a valley, this kind of thing. After the target was destroyed, and all ordnance was suspended, we would then go back on in and do our BDA[52] and then withdraw back over friendlies.

So the Mosquitoes provided on-call coverage in all corps areas every day from sunrise to sunset. We had a few missions that we flew after sunset, which were very interesting. When you're flying these missions in daytime, you get very absorbed in them, and you really didn't notice any antiaircraft fire coming up at you. But, at nighttime, all these "golf balls" were coming up, and you really got an idea of what you were flying through in the daytime!

After about twenty missions, we were placed on temporary duty with the Army as ground forward air controllers. I was assigned to the 1st British Commonwealth Division, 28th British Brigade. Here we got to see the war from an entirely different perspective. I spent most of my time at forward artillery observation posts with the New Zealanders, who provided the artillery support for the 28th British Brigade. I came away from the assignment with the greatest respect for the bravery and professionalism of these Commonwealth troops, and I say that and I really mean it. They were a wonderful group of people. Most of them were World War II veterans. They fought through the Western Desert, then they fought all the way through Europe, and they were back out there in Korea—and no complaints whatsoever because they really wanted to be there.

Shortly after returning to my squadron, I was sent to Johnson Air Base in Japan for survival school. We had no survival training before being shipped to Korea. The topics at Johnson, in addition to survival, were escape and evasion, and prison camp organization. We were all young pilots with about seventy-five missions to go on our one-hundred mission tour, and I guess the feeling was that some of us would be able to put what we learned at survival school in pretty good use before our tour was over!

After seventy missions, I was made commander of one of the two flights in our squadron, and I was also made an instructor pilot. In this capacity, I got to work with the new pilots coming on into the squadron. They came from all kinds of flying backgrounds. Some of these guys had really good World War II experience as fighter pilots. In fact, a lot of them had World War II service and had been recalled from civilian life. These were guys that had fought in World War II, had gone back on the GI Bill through college, or maybe got married and started a family, and—bang!—five years later, they're recalled, and they're in Korea. But others, of course, like myself—second lieutenants, first lieutenants—were getting our first taste of action. All the pilots in my squadron, except for myself and one other pilot, were Reserve officers. I received a regular commission on graduation from the Naval Academy, and the other pilot had been augmented. But everybody else was a reserve, real civilian soldiers, the kinds of guys that Tom Brokaw talked about in his book, *The Greatest Generation*.[53]

In spite of the fact that we were flying the lowly T–6, while our buddies were flying the new jets, morale in our squadron was always high. This was because the mission was so satisfying. We knew that what we had was an important job, and we could see the instant results of our work. There's nothing like seeing the top of a ridgeline just blow up, or providing timely, life-saving air support. In one case I remember, the Army requested a strike fifty yards from friendlies. I tried to talk them out of the strike because it was too close and thus too risky. I got the reply, "If you don't give us some help with the F–51s, we're going to get overrun!" So we put these F–51s in fifty yards from friendlies and we took care of them. That's professionalism.

It's not well known that, in addition to our work at close air support, we had an air-to-air mission! The enemy had a vintage, fabric-covered biplane we called Bedcheck Charlie.[54] He had a nasty habit of sneaking in at night and dropping grenades on the F–86s at Kimpo, outside of Seoul. Flying low and slow, with a low radar cross section, he was a real challenge to our air defense jets: indeed, instead of "out-flying" the jets, Charlie "under-flew" them! The Mosquitoes answered this challenge by slinging two .30-cal machines guns under the wings and taking up nighttime alert at Kimpo. Of course, everyone was salivating to become a fighter ace by shooting down Bedchecks! I drew this duty a couple of times, and, although I didn't have any victories, it was always a kick to taxi into the alert area of Kimpo, park our T–6s next to these F–86s, and tell the F–86 pilot sitting on alert there, "Okay, guys, go get a good night's sleep. We'll take it from here!"

In this month's Smithsonian *Air and Space* magazine, the centerfold depicts the aircraft of the Korean War.[55] Of course, the F–86 is there. Even Bedcheck Charlie is there. The T–6 Mosquito isn't there. But the Mosquitoes have a proud record. During the war, we flew 40,354 combat missions and more than 120,000 combat hours. The 6147th received two U.S. and one Korean Presidential Unit Citations. One hundred of our people were listed as KIA, MIA, or POWs. Fortunately, nineteen of our POWs were repatriated at war's end. Today, we have a really great Mosquito Association to keep the memory of our unique organization alive. We were the only unit—the only combat unit of the Korean War—to march as a unit in the Korean War Memorial Parade. And the one and only airman statue at the Korean War Memorial is that of a Mosquito forward air controller. Thank you.

GENERAL SHAUD: Thanks, Phil, for that excellent presentation. Yes, sir?

GENERAL DOUGHERTY: There's a footnote that needs to be added to the T–6 story. Early in the Korean War, Maj. Gen. Partridge, commander of Fifth Air Force, and Gen. Walton Walker, who was the Eighth Army commander (and later killed in a Jeep accident), used to load up every night in a T–6, with General Walker in the back and General Partridge piloting it. They'd fly all around the combat zone, and Walker is even alleged to have said, "I learned more from those flights than from all my intelligence officers put together." It got so bad and so frequent that it scared us all to death. Here were the two major combat commanders flying around in an airplane and going very close to enemy units! Finally, I understand—I don't know this—that the senior Army and Air Force leadership got together and issued a message saying "Knock it off. No more flights together!" So Partridge and Walker each awarded the other an Air Medal and quit flying the T–6!

GENERAL SHAUD: Thank you, General. For our next speaker, we have Jesse Jacobs. Let me talk about him just a little bit. The first point I'll make is he's a World War II veteran who, as Phil just discussed, was part of these outfits. Jesse was in B–17s in the Second World War. Now what he'll have to explain to us is

Air Pressure: Air-to-Ground Operations in Korea

how he flew both transports and F–80s in the Korean War! So sir, if you'll get into that a little bit. The other part you need to know is that he went through the Empire Test Pilots School at Farnborough, England.[56] Later, he test-flew the Lockheed C–5A Galaxy—which was very impressive to me. He also has the distinction of having flown a six-engine Boeing B–52 having two test J75s replacing the standard twin-engine outboard pods. Colonel Jacobs, it's great to have you here, sir.

COL. JESSE JACOBS: Well, thank you. This is probably going to be shorter than I had planned, because I didn't realize that we needed a break until I stood up! I told General Conley's daughter[57] earlier that "I'm everything." I've had the unique distinction—or honor or misfortune, however you want to put it—of flying combat in bombers, fighters, and cargo. I apologize to General Dougherty on my cargo flying in Korea, but I'll get to that in a minute. I think I first met Gen. Bryce Poe when I was a student at VPI, Virginia Polytechnic Institute, now known as Virginia Tech, and he was at Langley flying RF–80s. I had never seen jets flying before except in combat in Europe, when I was flying a B–17, and Messerschmitt Me 262s took a couple of passes at our formation on two missions, and also a Messerschmitt Me 163 one day. The 163 wasn't a jet, but rather a rocket.[58]

But somehow or another, they figured out after I graduated from VPI that, since I had had a course in industrial accounts and costs, I ought to be a wing air comptroller at a single-engine jet fighter base at Misawa, Japan, with the 49th Fighter Wing.[59] So I wound up over there with a four-engine MOS[60] which converted to AFSC[61] for those of you who were on active duty in 1973. So I was a four-engine pilot at a single-engine fighter base. We actually had one squadron of F–51s (the 8th Squadron), and the 7th and 9th Squadrons had F–80As when I got there in May 1949 but changed shortly after that to F–80Cs. The wing commander was Col. Brooks A. Lawhon, who was a fairly senior colonel, a former World War II commander of a B–24 outfit in North Africa. I think he was relieved by Col. Jack S. Jenkins just before we started the Korean War. I knew that Colonel Lawhon, who had been a four-engine pilot and now ran a fighter wing, would be somewhat sympathetic to me wanting to fly a fighter. I'm one of these pilots that flies fighters and isn't a fighter pilot, you know—at least some people look at me that way!

However, the reason I was a four-engine pilot was that I was a "boy aviator" in World War II. You've got to look at me and tell that, you know. Actually I don't feel as old as I look until I look in the mirror, and then I feel that way! But, at any rate, I chose four-engine all the way through flying school, and the reason I did is that I didn't want to wind up in the right seat of a four-engine airplane, and that's where ninety percent of all of my vintage were going![62] I was in Class 44B, which graduated in February of '44. So I figured I'd outsmart them and get what I wanted—so I got B–17s. When I was at VPI going to school, I was flying with the Reserve down at Roanoke and Richmond, Virginia, and they had some P–51s down at Richmond. I said, "Hey, how about checking out in a –51?" "How much previous fighter time you got?" "None." "Sorry, we can't do anything for you." And this is what I'd hear every place I'd go. By the way, I was an IP[63] and made senior pilot as a first lieutenant. So you can see what kind of flying experience I had.

But, at any rate, Colonel Lawhon and I were sitting having a hamburger at Itami Air Base one Sunday afternoon, waiting on the husbands to come to the airplane, and I told him this story. I could see he was taking it in, and the next day, Monday, I couldn't believe it—I came out on orders assigned to the 9th Fighter Squadron! Here I am wing air comptroller, and I've still got to line up some affairs for that. So I went ahead and started flying with the 9th Squadron, in F–80s. That was the first time in my life that I had ever flown an airplane where they'd pat you on the butt, stand over you while you were starting it, wait as you read the book and fill out a questionnaire, and watch you go off with a chase pilot.[64] We didn't have any T–33s[65] while we were there, at least until after the Korean "War" or "conflict," or "police action" started. So I got thirteen flying hours in an –80 before I ever saw the inside of a T–33.

In March or April 1950, FEAF decided they were going to get rid of the C–46s.[66] We had two or three C–46s at Misawa, and I was an IP in a C–46, so they said, "Take that airplane back to the States and pick up a C–47 and bring it back." Well, I did, and, as a result, I was gone the entire month of May. I think I got 130 flying hours that month before I came back. The airplane was in for an acceptance inspection, there was no training for anybody on the base after we got back, and about that time the red flag went down in Korea. So I got a call about 10:00 or 11:00 one night saying, "Jake, go take that C–47 and go pick up Col. Phil Cage down at Tachikawa and go on down to Ashiya." And so I went to Ashiya, and I started flying in and out of Pusan and Taewon, flying combat cargo. Every day I'd come back with the same litany: "I'm a fighter pilot assigned to the 9th Fighter Squadron, so I've got to get back to my unit!" Mind you, I had thirteen hours' total fighter time. It took me about ten days before I got back to Misawa. Well, then they decided that they were going to train me a little. So I got one gunnery mission, fired two guns out of six,[67] a total of 220 rounds. I fired two 2.75-inch rockets, and off I went to war. My squadron, the 9th Squadron, had already been in combat. They were at Komaki Air Base at Nagoya on maneuvers when the war started, and they went down to Itazuke, flying with and supplementing the 8th Fighter-Bomber Wing. So I trained with the 7th Squadron at Misawa until the 9th came back. I went back down with the 9th and flew combat out of Itazuke in the F–80.

Earlier in the war, I had landed at Taegu (K–2) while I was flying the Goon[68] when the ROK[69] pilots were flying their F–51s out of there, and they had nothing except sod. It was just a grass field. When we got over there in the –80s, we were the first jet outfit to physically locate in Korea, and we went to K–2. But now they had a 5,700-foot runway fabricated from pierced-steel planking (PSP). We didn't know anything about takeoff speeds, refusal speeds, or refusal distance, critical field lengths, anything like that. We used the runway, and that was it, and we had about five hundred feet of dirt overrun on the end.

Air Pressure: Air-to-Ground Operations in Korea

In order to get more range out of the –80s, we modified the 165-gallon wingtip jettisonable fuel tanks. Mind you, I'm sure that most of you who have ever seen an –80 haven't noted (unless you've looked at a picture real close) that it has underslung tiptanks. Lockheed centerline-mounted tiptanks on the T–33s later, but, for the F–80s, we had bomb shackles that were faired in with the wingtips, with the tanks hanging under them.[70] Then "Rabbit" Johnston from the 8th Squadron and "Foots" Eckman in the 9th Squadron designed a bigger tank.[71] They used the Lockheed tank's nose and tail joined to two cylindrical center sections from longer Fletcher tanks, with a rod that went all the way from the tail cone to the nose cone, and with no baffling. These modified tanks were about seventeen feet long and carried 265 gallons. We eventually quit using these because they would fail under load, sometimes wrapping themselves around the wing, and, on gunnery, the fuel could shift due to the lack of baffling, leading to wing failure, especially if you had any fuel left in them.[72] So, at any rate, that's how we got the range.

I was there when the 27th came over from Bergstrom to K–2, with Colonel Packard[73] leading them, and I was there when Colonel Eagleston, Jabara, and the rest of them in the 4th came as well.[74] Before they got over there, we would escort the reconnaissance flights up to the Yalu. Later, we would do it with two airplanes. We'd have guns, so theoretically we were supposed to beat the MiGs off and let the RF–80 get back with its pictures. I saw MiGs taking off on an airstrip at Antung when we were up over the Yalu River. Now mind you, K–2 is what? Roughly 110 miles south of Seoul or thereabouts? So we had to have pretty good range.

Speaking of range, when I heard General Braswell talking today, West Point Class of '48, it seemed to me like Alton H. Quanbeck was also Class of '48 at West Point, and he was in my group at K–2. He and a guy named Diefendorf were the two pilots who got court-martialed for strafing Vladivostok.[75] Col. Stanton T. Smith, the 49th commander, got fired and promoted up to Fifth Air Force Advanced and was heading up the Joint Operations Center. And they didn't say that my squadron commander got fired, but he did, too. At any rate, we had given those guys up for lost. They were out for three hours and thirty-five minutes on that flight and been down strafing, having a lot of fun destroying P–39s and P–63s up in Vladivostok.

But that was pretty much how I got combat time in both cargo and fighters. Then after I had about thirty-five missions, in October 1950, the Reserves had been called up. They brought the C–46s back over to the FEAF and were flying combat cargo in to and out of Taegu. The pilot of a Reserve C–46 showed up sick one day, and I had to put him in the dispensary. His copilot was not checked out in the airplane, didn't have an instrument card or anything, and so they said, "Jake, you go take that C–46 and fly it around Korea until this guy gets well enough to fly the airplane again." So I did that. So I had a period of flying fighter and cargo at the same time, three different types of airplanes—the C–46, C–47, and F–80—over there.

Silver Wings Golden Valor: The USAF Remembers Korea

The –80 was originally designed to carry just under sixteen thousand pounds max gross weight, but we were grossing out at over twenty thousand pounds. My favorite weapon in air-to-ground operations was napalm. We used lots of napalm. We skip-bombed with it, using the nose of the airplane as the gunsight. As soon as the target disappeared under the nose, we'd pickle the napalm tanks off, and it would get into foxholes and everything else. I went as a forward air controller with the 187th Regimental Combat Team in January of '51. We were the rear guard off the Han River during the second retreat, and I thought I was going to be swimming when I left Korea. One thing, since I wasn't used to being in ground war, I never learned to tell the difference between incoming and outgoing artillery. Of course, I was petrified! But those guys didn't want anything to do with my job either. They were petrified of flying. I went down to K–2 when I had a break one afternoon, drove down there in a Jeep, packed up all my things in a footlocker, and gave it to a guy named Jesse Green to put on the first C–54 going to Misawa. By the way, speaking of Jesse Green, he had the best eyes of anybody I ever flew with. He could spot a truck from thirty-five thousand or thirty thousand feet moving down the road, and, the next thing we'd know, he'd go down there, and we'd have at them.

I've rambled enough. I know you all want to break. I'm trying to think if there's anything else that is of interest. We were fighting trying to justify the Korean police action, and Chappie James[76] was a captain, flying combat with us in a T–33 with a photographer in the back seat taking pictures of what we were doing, so they could bring it back here and try and convince John Q. Public, I suppose. Some of the –80s had cameras that looked like a 37-mm cannon mounted in the leading edge of the wing, just outboard of the wing root. Anybody who knows anything about aerodynamics knows how just a little piece of aluminum can change the stall characteristics of an airplane. Test pilots call them stall strips. You know, it's a wonder we didn't kill ourselves.[77] I'm through!

GENERAL SHAUD: Thank you very much, Jesse. The last speaker on our panel is Gen. Bill Smith. As I mentioned before, he was both a forward air controller, then flew with the 49th Fighter-Bomber Group, and, of course, later on became a four-star general in our Air Force, spending a lot of time in Europe. With that, General Smith, sir?

GENERAL SMITH: Thank you very much. When the war began in June of 1950, I was in one of the two combat-ready fighter-bomber groups in the United States, the 20th Fighter-Bomber Group at Shaw Field, South Carolina. Being one of the two combat-ready groups, we expected we would go to Korea. But we were told we were going to England instead, because our intelligence services were convinced what was going on in the Far East was merely a feint. The real war was going to be fought in Europe, and we had to get there and be prepared to resist a Soviet invasion of Western Europe.[78] We stayed there several months, and then we were relieved.[79] I came back to the United States in the spring of 1951 and went to Korea, first assigned to a Strategic Air Command [SAC] unit. Now that's unusual

Air Pressure: Air-to-Ground Operations in Korea

for a fighter pilot! We didn't have anything to say about it; we were attached to the 27th Fighter-Escort Wing, under the authority of the Fifth Air Force.

Our aircraft was the straight-winged Republic F–84G Thunderjet, a forgotten aircraft in a forgotten war, but it was a good aircraft.[80] I saw one bounce off a mountain, fly home, and, after repairs, it flew again. Now, you know, you can't complain about an aircraft like that! So we really liked it. In April and May of 1951, we flew primarily close air support and battlefield interdiction. We got pretty good at both, and this was just the beginning. We used forward air controllers on the ground. I think I may have flown one mission in a Mosquito aircraft as I was going forward in early June of 1951 to be a FAC with the 25th Infantry Division. I worked with the 64th Artillery Battalion of the 25th Infantry Division.

Shortly after I got there, the stalemate developed, so it was fairly quiet. That spring, we worked very closely with the Army in our close air support missions. We had a pyramid method of identifying the targets we could hit in front of the front lines. The ground forces would put out bright fluorescent panels. This worked quite well, because then we knew what we had to be in front of, and they knew what they had to be behind. We got quite good. In fact, one time we were told after we completed our mission that we had killed about thirty to one hundred North Koreans or Chinese. We were quite pleased. But then, a couple of weeks later, one of the Army units came down and said when they had advanced it turned out that rather than thirty to one hundred, we had killed closer to eight hundred to one thousand. So close air support really worked, and, when we got the Mosquitoes operating, it got even better, really establishing good relationships between the Army and the Air Force.

We got pretty good at battlefield interdiction—trying to catch Chinese troops moving south during daylight, which they didn't like to do and which they didn't do very often, unless forced to do so by the pace of combat. On many occasions, we would catch these units moving down these roads, and they became just sitting ducks. The roads were narrow, the shoulders were narrow, and the ditches were not deep enough, so they just couldn't hide. We could respond quickly. If we got a report that the troops were moving, within thirty-five to forty-five minutes we could be overhead, either because we had people on alert or already in the air. And within thirty-five to forty-five minutes, units couldn't move that much. So we became quite good, and we were proud of what we were doing. Overall, during the time I flew with the 27th Fighter-Escort Wing, I'd say seventy-five percent of my missions were close support and battlefield interdiction.

We did some other interesting things as well. Being part of SAC, we had to escort bombers, and so more than once we escorted B–29s on their raids into North Korea. You know, when you try to get fast jet aircraft assembling with slow propeller-driven aircraft, using assembly and formation tactics dating from World War II, let's just say it was instructional! It worked out, it just wasn't perfect, but it worked out. We also ran fighter sweeps, and I remember one to Sinuiju with over three hundred aircraft. We had the Marines included in this one, as there had been an intelligence report that the Chinese were going to move some fighters south of the Yalu in order to increase their zone of influence over North Korea. Our job was to have all these Air Force and Marine fighters attack that airfield, destroy those aircraft, and just wreak havoc. Well, we did wreak havoc! There weren't many aircraft there—I don't know whether the Chinese may have learned we were coming. Our job was to cover some of the F–51s that were doing attacks on the ground.[81]

We also hunted MiGs. Now, if you look at it rationally, that wasn't the best mission in the world for the F–84G, which didn't stand a chance against a MiG, but we were more willing to do things than we were clever of understanding why we shouldn't! So we didn't mind. I reviewed some notes I kept during that time, and I said, "I want to get a shot at one of those MiGs sometime, and I'm just waiting." I did once. He was flying straight up, and I was trying to fly straight up. That wasn't very successful!

During the time I was on forward controller (which was from June through August 1951), it was fairly quiet; the first couple of weeks, there were a couple of Chinese attacks on the 25th Infantry Division, but after that it was fairly quiet. Just sporadically throughout the rest of that year was there ground action that called for very much close air support or battlefield interdiction. So when I joined the 49th Fighter-Bomber Group in September of 1951, we were doing primarily interdiction—that is, railroad interdiction trying to stop the Chinese and North Koreans from supplying their forces on the front line. We got pretty good at it. I was acting as assistant group operations officer in the absence of the group operations officer, who wasn't there for that period of time. So I got some statistics. How did we do to compare with World War II? We did, I would say, twenty-five to thirty-five percent better, and I just saw that subsequent histories have borne this out.

So we really were able to stop the Chinese and help impede their delivery of goods and supplies to the front line. If you were in that situation, what would you do? You'd build up your defenses, and that's what the Chinese did. As Arnold Braswell will know and Clark will know, we took a lot more losses in the fall and winter of 1951, because the Chinese air defenses of their supply lines improved. Also, they were clever enough that, if we stopped the flow of supplies on the rail track between A and B, they would just truck it at night that distance and put it back on the tracks further downstream. So they really did have a considerable effect on our ability to keep them from getting their supplies to the front. But the main reason was that they didn't need many supplies. They could judge when they were going to use them, and, though it was a good idea and we did a good job, we could not stop the flow of goods to the front line.[82]

Let me tell you some lessons that I took away from the Korean War. Some of these have not always been universally agreed by everyone in the Air Force, but a little diversity is not bad.

Air Pressure: Air-to-Ground Operations in Korea

I really believe that close air support was important and that it was important for us to work with the Army. Part of that came from my experience in Korea, but I really always felt that the Air Force can and should provide close air support for the Army.

Another lesson I took away is interdiction works, but it is a never-ending job and alone cannot isolate the battlefield. You can help, and you can do good, but we ought not expect too much of interdiction. It's another important tool, and we have to keep trying to do it well.

The next lesson is that air superiority is essential. We didn't have total air superiority when you could have a Bedcheck Charlie. That was important, and it got a lot of attention and got a lot of people worried. Before that, we had control of the air from about thirty or forty miles south of the Yalu; but, above that, the MiGs were there. And so we didn't have complete air superiority over all of Korea, and we had to operate accordingly. Even on our interdiction missions and particularly later in 1951, we had to be careful lest there be some MiGs around. So, though we gave complete protection to the ground forces down where they were, we could not give complete protection to the air forces where they operated. That just underscored for me the importance of having air superiority so everyone can operate freely and without impediment.

Another lesson that I took away is that training is critical. Today, the Air Force really appreciates that. In Korea, we didn't go in very well trained. Training is important not only before you get to the combat zone but in the combat zone; you can't underestimate the value of training. It was brought home to me the one time I really needed to draw upon it. I was in trouble. Fortunately, I knew what the aircraft could and couldn't do, and I knew exactly what I had to do to make the best of the situation I was in. I got through it because I had been properly trained. It really made an impression on me that we've just got to have the right kind of training. We can never give up, and we may never fully master it, but training is essential to a successful air force.

Bryce Poe and I both had some experience in logistics, he a lot more than me. I remember that, in Korea, we didn't have a full wing of aircraft. We were supposed to have seventy-two but probably had less than sixty. We could send up only twenty-four aircraft in a day! That's all we could send up unless we had an all-out mission, because we just couldn't keep them supplied. Engine problems and maintenance posed serious challenges. If you're really going to have a successful operation, you've got to have a successful logistics system, and, to be quite honest with you, that's something that we are still learning. It's even more important now than it was then because of the complexity of our newer equipment.

We made a lot of advances in medical support during that period—and I also know this from personal experience—in terms of taking care of the wounded and making them feel they were still part of the service, still important and deserving of proper treatment. I really think that we made some real advances here that are not appreciated enough by a lot of people. For those of us who went through it, it meant a lot.

Finally, and there was a little discussion about this—Clark knows this as well—in the 49th when we were there, we decided that no pilot would go down behind enemy lines without air cover until the helicopters came there to pick him up. Now there was a time when some said, "We're not going to fly helicopters anymore." So we called up and said, "We're going to come and pick up those helicopters. We're going to bring them back and train our people to fly them, because we're not going to send our people behind enemy lines unless they can be picked up!" So after this they said, "Okay, we'll fly!" To have a successful unit and have fighter pilots have confidence, they've got to have the assurance that if, they are alive and seen on the ground, someone is going to be there to pick them up. That was another important lesson I took away from Korea.

Finally, what makes this whole thing work is the people. You've just got to have good people, people who think they belong, who think they are part of one force working together. We had that in Korea. One thing that I learned, to have a successful force, you've got to have good people who are willing to make sacrifices and do the job and think not of just themselves but what's good for the larger organization that they're in and what's good for the country. Thank you.

GENERAL SHAUD: We're already getting into Dr. Wayne Thompson's time here, but I'll tell you, this last panel is incredibly important. The buzzword over here on the Hill right now has to do with transformation. What has happened since Korea is that we transformed from air power in Korea to aerospace power in Kosovo. It really is a seamless transition, and it's going on right now. I am convinced of that, and it's working.

Let me finish up this way. It's a rare treat for us to be able to hear from these veterans of Korea. I have one question that I'd like to pose to each of them in turn, and I think it will help us move into the next panel. The question is this: what was the most effective use of air power during the Korean War? General Dougherty, what would you say, sir?

GENERAL DOUGHERTY: Let me think about it a minute, Johnny. Let me think about it.

GENERAL SHAUD: Bryce, the most effective use if you could pick one?

GENERAL POE: I believe in my time it was air-to-ground, like you said. You take some hits, but they're worthwhile.

GENERAL SHAUD: Air-to-ground. Okay. Thank you. Phil?

MAJOR GENERAL CONLEY: Well, like I said, I was a second lieutenant with less than three hundred hours and what did I know? All I did was close air support, but I thought we were damn effective at doing that. When I told about putting those F–51s in that day fifty yards from friendlies, and as I made a low reconnaissance at twenty-five feet or so, I could see these Chinese coming off this hill and everything. I could see our guys were in dire straits, and they were going to get overrun if we didn't do something. And those –51s that day, they went on in, and they cleaned their clock!

GENERAL SHAUD: Sam?

COLONEL DICKENS: I think, in the beginning, the different elements of air power were being used almost separately or piecemeal. So each one was effective in its own role. So it's sort of a difficult question to answer, because I think what we learned during the Korean War is effective control of all the different elements of air power—being able to coordinate adequately for their greatest effectiveness, because each one did certain things. That's the way I look at it.

GENERAL SHAUD: Jesse?

COLONEL JACOBS: All of the other guys have skirted around what I was thinking. I think the most important thing depends on the time that we're talking about, what phase of it. When we first started out, General Dougherty's was the most important because he had to evacuate the people. When I first got over there in fighters, the most important thing was close air support, because we were getting the devil kicked out of us, and it really was effective against the enemy, especially once we started using napalm. Then, when the MiGs got into it, then the 4th was very important. Of course, the MiGs weren't bothering us down where the fighting was going on with the ground troops, but they could have been if they would have had the range, and it would have been very important to have somebody there who could give us some air superiority to keep them off our backs. So we were all effective. It just depended on what phase of the war we're talking about.

One thing that I got in reading all this material that you sent me before I came out here was it's very important to have one commander of all air, to coordinate the whole thing and knock some heads together and make them do it, instead of having the Marines and the Navy going their separate ways.

GENERAL SMITH: They particularly did then. We got along better than we could expect. Of course, it's an unfair question, and, as you know, I'm partial to close air support, but, let me tell you, if you look in terms of effective, in terms of doing the job, and in terms of building the reputation of the Air Force and giving it a firm foundation on which to build, you have to look at what the F–86 did against the MiGs. That's taking it over the long term. That's something we haven't equaled since then, and it's more impressive the more we learn about it. Now, having said all that, I still think close air support is very important! [Laughter]

GENERAL SHAUD: Go ahead, sir.

GENERAL DOUGHERTY: I think there were as many phases as described, and each one of them had its own requirements, but the consistent one that ran through it all was close air support. The B–29s did a pretty good job with a very limited target system. But it didn't keep the enemy off your back. Air superiority was very effective when we were working against the MiGs during a part of the time, but it still didn't keep the enemy off our back. It was a ground war, and the enemy was there all the time and has stayed there. They're still there. I'm not sure we did anything completely, but we did some spectacular bits and pieces. I agree with Bill Smith. This was a war where close air support had to be, but, if they hadn't gotten close, we wouldn't have had a close air support problem. We couldn't keep them from getting close. We couldn't stop them. So I think the main thing we did was learn our lessons. You've got to keep them from getting close because, if they get close, they've got you outnumbered. They can usually out-fight you because they've got a lower standard of dying than you have. So you've got to keep them from getting close, and we couldn't do that.

GENERAL SHAUD: Let me wrap up with this. General Heflebower, as you sit there representing our active-duty Air Force of today, one of the things that absolutely astounds us with the permanently blond hair at this table is the terrific way your airmen are trained today and the way they performed in Operation Allied Force over Kosovo. Our hats off to you, and thank you very much.

Notes

1. Recce: reconnaissance, also sometimes abbreviated as recon.
2. As mentioned by Senator Campbell earlier, these were primarily two-place Polikarpov Po–2 training biplanes, roughly equivalent to a World War II Stearman trainer, used for harassing attacks.
3. The Douglas C–54 transport, a four-engine heavy airlifter, equivalent to the civilian DC–4 airliner.
4. Haneda International Airport, Tokyo.
5. Nickname for the Douglas C–47 Skytrain, the military version of the legendary Douglas DC–3 twin-engine airliner and transport.
6. Instructor pilot.
7. The Douglas B–26 Invader, known originally as the A–26 (and redesignated as such for the Vietnam War), a fast (and superb) twin-engine medium bomber, not to be confused with the Martin B–26 Marauder of World War II. The unit was the 452d Bombardment Wing.
8. This transport, from the 1503rd Air Transport Wing, suffered damage on June 24, when a laborer drove a forklift into an aileron. Two North Korean Yak–9 fighters strafed it the next afternoon, damaging it. Then six others strafed it subsequently; it burned after the second attack.
9. Noncommissioned officers.
10. A reference to the garrison uniform of the day.
11. Professional kits.
12. Pilots navigate by visual flight rules (VFR, "eyes only") and/or instrument flight rules (IFR, cockpit instrumentation plus radio-navigation techniques). Until the advent of the vertical omnirange (VOR), airmen navigated IFR by a four-course radio range, which generated four monotone beams called equisignals formed by the overlapping Morse code signals of the letters A and N. Pilots flying the equisignal were flying "on the beam." Pilots flying VFR sometimes jokingly stated that they flew IFR, too: "I follow railroads." The "iron beam," thus, is a humorous reference to following the stark trace of a railroad line to one's destination.
13. Airmen nicknamed the west railroad bridge at Seoul over the Han River the "elastic bridge." Attacked continuously over the month of August 1950, the bridge was repeatedly dropped and rebuilt until finally downed for good on August 19–20, 1950, due to concentrated attacks by Navy aircraft and Air Force B–29s. Theater commander Gen. Douglas MacArthur presented trophies to both the Navy's Carrier Air Group 11 and the Air Force's 19th Bomb Group for destruction of the bridge. The FEAF commander, Lt. Gen. George E. Stratemeyer, went one better by presenting both CAG–11 and the 19th BG with a case of Scotch.
14. The single-engine, propeller-driven Chance Vought F4U Corsair, affectionately nicknamed the "Okinawa Sweetheart" by Marine infantrymen for its close air support during that savage World War II campaign. U.S. Navy and U.S. Marine Corsairs went on to do excellent service in Korea, particularly during the opening stages of the war and, especially, covering the withdrawal of Marine forces from the Chosin Reservoir.
15. Maj. Gen. Earle E. "Pat" Partridge, commander of Fifth Air Force, a subordinate command of Lt. Gen. Stratemeyer's FEAF. The reading referred to is Richard H. Kohn and Joseph P. Harahan, eds., *Air Interdiction in World War II, Korea, and Vietnam* (Washington, D.C.: Office of Air Force History, 1986), one of a number of publications sent to the panelists for their review prior to the symposium.

Air Pressure: Air-to-Ground Operations in Korea

16. General Partridge wrote, "I had an intelligence unit headed by an American major—a crazy man. He had about sixty or eighty Koreans. He was funded by the Far East Air Forces headquarters, and he was a one-man intelligence section, I'll tell you. We wanted to find out how many airplanes the North Koreans possessed. I told him what the mission was, and he came back in about a week or two with one of the most beautifully hand-drawn maps you ever saw, pinpointing where the airplanes had been found in North Korea." (Kohn and Harahan, *Air Interdiction*, p. 50).

17. Special Security Office. Additionally, much of the intelligence-gathering activity supporting the air campaign at this stage of the Korean War fell under the purview of "that very superior officer" (in the words of General Stratemeyer), CWO (later Capt.) Donald Nichols, a remarkably effective individual noted for his ability to run covert operations. See William T. Y'Blood, ed., *The Three Wars of Lieutenant General George E. Stratemeyer: His Korean War Diary* (Washington, D.C.: Air Force History and Museums Program, 1999), 205.

18. During the Korean War, building on the experience of World War II, the Air Force employed both airborne forward air controllers (FACs) and ground-based FACs. The former flew in modified North American T-6 Texan trainers dubbed Mosquitoes. The latter traveled in radio-equipped Jeeps operating at the forward line of troops.

19. Brig. Gen. John P. Henebry, who, at the time of Korea, was the youngest general officer in the Air Force. General Henebry, a bomber veteran of World War II, succeeded the legendary Maj. Gen. William H. Tunner, of Hump fame, who had done a brilliant job in his own right running Korean air logistical support. Combat Cargo had existed as a temporary command; but, on General Tunner's recommendation, FEAF discontinued it on January 25, 1951, activating the 315th Air Division under General Henebry. By war's end, Combat Cargo had carried 697,000 tons of cargo and 2,650,000 passengers; air-dropped 18,000 tons of cargo; and air-evacuated 314,000 patients, the greatest continuous medical air evacuation in military history. See William M. Leary, *Anything, Anywhere, Anytime: Combat Cargo in the Korean War* (Washington, D.C.: Air Force History and Museums Program, 2000), and Capt. Annis G. Thompson, *The Greatest Airlift: The Story of Combat Cargo* (Tokyo: Dai-Nippon Printing Company, May 1954). The latter is an excellent commemorative history issued by the 315th Air Division.

20. Gen. Matthew B. Ridgway, U.S. Army, who had succeeded Lt. Gen. Walton Walker as Eighth Army commander on December 26, 1950, following Walker's tragic death in a road accident. On April 11, 1951, General Ridgway succeeded Gen. Douglas MacArthur as commander-in-chief of United Nations Command and Far East Command of UN forces following President Harry Truman's well-publicized relieving of the legendary MacArthur.

21. The Lockheed Constellation, an elegant (and large) four-engine airliner that served in the U.S. Air Force as the C-69 and C-121, not at all suited to landing on a short strip.

22. The Lockheed RF-80A Shooting Star, a photoreconnaissance derivative of the F-80A fighter with cameras replacing its six .50-cal machine guns. For a survey of the RF-80A, see Doug Gordon, "Flying 'Eye:' Lockheed's RF-80A Shooting Star," *Air Enthusiast* 99 (May–June 2002): 33–43.

23. A reference to the two-place, Vietnam-era McDonnell Douglas RF-4C Phantom II, which had a backseat reconnaissance systems officer/navigator. At certain times in Vietnam, RSO/nav backseaters were scarce and much coveted.

24. FEAF commander from April 1949.

25. That morning in appalling weather, then-Lieutenant Poe went aloft alone to photograph the leading elements of the North Korean forces. It was the first reconnaissance sortie flown in the Korean War and the first jet reconnaissance combat sortie ever flown by the Air Force.

26. After Poe reported the locations of Korean forces and that air attacks could be prosecuted, FEAF swung into high gear. B-26s from the 3d BG hit the railyards at Munsan, then strafed and rocketed advancing NK forces; F-80s strafed targets north of Seoul, leaving fires visible for fifty miles; F-82s flew top cover for transports; and B-29s attacked road and rail targets. Many of the low-flying B-26s were damaged, but only one was damaged so badly as not to be repairable. Another B-26, sadly, crashed during its landing approach at Ashiya, due to losing sight of the runway in the terrible weather.

27. Jettisonable fuel tanks were a scarce item early in the Korean War, but the necessity of minimizing drag and weight to maximize performance—particularly for reconnaissance aircraft deep in hostile territory—overruled traditional logistical concerns.

28. The heavy cruiser USS *Helena*, undertaking 8-in. and 5-in. naval gunfire support missions off the Korean coast.

29. FEAF RF-80 photo reconnaissance was critical to the success of the Inchon landings. To quote the official history, "the Navy sorely needed to know the exact high-and low-tide heights of the sea walls which would have to be scaled at Inchon. Four precisely timed photo missions were assigned to the 8th Tactical Reconnaissance Squadron and within two days the needed photography was delivered to the Navy. These oblique photographs, taken by low-flying RF-80 photojet pilots, not only provided the basic information that the Navy wanted to know, but they proved to be just what the Navy needed to orient its landing crews. In less than a day, 2,100 prints of the oblique photos were delivered to the naval task force at Kobe." Futrell, *USAF in Korea*, 157, citing Col. R. W. Philbrick, *Report on Some Problems*

in the Production and Utilization of Air Reconnaissance in the Korean Campaign (26 Oct. 1950), 15–17.

30. The latter in reference to the linking-up with forces breaking out northward from the Pusan perimeter, advancing on the heels of the disintegrating North Korean resistance.

31. Later in the war, the Navy and Marines operated small detachments of Grumman F9F–5P and McDonnell F2H–2P recce aircraft from carriers. Additionally, the Marines operated F2H–2Ps ashore, undertaking deep reconnaissance missions over communist territory, including Manchuria.

32. This is a reference to the color of naval aircraft at the time. During the Korean War, all combat naval aircraft featured a "wraparound" dark-blue color scheme. After Korea, the Navy changed to a gray-and-white scheme (gray topsides, white undersurfaces), in part because the service had found the all-blue scheme made it difficult for pilots in formation to spot combat damage and fuel, oil, coolant, and hydraulic leaks. Thus, pilots often lost the critical time to declare an emergency and leave enemy airspace before the plane was perhaps catastrophically stricken. Later, after Vietnam, the Navy (like the Air Force) adopted an all-gray scheme, in part to reduce visibility and help defeat infrared-guided missile threats.

33. The Fairchild C–119 Flying Boxcar, a distinctive twin-engine, twin-tail boom design extensively used in Korea to drop troops and supplies. During the retreat from the Chosin Reservoir, C–119s dropped supplies and evacuated wounded, as well as bridge sections to permit the Marines to bridge a gorge, allowing them to continue to use their vehicles to extract their people.

34. For an excellent survey on supportability and "make do" issues, see Gen. Bryce Poe, "Korean War Combat Support: A Lieutenant's Journal," *Air Force Journal of Logistics* XIII:4 (Fall 1989): 3–7.

35. One of the pioneers in aerial reconnaissance, Colonel Polifka had commanded the Mediterranean Allied Photographic Reconnaissance Wing (MAPRW) during World War II. Not content to fly a desk, he went on numerous extremely hazardous missions piloting unarmed Lightning reconnaissance airplanes. Brig. Gen. George W. Goddard, considered by many the father of American aerial reconnaissance, noted in his memoirs that "of all our World War II recce pilots there is no doubt that Pop Polifka was the most outstanding.... A heavy set, square-faced blond tiger with Slavic features and no visible nerves . . . a pilot par excellence and a flight commander who inspired tremendous respect and loyalty from his men." See Brig. Gen. George W. Goddard, USAF (Ret.) with DeWitt S. Copp, *Overview: A Life-Long Adventure in Aerial Photography* (Garden City, NY: Doubleday & Company, 1969), 300. In 1950, Goddard made an inspection trip to Korea to study the reconnaissance situation, and, on his recommendation, General Stratemeyer made a by-name request for Polifka. He arrived in Korea in January 1951 and activated the 67th Tactical Reconnaissance Wing on February 25, 1951. Sadly, Polifka was shot down on July 1, 1951, flying an RF–51, losing his life while trying to bail out of his stricken plane. Polifka was so highly regarded that the Air Force leadership tried, unsuccessfully, to have him promoted posthumously to brigadier general.

36. Constance Babington-Smith, *Evidence in Camera: The Story of Photographic Intelligence in World War II* (London: Chatto and Windus, 1958). Babington-Smith, who died in 2000 just prior to the sixtieth anniversary of the Battle of Britain, was herself one of the most decorated of Royal Air Force wartime photo-intelligence interpreters, being noted particularly for her legendary role in detecting the existence of German V-weapons. The American edition of this work was entitled *Air Spy* (New York: Harper & Brothers, 1957).

37. Using the pseudonym "Lieutenant Jones," a ruse that fooled few. See Babington-Smith, 168.

38. An airplane with a relatively thick and high-aspect-ratio straight wing, the unarmed RF–80 was limited to just over eighty percent (Mach 0.8) of the speed of sound before transonic drag rise and shockwave formation would result in pronounced buffeting and potential loss of control or even structural failure. In contrast, the swept-wing and lower-aspect-ratio MiG–15 could reach Mach 0.92 before experiencing the same difficulties. This translated into about a fifty to sixty mph advantage (depending on altitude) in favor of the MiG.

39. FEAF originally planned to replace the RF–80 with the Republic RF–84F Thunderflash, a photoreconnaissance variant of the swept-wing F–84F Thunderstreak jet fighter. But the F–84F, and its reconnaissance stablemate the RF–84F, underwent prolonged gestation, and neither entered Air Force service until well after the Korean War. In November 1951, alarmed by the danger the MiG–15 posed to even escorted RF–80 operations north of the Chongchong River, the 67th Wing requested that two F–86As destined to be returned to the United States be instead modified as recce aircraft. A visit by Gen. Hoyt Vandenberg, the Air Force chief of staff, to Korea the next month accelerated interest and expanded the project. FEAF assigned six airplanes (48–187, 48–195, 48–196, 48–217, 48–246, and 48–257) to be modified by Far East Air Materiel Command (FEACOM, later reorganized and redesignated as Far East Air Logistics Force, FEALF), under the project leadership of CWO Lawrence K. Redmond. The modification effort was designated Project Ashtray. FEACOM installed a K–22 forward oblique camera and two K–24 split vertical cameras in the first modified Sabre, 48–217, dubbed Honeybucket. The K–22 installation worked fine, but the K–24 installation was "greatly inferior to subsequent modifications . . . [and was] not being used." The other five Sabres received a K–22 nose oblique camera and a K–22 vertical camera. The latter actually was installed with its photo axis parallel to the axis of the

Air Pressure: Air-to-Ground Operations in Korea

wing, but then used a 45-degree mirror to shoot a vertical image. Thus modified, the RF–86A was judged "an excellent aircraft to use for nose oblique photography," and, by the summer of 1952, RF–86As were flying all Fifth Air Force nose-oblique photography missions. But, even after subsequent modifications, it was "not a good reconnaissance aircraft" for vertical photography because of the camera space limitations; its 9-by-9-in. format K–22 vertical camera was not as satisfactory as the 9-by-18 K–38 used in the RF–80 and the U.S. Navy/Marine McDonnell F2H–2P Banshee; indeed, a Sabre needed twice as many sorties as the RF–80 to cover the same area. The RF–86A's major advantage over these other aircraft was its speed, both to evade MiG–15s and enemy ground fire. Subsequently, in the much more extensively modified (Project Haymaker) RF–86F—with distinctive "cheek" bulges on either side of the cockpit for two vertical K–22s, as well as a K–17 vertical camera in the belly—supplanted the RF–86A in the recce role. See CWO Lawrence K. Redmond, "Project Ashtray (RF–86A) Report," in 67th TRW, *Special Projects* (July 1952), I-1 to I-9, an appended report to the 67th TRW, *A History of the 67th Tactical Reconnaissance Wing, Period 1 July to 31 December 1952* (Kimpo AB, 67th TRW, 10 Feb. 1953), copy in the files of the Air Force Historical Research Agency, Maxwell AFB, Alabama, catalogue number K-WG-67-HI Jul–Dec 1952.

40. From an old expression about "dicing with death," that is, gambling with one's life.

41. See USAF, *Flight Handbook USAF Series RF–86F–30 Aircraft*, Technical Order 1F–86(R)F–1 (30 Apr. 1958 ed.), 4–1, for details.

42. "Tech reps" were civilian technical representatives from the aircraft manufacturers working with Air Force units flying their designs, in this case from North American Aviation, Inc.

43. Nickname for the previously cited *Flight Handbook*. Its colloquialism arises from the –1 suffix to the technical order number, which indicated flight manuals.

44. The temperature of an exhaust flow is a direct measurement of its energy, and, thus, engine performance. "Rats and mice" were flow constrictors to help improve nozzle effects and increase the ambient temperature of the exhaust.

45. That is, the launching of defensive interceptors; in this time period, typically Lockheed F–94Bs.

46. During the Korean War, Soviet radar technicians had dramatically increased radar coverage on the Korean peninsula and along the Chinese and Russian coastlines. The leading Soviet radars in use at this time were RUS–2, a 65–85 megacycle truck-mounted early warning radar, and a fixed-base derivative, the P2M Pegmatit; Dumbo, a 65–85 megacycle EW and limited-use ground-controlled intercept (GCI) fixed-base radar, and an improved derivative dubbed *Kniferest*; and *Token*, a 10-cm EW and GCI radar first detected at Antung (now Dandong), Manchuria. In the Korean era, Soviet radar technology generally lagged that of the West, and, indeed, the Soviets made use of imported British radars, copies of the American SCR–584 (dubbed *Whiff*) and perhaps even captured Nazi Freya and Würzburg systems. For more on Soviet air defense radar development at this time, see "Round-Up of Red Radars," *Air Intelligence Digest* VII:8 (Aug. 1954): 20–27, copy in the archives of the Air Force History Support Office, Bolling AFB, D.C.

47. An intelligence summary at this time credited the Soviets with no less than 77 operational airfields in the Far East, most concentrated in the Vladivostok-Khabarovsk region; North Korea had an additional 14, Manchuria approximately 40, and China 31 with "several hundred" others not in use or under development.

48. The MiG–17 (NATO identification name Fresco) was a much more refined derivative of the MiG–15, featuring better transonic performance, a new semi-crescent wing configuration, and a more powerful engine with an afterburner. Overall, the MiG–17 could outperform any of the early Sabre family, with the possible exception of the F–86H and the Navy's F–86-derivative FJ–4 Fury. The F–86 had itself led to a next-generation North American fighter, the F–100A Super Sabre, America's first supersonic jet fighter, a better match for the MiG–17 than the F–86, but the Soviets matched this development with their own first generation supersonic jet fighter, the MiG–19 Farmer.

49. Maj. Gen. Emmett "Rosie" O'Donnell, Jr., a distinguished bomber commander from World War II, appointed as commander of FEAF Bomber Command on July 8, 1950. Prior to that, he commanded Strategic Air Command's Fifteenth Air Force.

50. FAC. a forward air controller.

51. The North American T–6 Texan, an excellent and much-loved two-seat advanced trainer that evolved from the pre–World War II basic training BC–1. Powered by a single 600-hp Pratt & Whitney R–1340 radial engine, the T–6 was a reliable and surprisingly agile airplane, with a top speed of 210 mph and a cruising speed of 145 mph—but terribly vulnerable to light flak and automatic weapons fire.

52. Bomb damage assessment.

53. Tom Brokaw, *The Greatest Generation* (New York: Random House, 1998).

54. See note 2. Primarily these were two-place Polikarpov Po–2 biplanes but sometimes were other more modern light aircraft and trainers.

55. Harry Whitver, *Air and Space Smithsonian* XV:2 (Jun–Jul 2000): 46.

56. Although initially located at the Royal Aeronautical Establishment, Farnborough, the ETPS later relocated to the Aeroplane & Armament Experimental Establishment (A & AEE) at RAF Boscombe Down, Wiltshire.

Silver Wings Golden Valor: The USAF Remembers Korea

57. Col. Kathleen Conley, USAF, a C–17 pilot commanding AF/CVAM, Special Air Missions.

58. The Messerschmitt Me 262 *Schwalbe* (Swallow), a twin-jet, 550-mph fighter armed with four 30-mm cannon and unguided rockets, used in the latter stages of the war in a desperate attempt to stop the Allied day bomber offensive. The Me 163 *Komet* (Comet) was powered by a single liquid rocket engine and armed with two 30-mm cannon. Although the 262 had tremendous combat potential and posed a real threat to Allied air superiority, the flashy 163 had negligible impact, and, indeed, was far more dangerous to its pilots than to the Allies.

59. Redesignated the 49th Fighter-Bomber Wing in February 1950.

60. Military occupational specialty.

61. Air Force specialty code.

62. That is, the copilot's seat. The reference is to pilots who chose other preferences, typically fighters, and then were instead "drafted" to bombers. Jacobs chose the four-engine track voluntarily, which put him in line for pilot in command (left seat) of a bomber or transport.

63. IP: instructor pilot. Such rapid progression indicated extensive flying experience in diverse and challenging conditions and circumstances.

64. That is, there was no two-place conversion aircraft for familiarization flying before going solo.

65. The Lockheed T–33A Shooting Star, a two-place, armed trainer variant of the F–80 jet fighter (originally designated the TF–80C), which was eventually used as a transition aircraft to train pilots for F–80 conversion.

66. The Curtiss C–46 Commando, a twin-engine transport that was larger and heavier than the famed Douglas C–47 Skytrain. Although rugged and powerful, it was neither as reliable nor as well liked as the smaller "Gooney Bird."

67. The F–80C had an armament of six .50-cal machine guns.

68. Goon: Gooney Bird, that is, the C–47.

69. Republic of Korea. This is a reference to Project Bout-One, a hastily assembled composite American-Korean fighter force flying ten F–51 Mustangs, under the leadership of then-Major Dean Hess, USAF.

70. As designed, the F–80 did not have integral tiptanks to extend its range. Instead, it had provisions to carry two 165-gallon jettisonable tanks, each one hanging from a bomb shackle at the very wingtip of the airplane. Ironically, this tank arrangement actually improved the lift-to-drag ratio of the F–80 compared to an F–80 in "clean" (that is, tank-free) configuration. Clean, the F–80 had but a 100-mile radius of action; with two tanks, it had a 225-mile combat radius. If necessary, F–80s could also carry a single 1,000-pound bomb from each wingtip in place of the tanks and did so in Korea.

71. Lt. Edward R. "Rabbit" Johnson, 8 FBS, 49th FBW; and Lt. Robert "Foots" Eckman, 9 FBS, 49th FBW. The tank development program was undertaken at the request of General Partridge, who assigned it to the 49th Wing. The modified F–80 tanks were called "Misawa tanks" and increased the F–80's combat radius to 350 miles. See Futrell, 59–60.

72. During a diving gunnery pass, fuel could slosh forward in the tank, increasing the amount of backstick pressure the pilot needed to control aircraft trim. Then, on recovery, the fuel would slosh toward the rear of the tank; unless the pilot compensated rapidly, the plane could pitch up rapidly, overstressing the tanks and leading to disastrous asymmetrical or symmetrical failures of the tanks and/or wings.

73. The 27th Fighter-Escort Wing, equipped with Republic F–84 Thunderjets, and commanded by Col. Ashley B. Packard, left Bergstrom AFB, Texas, for San Diego, and then, in mid-November 1950, had its aircraft shipped via aircraft carrier and a tanker to Korea. It flew its first mission from Taegu on December 6.

74. Lt. Col. Glenn T. Eagleston, commander of the 334 FIS, and Capt. (later Maj.) James Jabara, 334 FIS, a future triple ace, members of the 4th Fighter-Interceptor Wing, commanded by Col. George F. Smith and based at New Castle County Airport, Wilmington, Delaware. Like the 27th Wing, the 4th had its aircraft shipped to Korea via surface vessel. The 4th flew its first combat sortie from Kimpo on December 15 and shot down its first MiG–15 on December 17.

75. On October 8, 1950, 1st Lt. Norvin Evans, Jr., 1st Lt. Alton H. Quanbeck, 1st Lt. Allen J. Diefendorf, and 2d Lt. Billy B. Watson were ordered to attack Ch'ongjin airfield. Due to engine problems, Watson aborted prior to takeoff. Evans had engine trouble after takeoff, aborted, and turned the flight over to Quanbeck. Now a two-ship, Quanbeck and Diefendorf pressed on in the midst of increasingly poor weather and obscuring cloud, climbing on a magnetic heading of 005 degrees. More than an hour later, believing themselves in the vicinity of their target, they let down through clouds, spotted an airfield with approximately twenty aircraft (which they identified as Bell P–39 Airacobras, but which might have also been Bell P–63 Kingcobras), and attacked it in three strafing passes, destroying some planes. Quanbeck suddenly realized the terrain features did not correspond with what he had been briefed, broke off the attack, and, together with Diefendorf, returned to Taegu. In fact, they had attacked a Soviet seacoast airfield at Sukhaya Rechka. The Soviets protested the attack, and General Stratemeyer, already angry over an earlier border violation by a B–29 crew, relieved the commander of the 49th Wing, Col. Stanton T. Smith, and ordered a court-martial for Lts. Quanbeck and Diefendorf. The court-martial subsequently refused to convict the two young airmen, who went on to further distinction (if in

less spectacular fashion) in the Air Force. Colonel Smith was brought to Seoul to direct combat operations for Fifth Air Force. See Y'Blood, 226–231, and Futrell, 149.

76. Capt. Daniel James, Jr. One of the Tuskegee airmen, "Chappie" James earned his wings in 1943. He flew 101 missions in Korea in F–51 and F–80/T–33 aircraft, flew 78 combat missions over North Vietnam, and rose to four-star rank as commander in chief of North American Air Defense. A highly respected fighter pilot and charismatic and inspiring commander, he retired in February 1978, sadly dying suddenly days later.

77. In aerodynamics, little things can mean a lot. Stall strips are small pieces of metal attached to the leading edge of a wing of some aircraft to ensure that they have predictable stalling characteristics. The point made here is that, in the field under emergency conditions, individuals often undertook hasty modifications without adequate thought being given to the effect that these could have on aircraft handling qualities. For example, the asymmetric protruding camera installation on the leading edge of the F–80's wing could have disrupted the local airflow, triggering a premature stall of that wing, and leading to a departure from controlled flight, possibly with disastrous consequences.

78. This constituted a reasonable assumption. Exploiting Western air power was always the lynchpin of NATO strategic thought, and the USAF was, in turn, the lynchpin of this air-rooted strategy. The very first NATO planning document, DC6/1, approved by the North Atlantic Council on Jan. 6, 1950, stated that, in the event of war, NATO's first undertaking would be to "insure the ability to carry out strategic bombing by all means possible with all types of weapons, without exception." This was understandable, given the force disparity already evident between the West and the Soviet Union. In December 1949, the Chiefs of Staff Committee of the Western Union noted that the Soviets could immediately attack Europe with 25 divisions, 5,000 tanks, and 2,000 aircraft, these figures rising to 75 divisions and 5,000 aircraft within an additional 30 days. In response, the North Atlantic Alliance could field only seven infantry divisions (only two of these were considered combat ready), four armored brigades, and 294 aircraft. The goal of air planners in those early days, and later as well, was to break any Soviet attack by interdiction strikes against railroad and road targets. Over the long watch of the Cold War, interdiction, second only to air superiority, was the central core of NATO's attack strategy. For more information, see Eduard Mark, *Defending the West: The United States Air Force and European Security, 1946–1998* (Washington, D.C.: Air Force History and Museums Program, 1999).

79. The 20th Fighter-Bomber Group went to RAF Manston, supporting SAC's 3d Air Division.

80. The Republic F–84 Thunderjet was the Air Force's first post–World War II jet fighter. It had one of the first axial-flow turbojet engines, the Allison J35, which gave it a slender fuselage by the standards of then-contemporary jet fighter design. Like the Navy's straight-wing F9F Panther, the F–84 had the distinction of spawning a swept-wing derivative, the F–84F, produced too late for Korean service. The F–84 initially had to overcome a bad reputation for wing failure triggered by inadequate structural stiffness, a problem cured by increasing the thickness of its wing skins and adding fins to its tiptanks to help inhibit tank flutter at transonic speeds. With these problems solved, the F–84 went on to a highly successful career, regarded as a rugged and reliable fighter-bomber in the tradition of its predecessor, the World War II Republic P–47 Thunderbolt. Both the straight- and swept-wing F–84 family saw extensive service, particularly with NATO's air forces.

81. On May 9, 1951, 312 Air Force and Marine fighters attacked Sinuiju airfield in relays, in response to intelligence indications that the communists had moved some 38 aircraft, comprising Yakovlev Yak–9 and Lavochkin La–5 fighters, and Ilyushin Il–10 attack aircraft, into revetments at the field. F–86s from the 4th Fighter Wing, F–84s from the 27th Fighter Wing, and F9Fs from the 1st Marine Air Wing (MAW) furnished top cover, fending off some desultory passes from 18 MiGs that attempted to interfere. F–80s from the 8th, 49th, and 51st Fighter Wings; F–51s from the 18th Fighter Wing; and Marine F4Us from the 1st MAW bombed, rocketed, napalmed, and strafed the field, striking a series of pre-briefed targets in a ten-square-mile area, destroying what aircraft were on the field, together with more than one hundred buildings, a fuel dump, and other ammunition and supply dumps. Only one aircraft, an F–84, suffered enemy damage, and it returned safely. See Futrell, *USAF in Korea*, 302–5.

82. In the conditions of largely static warfare under which Korea was fought from mid-1951 until the spring of 1953 (before the final occasionally savage fighting that preceded the armistice in July), enemy usage of supplies was relatively low. Thus, even though interdiction accounted for large numbers of destroyed supplies, the amount that did get through was more than sufficient to meet frontline needs. Later, when the tempo of fighting increased in 1953, UN forces noted for the first time that the Chinese and North Korean forces began to be far more conservative in firing their weapons, as the frontline consumption was now so great that the results of the UN air campaign against supply lines and depots was beginning to clearly be felt by the enemy.

Chapter 7

FROM KOREA TO KOSOVO: LEARNING FROM THE PAST FOR THE CRISES OF THE FUTURE

Dr. Wayne W. Thompson
Panel Chairman

MAJOR GENERAL MOSELEY: We're going to depart from the form that we had for this symposium for the first two sessions. In my opening remarks, I stated that we were building this symposium around the American veteran, the veteran of the Korean War, and the contributions they made. The last panel is different. The last panel addresses the legacy of the Korean War. We're basically looking at the subject of Korea to Kosovo, aerospace power in the world today, the lessons of Korea.

Our chairman is Dr. Wayne Thompson. Wayne is a different kind of historian. He's Chief of Analysis for the Air Force History Support Office [now the Office of Air Force History] at Bolling Air Force Base. He has been intimately involved in contemporary Air Force operations over the last decade, ranging from the Gulf War (where he worked with Checkmate in the Pentagon) to Operation Deliberate Force and onto Operation Allied Force and the analysis of Allied Force since the end of that conflict. Additionally, he has a book coming out on the air campaign over North Vietnam.[1] He was the senior historical advisor for the Gulf War Air Power Survey, and, since that time, as I've mentioned, he's turned his attention to air power and air operations in the Balkans.

Wayne has a very distinguished panel, including Dr. Dan Gouré of CSIS, and Dr. Chris Bowie of Northrop Grumman, who is an old colleague of Wayne and Dick Hallion's from the Secretary of the Air Force's Staff Group in the days of

Silver Wings Golden Valor: The USAF Remembers Korea

Don Rice. We are very fortunate to have as well Lt. Gen. Chuck Heflebower, who has come all the way from Korea to participate in this panel. He will put the Korean air war in the context of Korean operations and the challenge of Korean operations today. So, not to steal any of Wayne's thunder—Wayne, I turn it over to you.

DR. WAYNE THOMPSON: It's been quite a day. I have really enjoyed it; it's been a privilege. The reason we do these after fifty years is that the people eventually go away, and we can't get the benefit of their experience. If we don't do it now, we might not be able to do it later. All of you have shared with me this privilege. I'm sure you feel the same way I do—very special. Now you'll notice the people we've got up here are younger; the average age has gone down; our practical experience of the Korean War is very, very slight, and we were all toddlers at best. Our perspective is obviously a little different.

As an official historian, I deal every day with the question of what in the past is relevant to the problems we're dealing with now. As I was listening today, that's what was going through my mind. I know there have been tremendous changes in the last fifty years, and I also know there is something here that is still gripping, that still relates. So I think our challenge here in our final panel is to begin to try to sort that out a little bit for ourselves at least. What's still relevant? What's different? The changes have been enormous.

A few days ago I sent my fellow panel members a list of questions about what has changed in the last fifty years. I don't know whether we'll really get to discuss many of them. We don't have that much time, and my fellow panelists will each have their own thrust. They'll each make an initial pitch, and we will have a chance for interchange. We want to get all of you involved with your particular questions, but I thought I would throw my questions out front here, and, if I get a chance later on, I may bring some of them up again.

My first to the panel is "Has the development of precision-guided bombing since the Korean War fundamentally changed the nature of air power?"

My second question is "What is the best defense against precision bombing?"

My third question is "Is there still a role for area bombing?"

My fourth question is "Have Americans become too squeamish about casualties, whether among their own people in uniform or among enemy civilians?"

My fifth question is "A new factor in air defense since the Korean War is surface-to-air missiles. How well have we done against SAMs?"

My sixth question is "What is the most serious threat to American air dominance?"

My seventh question is "Which are most important to the future of aerospace power—manned aircraft, or UAVs, or space vehicles?"

My eighth question is "What have we learned over the past half century about working with allies?"

My ninth and final question to bring us home is "What do you think is the most important legacy of the Korean War?"

From Korea to Kosovo

We have a first-rate panel, and I'll introduce them just before each of them gives his initial pitch. We're going to start with Lt. Gen. Charles "Chuck" Heflebower, Commander of Seventh Air Force. He's come all the way from Korea to be with us. It makes me wish when we titled this panel that we had called it "From Korea to Korea." We called it "From Korea to Kosovo," but "Korea to Korea" might be the better title, because we're still there.

General Heflebower has spent many years preparing himself for this very special responsibility. He's a graduate of the Air Force Academy and the National War College. He has a master's in international relations from the University of Arkansas. His combat experience goes back to Vietnam. He was an RF–4 pilot and later an F–16 pilot.[2] There's nobody better qualified to tell us about the contrast or the comparison between Korea today and Korea fifty years ago. General Heflebower, sir?

LT. GEN. CHUCK HEFLEBOWER: Thank you. I'm not going to address each of those questions individually. I'm going to allow the Q&A period to really take that, but I want to talk a little bit about the differences between Korea today and Korea when the gentlemen who you heard talk earlier had to go over there and really come up to scratch from scratch.

It is amazing for me to sit out there. One of the great things about serving in the military, any occupation, is you never quit learning. When you do, you quit developing. I learned more today probably in the six hours or so that I listened to these gentlemen talk than I have in probably a couple of years. So I probably got more out of this than I can take back with me, or you can imagine.

Many of the fundamentals haven't changed. We still have to gain and maintain control of the air. That's job #1. So that's still very important to us. Without it, you can't win. With it, you can't lose. Clearly close air support is important today. The structure that was developed and really and truly pioneered during the Korean War built on some of the lessons first learned during the North African campaign in World War II and later.[3] In turn, the close air support structure that we have today was one that was fundamentally set up by folks like General Conley who went over to Korea and built it up then. We're perhaps a little more sophisticated at it now, and we train at it better along with our Army and Marine colleagues, but it's basically the same takedown and escapes. We just practice it a lot more, and, hopefully, when we have to do it for real, we'll be prepared to. We are still doing reconnaissance. We're doing it a little differently. We still do reconnaissance in all three dimensions. Sometimes we do it a little higher with space vehicles. We also do it with manned vehicles, and we do it with unmanned vehicles. So the basic fundamentals and the things you heard about today still apply, even if how we do them is a little different in some cases.

What's different in Korea, of course, is, unlike on June 25, 1950, we have sizeable American forces in place on the ground. As we speak, we've got 37,500 Americans stationed in Korea. We've got a division minus north of the Han River, a very capable division, the 2d Infantry Division, and we've got around ten thou-

Silver Wings Golden Valor: The USAF Remembers Korea

sand American airmen who are there maintaining two main operating bases with both F–16s and A–10s.[4] We fly U–2 surveillance missions every day.[5] Then we also have American airmen stationed at what we call "colocated operating bases," whose mission is to receive follow-on forces very quickly. So, if war breaks out, we're prepared to get back into Korea with additional reinforcing forces in a hurry.

Clearly, there are a lot of things different with regard to the Republic of Korea forces. At the beginning of the Korean War, there was no Korean air force to speak of. Today, it's a very capable jet air force with almost eight hundred airplanes. The predominance of air power there on a day-to-day basis is embodied by the South Koreans themselves. They now build their own F–16 variant, and they have F–16s and F–4s and F–5s.[6] They're very capable and very well trained—mostly by Americans, I might add. The story of the South Korean air force is one of great heroism, as they literally developed their air force under fire. We also have a very capable Korean army and a very capable navy as well. So the state of affairs in South Korea in terms of readiness and preparation is a lot different—happily— than it was when these gentlemen we've heard from today had to go and fight in harm's way.

You heard these veterans emphasizing training today, and that is so very true. The American airmen and soldiers and sailors and Marines are as well trained today as they ever have been. We put a lot into that institutionally, and we put a lot more in when they arrive in Korea. In terms of motivation, I probably have one of the easiest jobs there is in command, because, when people arrive, we take them up to Panmunjom, the demilitarized zone, and put them face to face with the North Koreans. Then, for the next year, motivation is not particularly difficult; they understand what they have to do. Ninety-five percent of the Americans over there are unaccompanied, without their families. So the focus on the mission is unique compared to other locations around the world.

We also hand them their chemical equipment, teach them how to use it right away, and so, within a couple of days, they're ready to fight. We say—and I emphasize it over and over—we have to be ready to fight tonight. I can tell you that the American forces and our Korean forces there are ready to fight tonight. That readiness came from the lessons you heard about and discussed today—that's where we learned to be ready to fight tonight and not be unprepared.

That state of readiness and that state of preparation can be very fleeting. It's not one that is easy to maintain. Of course, we turn over all our people every year over there, and so there's a constant training problem, a constant training challenge for all of the commanders and supervisors over there. But I can tell you that the people we have to train, the young airmen, soldiers, sailors, and Marines, are high quality and do a terrific job. Overall, the cards dealt are pretty good, and certainly we're dealt a better hand today if we have to do this thing for real than folks were dealt fifty years ago. I'm going to yield the microphone so we can get on with the other comments and then perhaps get into some questions and answers. Thanks very much.

DR. THOMPSON: Next we'll move to Chris Bowie. I've known Chris a long time. For years, he was with the RAND Corporation. He has his doctorate from Oxford. Since he joined Northrop Grumman, he's become the "stealth man." Whenever I think of a B–2, I think of Chris. Today he tells me he wants to talk about precision. So, Chris, it's all yours.

DR. CHRISTOPHER BOWIE: Thanks, Wayne. Wayne had sent out the list of questions, and I picked the first one, which was precision. I think it has fundamentally changed air power. I think also, looking at it historically, you find the difficulty of coming to grips with the implications of precision weaponry because I have a lot of trouble trying to figure out what it really means. Ed Luttwak always has a good descriptive name, and he calls this the "implications of routine precision" when it's a normal attribute of combat operations.

Air-delivered precision-guided weapons were dropped in Korea by the B–29s, and continued R&D led to the fielding of additional weapons. We saw the first laser-guided bomb used in combat operations in 1968 in Vietnam.[7] About twenty-seven thousand laser-guided bombs were dropped during Vietnam, 1968 to 1973, but finally we just thought of that as sort of an extension of tactics. Just before the Gulf War, when I was serving on the Air Staff, a popular Air Force saying was, "A smart airplane is preferable to a smart bomb because a smart airplane can make a dumb bomb smart, and a dumb bomb costs about the same per pound as hamburger." Smart bombs were viewed as too expensive. So, on the eve of the Gulf War, out of a force structure of about three thousand Air Force combat aircraft, only two types, representing just five percent of the force, could self-designate and self-deliver laser-guided bombs.[8] Now, after the Gulf War, we suddenly realized that those weapons had a profound impact on the nature of the Desert Storm air campaign and are often considered to have redefined the meaning of "mass" in warfare.[9] It's ten years later now, and most if not all of the force we have can deliver precision-guided weapons, and we've also used for the first time in combat a satellite-guided, all-weather precision bomb, the joint direct attack munition or JDAM.[10]

But I still wonder if we really understand what it means. If you'd asked me ten years ago, or even a year ago, or just six months ago about the idea of delivering concrete by guided weapons from aircraft, well, I would have thought you were crazy. That's what we're now doing in Operation Northern Watch. In order to attack Iraqi air defenses without collateral damage, our forces have on occasion employed concrete-filled inert guided bombs. What the Iraqis tend to do is park their air defense sites near a mosque or some cultural area, and, if you drop an explosive weapon on it, you'd cause a lot of damage. So what we now do is drop five hundred pounds of concrete traveling at five hundred miles an hour, and that will knock out a radar. But, again, it's not exactly what I would have come up with when talking about precision first off.[11]

There's been a lot of discussion here about close air support and the vital nature of close air support in the Korean War. I think one of the implications of precision is that we need to rethink how we do it, our whole concept of operations. The traditional notion, as General Heflebower has described, really dates back to what we did in the '50s, when we set up orbits of aircraft with a forward air controller to mark the area and deliver weapons against it.

But try this for a concept—you simply take a big airplane with a long loiter time, like a B–52 or a C–130,[12] and park it ten or twenty miles behind the front lines. The longer the orbit the better. Then, on this airplane, you put dozens of small GPS-guided[13] weapons. In fact, we've already tested such weapons at the Air Force Air Armament Center at Eglin Air Force Base, with little wings that come out so you can get, say, a sixty-mile range. The Air Force special operations controller is on the ground and equipped with a GPS pack and a laser rangefinder so he can precisely fix the target with GPS coordinates. He lazes the target, passes the coordinates back to the aircraft overhead, and, within a few minutes, you could have dozens of weapons delivered on the enemy.[14] Is that the sort of thing that would normally come to mind when you think of precision? You've basically turned your infantry into Thor the God of Thunder, delivering lightning bolts with precision anywhere they can see.

Now, if you adopt this concept, you would not only change the way you think about close air support, but it could radically decrease the logistical tail required for fire support of combat forces. Right now we haul in massive batteries, really heavy batteries, of artillery and MLRS [multiple launch rocket system] rounds.[15] I was told by an artillery officer that the CEP[16] of an artillery round is about forty yards, so you typically have to deliver a large number to hit the precise spot, whereas you can get within several yards with these new GPS-guided weapons. So, instead of using artillery or rocket launchers, you could provide fire support from aircraft orbiting overhead and based hundreds or thousands of miles away. These are adverse-weather weapons, so weather is less of a concern. Again, speaking of the implications of precision, maybe these precision weapons are a means of making powerful ground forces much more strategically agile. I'll stop there. Thank you.

DR. THOMPSON: The final pitch will be made by Dr. Dan Gouré, who's from the Center for Strategic and International Studies. His doctorate is from Johns Hopkins. For a long time he was with the Arms Control and Disarmament Agency. He's worked with the Office of the Secretary of Defense, and I first became aware of him a few years ago when he and Dick Hallion and some others put together a wonderful study group, whose report was published as *Air and Space Power in the New Millennium*.[17] If you haven't seen that report, it's very germane to what we're talking about here today, and so we're very pleased to have Dr. Gouré.

DR. DAN GOURÉ: Thank you. I appreciate the introduction. Thinking about the topic "Korea to Kosovo," I happened to notice the statistics, and I might as well start there because the differences are at least notable. I'm not entirely sure yet what they all mean, but let's just start with the data. You're talking about going from a three-year war in Korea to a three-month conflict in Kosovo, from thirty-three thousand dead at least on the U.S. side, hundreds of thousands of allied forces lost in Korea, to essentially close to zero on the U.S. side in Kosovo. Sixty-five percent of the U.S. combat casualties in Korea were to the Army. In Kosovo, the Army lost two dead, but that was in training and other accidents: nobody in combat. Then, if I understand the statistics, something like less than two percent of the munitions in Korea were precision, certainly a slight number. Now, with Kosovo, I think the number was about twenty-five percent precise. So we have some really distinct characteristics, if I can call them that.

But what is it that's really changed? What does all that mean? I've spent some time thinking about that and have at least a couple of ideas. Let me just throw them out to be provocative.

It seems to me the first thing we've done in this period of fifty-plus years—and listening a bit to the panel before, to sort of confirm this idea—is that we've gone from "seat of the pants" to "state of the art" in terms of putting all this together. I don't mean that as pejorative, but it was just new stuff. We were inventing a lot of this. Some of it came from World War II. We can even go back and say we were inventing it in World War II and then added to it postwar inventions as we went along—for example, jets and other things. This created today's "state of the art," particularly when it comes to putting all the pieces together. An earlier panelist made the comment that you can't decide which was more important, for everything played a role. More interestingly, of course, is that we can now coordinate all those roles, whether it's in sequence in time, or time of the day, or place on the battlefield. That's awfully important, I think.

Perhaps even more important than that, I would argue—and have for several years now—that what's different between, say, Korea and Kosovo, or World War II and Kosovo, is that air power can now deliver on its basic promise, the basic Douhet[18] promise. Not only can we do precision, but now air forces can find targets rather reliably in pretty much all-weather conditions. They can hit what they aim at and can engage in the air rather precisely. We have created conditions where we can work with our allies to do it as well. The downing of a MiG–29[19] in Kosovo illustrates this: one of the MiGs Milosevic lost was downed by a Dutch F–16 vectored in by U.S. AWACS.[20] That's a fairly neat thing to do: the MiG left the runway and then it was gone, all within minutes. That's sort of the basic promise in terms of being able to certainly contest for air superiority, gain it if at all possible, do the surveillance both air-to-air and air-to-ground, and all the rest.

So, although people tend to focus on precision strike, it's really everything. In fact, I'm not sure that precision is the most important or significant piece, partly because we don't quite know what to do with it. The tendency is to still talk about it, and, with all due respect to the previous speaker, I'm not criticizing him, but I think we typically talk about it like we talk about artillery. We just talk about it now with things in the air delivering the firepower, which—the way I look at it—tends to be a mistake. The reason is, what you can do with the air now is in fact exercise strategic control as well as tactical control if done properly. If you can gain the air superiority, engage in the interdiction operations, strike some strategic targets, you can force the opposition, as we did with the air defenses in Kosovo to simply go to hiding, virtual attrition. Why? Because if they started shooting, you ran some risks, but they died, essentially. What's going on with Northern Watch over northern Iraq is the same thing. This is a turkey shoot—no disrespect to anyone out there. There are dangers, but, by and large, we've been dropping bombs every second or third day for a year and a half now. I forget the number of targets hit, but there have been a large number of targets hit. There's yet to be a single allied casualty: that's awfully significant in terms of strategic control.

That, I think, is sort of what's most important about the revolution in air power. We've gone from a place in which you had strategic air operations that were still in the service of, or support of, what was a ground war campaign. You had close air support, interdiction (again in support of a ground campaign), a ground/naval campaign, to a case in which, in fact, air power can define the strategic terms of a conflict. If the enemy comes out of hiding, it dies. In fact, more and more, if it's in hiding, we're able to see it, find it, put a bomb on it. And, sooner or later, the bombs are going to be good enough that, even if the foe buries himself, we can dig him out.[21] The question that may be most interesting, though, in this transition is "How relevant is this capability going to be?" Just as we get to the point of being able to use air power in its most strategic sense, the Cold War ended. The purpose, if you will, to which this thing was geared, was now gone. So to what extent is this capability going to continue to be relevant? And, of course, that also involves another question: "In what kind of conflict?" All of which leads me to a couple of sub-thoughts.

Now, at the end of the Cold War, will we continue to have the kind of threats or adversaries that require or cause us to want to use air power strategically rather than—if I may use the expression—conventionally? I think the answer is certainly "yes." We see it not only in Korea where we have an adversary who, if anything, is surprising all of us now in the foreign policy arena by getting better. We thought that the North Koreans were on their last legs. In the last couple of years, certainly the last year, they've turned up a bit in terms of what they're doing and how they're doing it. So we certainly have that threat. We have the emergence of people who are taking advantage of technology the best they can and, more importantly, are trying to "game our game" and figure out how to apply these asymmetric strategies, the "bury it, hide it, spread it out, use nuclear weapons or other weapons of mass destruction" mindset. So we certainly have the threats.

More problematic, in two regards, is the question of time. Air power continues to get better. But we don't seem to get better at (1) anticipating the conflicts, and (2) getting to them ahead of the game, either by preempting or simply deterring by the demonstration of power. It's been tried. It's very tough. So, in a sense, the timing issue is not any easier. That puts us into a difficult situation of having to move all our neat stuff into theater, do it in a way that doesn't create a threat, get it into combat in time to affect the situation, and then roll on through.

That leads to the third problem. We've got this spiffy tool, but will there be the will to use it? In that regard, there's quite a contrast—and not a good one—between Korea and Kosovo. In Korea, we engaged in what was a classic strategic, theater-level conflict. There were a couple of constraints—going across the Yalu was one of them—but, in terms of how we fought, what was south of the Yalu was pretty much a straightforward strategic campaign. There were rules of engagement. You weren't killing civilians for the sheer fun of it; in fact, we tried to avoid it as a rule. But, still, you were conducting a broad strategic campaign. We've got now into a situation in which the character of the constraint—for example, in time and in both friendly and enemy casualties—may be so daunting as to prevent us from being successful, whether it's air or any other kind of military power that's employed. It's a real question about whether we can use any of the modern instruments of force effectively enough, given the political constraints.

"Force protection" is an example of one of those things that is not only a need of the military but that also has a political dimension. The goal of "zero casualties" constrains what you can do even when the cause is just.

I know that there was a study coming out of West Point—a former colleague of mine, Don Snyder, wrote it with several other colleagues—about the question of whether or not the allied military and the native forces violated the laws of war by being so casualty adverse in the conduct of their operations that, in fact, they inflicted casualties that were unnecessary. This is sort of the Amnesty International argument, but I think it may have some merit. It's not a matter of the public being casualty adverse. It's the leadership being casualty adverse.

Another one is homeland defense, which, I suggest, may be an interesting area. What relevance does modern air power have to the problem of homeland defense? The reason I bring that up is not because the threat to the homeland is all that particularly great, but we run the risk of crossing a threshold the first time you have a major event. Take the reaction to the loss of TWA Flight 800, which was an accident.[22] You had major changes in airport security and behavior of people and all the rest. That was a sheer accident. We thought it was terrorists. But have your first domestic incident, and people are going to start to look at the military power, I think, potentially differently. I'm not sure what it means for what we're doing in air power, but we may end up with something that is hard to defend. We have something here that may be harder to defend in the context of what are you doing for the homeland than in the traditional context.[23]

So let me leave you with just a couple of thoughts. One is that, from Kosovo, at least, there are two types of lessons. One is the conduct of the military campaign, which was quite amazing: the character of this campaign, the kind of operations that were run, the air space that was managed, all the allied flights that were managed. It's truly amazing, and it stands out. I think that would be the way we would treat other air campaigns as we go along. So the conduct of the military operation was quite superb. But contrast that to the conduct of the political campaign which was, I don't know, the best word I would use is amateurish, ham-handed. Politicians choosing targets—not just U.S. politicians which, perhaps, would be bad enough, but a whole set of leaders from a whole set of countries trying to make arguments about what targets were legitimate, which ones go on the target list, and which ones do not. The problem has been, to a certain extent, that judgments about the effectiveness of air power have gotten mixed up with judgments about political decisions, and the two ought to be kept separate.

The constraints are not new. We've had constraints in all wars. In World War II, you know, the political leadership did some fair agonizing about how they were going to conduct bombing and when you were going to use it, for example, low-level fire bombing, saturation bombing, et cetera. Frankly, people pulled back after Dresden,[24] for probably a very good reason. But we're at a point where I'm worried that, in fact, air power may be defeated, if I can call it that, not by our adversaries and what they can do but by ourselves. This is going to be truly the case that we may run into: "Pogo's law."[25] The enemy may be us rather than the adversary. Let me end there.

DR. THOMPSON: Would any of the three panelists like to respond to the other?

LIEUTENANT GENERAL HEFLEBOWER: We traditionally tend to focus on the last battle fought, in our case, Kosovo, which was successful. The previous speaker adequately described that in any operation there are three circles of influence: the political, strategic, and operational. In the case of Kosovo, the political dimension was huge. That doesn't understate the military performance, but clearly we need to understand [that] we intervened in Kosovo because of perceived human rights violations associated with some number of civilians, pick a number, one thousand or less. That doesn't make it right or wrong. Those are the facts.

South Korea has roughly fifty million people, twenty-five percent of whom live around Seoul. Just north of the DMZ, within range of Seoul, our estimates are that the North Koreans can present three hundred thousand to five hundred thousand rounds an hour of artillery, both conventional and unconventional. There are a total of twenty-four divisions facing each other within about fifteen miles, backed up by another approximately twenty divisions. It is a whole different ball game. And so, when the statement is made about how precision has fundamentally changed air warfare, I'm not so sure I can agree with that, because I think in what will be a war, mass is still important. One of the speakers said earlier today there is still a certain quality in quantity, and I think that's as true today as it was in the past. What precision has done, without question, is made us far more effective.

I think the other thing is that around the world we're seeing our adversaries—and North Korea's a great example—try to take away the asymmetry that exists through American technology and air power. Almost the entire North Korean army, navy, and air force can go underground in hardened facilities. Their artillery sites are all underground. Their surface-to-air missile sites are underground and are elevator-served. They clearly have learned from the Korean War that air power can influence the outcome. They've also learned that they were outgunned by the United States Army once our forces got onto the peninsula, and so they've learned from that and introduced long-range artillery that can out-range our own, with the exception of the ATACMS[26] and MLRS. In terms of close air support, when you're dealing with a million men coming south, precision becomes a little less significant, and mass becomes a little more important. So I think there's a balance there. I can tell you nowhere in any of my plans is there a concrete-filled bomb! That doesn't diminish the ingenuity and the insight in developing that, and using it in an Iraqi kind of situation—don't misunderstand me—but I don't plan to use one. So there are some lessons learned from Kosovo that are applicable to Korea, and we've grabbed all we can. But I think you can also learn the wrong lessons if you're not careful.

DR. BOWIE: I guess I did cut off my remarks. I was going to go on and talk about with precision you also get smaller weapons that can do the job of larger weapons with less precision. Thus, you can get fractionation. You can fractionate the payload. For example, an F–15E[27] can carry four two-thousand-pound bombs. If we go to the small smart bomb, that same aircraft would carry thirty-two, and thus you can really get enormous effects out of that.

Now, after the Gulf War, there was a lot of debate about whether dumb bombs still had their place, and we still have that debate. In Kosovo, twenty-three thousand rounds were dropped by the United States. About seven thousand of those were precision, nearly one-third. Two-thirds were, thus, general-purpose ordnance mostly delivered by B–1s[28] and B–52s—five-hundred-pound rounds.[29] I would argue that, since we can now make each of those a precision-guided round, we can choose a target for each of those weapons. Given the cost of getting the sortie across the target, if you think in life cycle terms, it's always better to have the round go where you want it to go. Certainly I understand in Korea you need to fling a lot of ordnance and a lot of ordnance is coming back at you. But if you can make each ordnance round more effective, I think you can take advantage of the fractionation made available by precision.

DR. THOMPSON: I'd like to comment on that. There is an aspect to area bombing that you just don't get with any amount of precision. It has to do with a psychological impact of a whole lot of bombs going off all at once in your vicinity. Those of us who studied Vietnam know that the Viet Cong have said since the war—and some at the time—that area bombing was really shattering to them. We've heard that in other places.[30] Since the Gulf War, some analysts have suggested the Iraqi leadership in Baghdad was not too impressed with all those pin pricks. Instead, if we had gone to downtown Baghdad (where there was a heavy concentration of office buildings) with our B–52s, as we did in Taji, north of Baghdad, we would have made a lot bigger impression. So that sort of thinking is still out there, and I'm wondering if we get into a situation where the enemy on the other side is a little more competitive, that we might see a return of area bombing. I just throw that out.

AUDIENCE MEMBER: I spent a year in Vietnam in close air support operations with F–100s,[31] and the comments that you made are rather intriguing. I guess the first question I would come up with is what percentage of precision-guided bombs are not accurate? In other words, they don't hit where they're supposed to, for whatever failure in the system. That's extremely important to the Army, and we didn't have many short rounds even though it was eyeball-delivery with F–100s.

LIEUTENANT GENERAL HEFLEBOWER: It depends on the munition, and it depends on the situation under which it's released. Again, it varies, but it's a very low percentage. But there is a percentage, depending on the munition, that will either go long or short.

As a matter of fact, today we're doing close air support with precision, the Maverick missile.[32] You know, I would say that the 30-mm gun on the A–10 is relatively precise.[33] Where we're doing close air support with precision is not only in the munitions, but in the identification and location of the target. We do this through technologies, such as laser pointers, that data-link coordinates to a pilot, and target designating—for example, the Pave Penny pod[34] on the A–10 that can pick up a spot on the ground. The coordination between the ground forward air controller as well as the airborne forward air controller, particularly the ability to have secure communication between the two of them, assists in precision location. Add to that GPS and other things as well with the space-based systems that we have, the use of targeting pods and laser designating, and that kind of thing, means that we're far more precise in close air support than we have been before. Again, we can stand off a little better using targeting pods and those kinds of things to stay above the fray a little bit and still precisely deliver weapons where the Army in fact needs them.

So we're clearly going down the road with precision and close air support and everything else. I'm not sure that I would say that it has fundamentally changed the way we do business, but what it has done is make us do the business better and more effectively. Because each sortie is more effective, we can do more with fewer airplanes whether it's in close air support, interdiction, or even air-to-air.

AUDIENCE MEMBER: What about information operations and electronic warfare, then and now?

LIEUTENANT GENERAL HEFLEBOWER: Well, the answer is we do both. Electronic warfare is important today and will be important in the future. Some aspects of information operations are relatively new. Others are not. Clearly, as we see in watching the History Channel, a classic example of information operations was to decoy and convince the Germans we were going to attack Calais as opposed to Normandy. That was information operations in its most basic form.

We use it. For example, we've formed an information warfare flight that works within our command and control facility that has a principal input to the development of what we call our Integrated Tasking Order—known as the ATO[35] in other theaters. So that aspect of it exists, and, as information operations continue to develop and mature, they will be folded into the air campaign. In terms of electronic warfare, with the evolution of airborne platforms, electronic warfare pods, the ability to use the EA–6, standoff and do SEAD, suppression of enemy air defenses with HARM: we're still doing that today, and that will continue to evolve.[36]

DR. THOMPSON: You know that whole business with SEAD, it comes really out of Vietnam. We didn't have SAMs in the Korean War, and we started facing SAMs in Vietnam, and then we started worrying about jamming pods and Wild Weasels and Shrike missiles[37]—now we have HARM missiles. There's a big intervening story since the Korean War.

LIEUTENANT GENERAL HEFLEBOWER: Clearly the development—and almost a revolutionary development in terms of aircraft and other airborne platforms—has been stealth. One of the reasons the Air Force is advocating so hard for the F–22[38] is the ability of it to operate, relatively autonomously, over high-threat areas. The F–22 and other stealthy platforms, the B–2[39] and the F–117, are huge aids in that regard, particularly in a North Korea scenario.

AUDIENCE MEMBER: Technically, the Korean War is not over yet. Fighting ended in an armistice, which continues today, and, as historians and subject-matter experts, and, General, as a warfighter who lives in that AOR,[40] do you ever think that the Korean War is going to end? We've been there for fifty years. Do you perceive this going on for another fifty more years, with American forces being in Korea?

LIEUTENANT GENERAL HEFLEBOWER: What you say is accurate. There is an armistice. Interestingly enough because of the fiftieth anniversary of the Korean War, we're having a lot of veterans start to return, some of whom have not been in Korea since the end of the war. Frequently they'll ask was their sacrifice worth it? Was it in vain? And, of course, generally speaking, if they can spend a couple of days in South Korea, they know it was not in vain because you can't find a more vivid contrast in the difference between democracy and a totalitarian regime, even in terms of just economic growth, when the human spirit is allowed to flourish and develop as opposed to being suppressed.

I have a simple example. I fly at night up there. A couple of months ago, just south of the DMZ, my CAP [combat air patrol] point was a well-lit ski area in South Korea, and all around me were lights. Up north, there was not one light: it was completely dark. The contrast is stark, and, for the veterans who come over there, they see that, and it is amazing to watch the look on their faces. We take them up to the demilitarized zone; they look, and they say, "That's the Korea I remember!" because there are no trees. They've all been used for firewood, whereas, in South Korea, it's a garden.

So, while there is no peace treaty, it is an armistice. There are some hopeful signs. We're a week away, hopefully, from a summit. North Korean misbehavior has been kind of quiet here for the last year or so, but it was only about a year ago that they tried to infiltrate Special Operations Forces via submarine and got caught.

So they're the same old folks up there; but clearly they're approaching the Western nations in a more open fashion. They have no choice. Economically, they're desperate. They're not being supplied, certainly not by the former Soviet Union anymore, and the Chinese appear to be getting a little wary of them as well. So there is a lessening in attention, but I very quickly point out that threat in simple terms is an equation made up of capability and intent, and, in many ways, North Korea's capability has improved. The North Koreans have continued incrementally in an evolutionary way to do things to improve their offensive capabilities.

DR. THOMPSON: I might add that if you look back fifty years, of course, the big difference from today was North Korea's association with the Soviet Union and communist China. The way those relationships have changed is really critical in assessing where we are.

AUDIENCE MEMBER: I'd like to comment on one lesson from Korea that we need to be sure to keep in mind. The message is that we should always make clear to the world what our intentions are, and that it's appropriate to do so. In the case of Korea, we made it at least reasonably clear that our intentions were not to defend Korea, and that had a great deal to do with the beginning of the Korean War, the attack on South Korea. I'm referring, of course, to a famous speech by Dean Acheson. That's a political lesson, not a military lesson.[41]

DR. THOMPSON: We've made that mistake more than once, of course, most recently in the case of the Gulf War. We hadn't been entirely clear with Iraq how we would respond.[42]

LIEUTENANT GENERAL HEFLEBOWER: I think every CINC, to include the one I work for today, if he stays awake nights—and I know he does—is making sure that we have not miscommunicated our intent in Korea, either militarily or politically, to stand and fight. Our worst nightmare is if they misunderstand that. Clearly we miscommunicated in 1950, and the Acheson speech is a classic example. You're absolutely right. That's why even today, and when we were engaged in Kosovo, we were actually putting force onto the peninsula so there could not be any miscalculation, because of our concern in that regard.

AUDIENCE MEMBER: This may be a little bit off the subject, but your comment raises in my mind—is there much talk within your command if the Chinese decide to invade Taiwan, what we will do? It seems like most people think they'll never do it, and we never thought they would come across the Yalu. I'm just curious about that. Is there any preparation for it?

LIEUTENANT GENERAL HEFLEBOWER: Happily my theater is the Korean peninsula. Unfortunately, others have to worry about the Taiwan scenario, but clearly our concern is that—and I use Kosovo as an example, but you could use China or Taiwan or any other thing—the North Koreans miscalculate and think that they could achieve some sort of military advantage as a result of our being engaged somewhere else. I think that would be a mistake, but that's why we stay as ready as we do. As I said, they know that the fifty years of relative quiet in Korea, I think, are due entirely to the fact that we've got American forces on the peninsula and a stated willingness through a treaty to defend South Korea. That and that alone is the reason why North Korea has not come south.

GENERAL DOUGHERTY: The reason that General MacArthur got relieved is because he overstepped the bounds of civilian control of the military. He was interested in total victory. The President and others were looking at the interactions in Europe that were possible with the Red Army sitting there. One of the things MacArthur was asked was "What would happen if the Red Army jumps into Europe?" and he said, "That's not my theater." But we were experiencing something called a "limited war" over there, and I don't think those of us who were over there understood it. I don't think MacArthur really understood it. But Bill Mauldin understood it! He had a cartoon with Willy and Joe, a real classic, sitting in a foxhole full of cold water, trees shot up all around, you know, no foliage on the trees, Willy with a cigarette dangling down, Joe reading the New York Times. Joe says, "Hey Willy! Listen to this here editorial about limited war!" And Willy says, "I ain't much interested in limited war. Limited war ain't limited to those of us to whom it is limited!" That's a perspective that everybody has to be clear about. Now we've got a real problem in global strategy. I made a statement a while back that we cannot afford to let our enemies get close, but they are close over in Korea. That's why we have land mines. I don't know how you feel about that. Globally, I've fought land mines. We have land mines all around the world, and you can't do anything—you can't even build an airport—because of the land mines. But, in Korea, they are so close that we have to tailor our strategy to the situation. Is there any way that you see that we can reduce that confrontation?

LIEUTENANT GENERAL HEFLEBOWER: Of course, as you know, sir, one of the fundamental reasons why the United States didn't sign the Land Mine Treaty was Korea. One of the fundamental reasons why the South Koreans didn't sign the Land Mine Treaty was Korea. We could go all afternoon on that treaty and discuss it, but on the fundamental issues, you're right. I mean they are close. You don't need binoculars to see them. You said, "Don't let them get close." They are. You've got it absolutely right. The other aspect in Korea again is the use of Special Operations Forces by the North Koreans. They have over one hundred thousand, and there will be a second front. There's no question about it. In terms of whether or not there will ever be a lessening in the confrontation, I think we've seen some of that. How long it will last really depends on the North Koreans. I think the current South Korean government with the "Sunshine Policy," as they call it, has been pretty effective, and we're leading up to the first summit since the end of the Korean War. We might have had one before, but Kim Il Sung died before it could occur. There has been a steady dialogue both at the four-party talks bilaterally with the United States, and now potentially between the North and the South. There's an awful lot of aid going to North Korea in efforts toward economic development, but they really haven't taken hold. All I can say is, from a behavioral point of view, by our standards, the North Koreans seem to be behaving more rationally. We never could explain such things as the axe murders.[43] No Western leader could understand how someone could take an axe to another person over a tree, but it happened. I think that there will be a lessening of tensions when there is a greater dialogue between the North and the South and a certain degree of trust. How long that will take is anybody's guess. Clearly the strategic objective of the North Korean regime is to preserve the North Korean regime.

AUDIENCE MEMBER: That means continuing the potential of confrontation.

LIEUTENANT GENERAL HEFLEBOWER: Well, perhaps not confrontation, but certainly the confrontation has really led to a North Korean desire to reunify the South and the North under North Korean control. The North Korean objective since the very end of the Korean War is to have the United States off the peninsula. Every time we've had a discussion with them, they point out that the one thing that really inhibits the peace process is the presence of American forces, which is sort of another way of saying, "If you'd just get out of our way, we could reunify Korea, and everything would be okay." The South Koreans don't quite see it that way and understandably so.

So I don't hold any great optimism for a resolution to the Korean situation. On the other hand, I'm not without hope in that regard. I think that one way to assure that there will be a peaceful resolution is to keep American forces there and to ensure that all the forces there are ready to fight tonight, and then make military action a just intolerable outcome. Because, if there is military action, if the North Koreans come south, the North Korean regime will then cease to exist. The South Koreans and the United States have made it very clear we're not going to attack first, and the North Koreans believe it, and we're not postured to attack first. We have no intention of attacking first, no desire to attack first. The North Koreans, on the other hand, are postured offensively, not defensively, and they have been for a long, long time. The only reason they haven't acted, I think, is because they know they can't win. So I think that the only way that there will be a peaceful resolution is if a military option is just unacceptable to the North Koreans, and they choose to evolve and see that the only way they can develop economically is through more open dialogue with the Western nations, and trade, and the kinds of things that rational nations do. At the same time, they must see that this will begin the undermining of their own government, as we saw in the former Soviet Union as it became more open. There were a lot of things that led to that, but, as it became more open, the Soviet leadership lost control of the population. It's a lot different in North Korea, for North Korea is just an entirely closed society.

DR. THOMPSON: I'm getting a signal from the back that we're about out of time, and I see my boss, Dick Hallion, approaching the front of the room. One more comment.

GENERAL SHAUD: It's always great to watch a great panel chief working. The thing that I liked about where Wayne went with his panel is that we really are at a threshold concerning the use of force. Today, we have the emerging area of information warfare. Is precision an ability or an effect? It came with the idea of fractionalization—there just are a lot of weapons available quickly. Really, it races toward our trying to grasp the whole notion of effects-based targeting and particularly how important it's going to be for an air force that understands that and is able to make input into theater plans.[44] As General Dougherty said, we must be concerned not only with the theater aspect, but also global implications, and that is why it was good for this panel at the end to step in that direction. Effects-based targeting is clearly one of the most significant new issues to be addressed. We really have a face in this, and it's fun watching all you guys trying to get a grasp. Thank you!

DR. THOMPSON: I return the floor to Dick Hallion.

Notes

1. Published as *To Hanoi and Back: The USAF and North Vietnam, 1966–1973* (Washington, D.C.: Air Force History and Museums Program, 2000), and copublished under the same title by the Smithsonian Institution Press.

2. The McDonnell Douglas RF–4C Phantom II, a supersonic, twin-engine, two-seat reconnaissance variant of the F–4 fighter; the Lockheed Martin F–16 Fighting Falcon, a single-seat, supersonic, jet fighter-bomber.

3. For the North African roots of American close air support thought, see David Syrett, "The Tunisian Campaign, 1942–1943," in Benjamin Franklin Cooling, ed., *Case Studies in the Development of Close Air Support* (Washington, D.C.: Office of Air Force History, 1990), 153-192; and Vincent Orange, "Getting Together," in Daniel R. Mortensen, ed., *Air Power and Ground Armies: Essays on the Evolution of Anglo-American Air Doctrine, 1940-1943* (Maxwell AFB, Ala.: Air University Press, 1998), 1–44.

4. Northrop Grumman (originally Fairchild Republic) A–10 Thunderbolt II, a twin-engine, single-seat, heavily armored jet ground-attack aircraft.

5. Lockheed Martin U–2R reconnaissance aircraft, the lineal descendant of the initial U–2 of Francis Gary Powers fame.

6. Boeing (originally McDonnell Douglas) F–4 Phantom II, a supersonic, two-seat, twin-engine jet fighter-bomber (F–4E) or reconnaissance airplane (RF–4E); Northrop Grumman (originally Northrop) F–5 Tiger II, a supersonic single-or-two-seat light twin-engine jet fighter bomber (F–5E/F) or single-seat reconnaissance airplane (RF–5E).

7. Air Force use of precision munitions in Korea is generally not recognized. On August 23, 1950, the B–29-equipped 19th Bomb Group began dropping one-thousand pound VB–3 Razon bombs fitted with radio-controlled tail fins that enabled bombardiers to guide them by controlling *range* and *azimuth only*. A total of 489 Razons were employed through the end of 1950, of which 331 hit their targets, a success rate of nearly sixty-eight percent, roughly the same level of accuracy achieved by the first-generation laser-guided bombs used in Southeast Asia a generation later. Fully ninety-six percent of the last 150 fifty Razons dropped in 1950 hit their targets, excellent by the standards even of Desert Storm, Deliberate Force, Allied Force, or the air campaign in Afghanistan a half-century later. See AF History and Museums Program, *Steadfast and Courageous: FEAF Bomber Command and the Air War in Korea, 1950–1953* (Washington, D.C.: AF History and Museums Program, 2000), 18.

8. The two attack airplanes that made up this five percent were the General Dynamics F–111F, a two-seat twin-engine, variable-wing-sweep jet; and the Lockheed F–117A, a single-seat twin-engine jet, the latter the first stealth aircraft in Air Force service. Other aircraft could drop laser-guided bombs, if another aircraft "buddy-lased" the target for them. The small number of self-designating precision strike airplanes posed a serious challenge to air war planners during the Gulf War.

Silver Wings Golden Valor: The USAF Remembers Korea

9. Col. Phillip S. Meilinger, the first commandant of the School of Advanced Airpower Studies (SAAS) at Maxwell AFB's Air University, wrote in his *10 Propositions Regarding Air Power* (Washington, D.C.: Air Force History and Museums Program, 1995), 41, 45, that "Precision air weapons have redefined the meaning of mass.... The result of the trend toward 'airshaft accuracy' in air war is a denigration in the importance of mass. PGMs [precision-guided munitions] provide density, mass per unit volume, which is a more efficient measurement of force. In short, targets are no longer massive, and neither are the aerial weapons used to neutralized them."

10. First used in the Kosovo campaign, the JDAM was a two-thousand-pound bomb outfitted with a Global Positioning System (GPS) guidance package, aerodynamic strakes, and control surfaces. JDAMs proved extraordinarily significant in destroying key Serbian military facilities and targets, and, as well, in the counterterror campaign in Afghanistan in the winter of 2001–2002. As early as the Gulf War, B–52Gs launched GPS-guided cruise missiles, the AGM–86C CALCM (conventional air-launched cruise missile).

11. This innovative use of inert precision attack was conceived by Brig. Gen. David A. Deptula, the commander of Operation Northern Watch, and first tested in 1999.

12. Boeing B–52 Stratofortress, an eight-engine intercontinental jet bomber; Lockheed C–130 Hercules, a four-turboprop engine transport and (in the AC-130 Spectre/Spooky variant) special operations gunship.

13. GPS: Global Positioning System, a reference to the orbiting constellation of Air Force-developed navigation satellites that, since the late 1980s, furnishes precise spatial coordinates for modern military and commercial air operations.

14. This indeed was precisely the mode of operation followed during the counterterror air campaign in Afghanistan in the fall and winter of 2001–2002. On numerous occasions, Air Force special operations controllers working with Army Special Forces teams or Afghani resistance forces designated Taliban and al-Qaeda forces for destruction from orbiting B–52s and other aircraft dropping JDAMs and other munitions.

15. MLRS: Multiple Launch Rocket System, a tracked battlefield rocket launcher first deployed in the early 1980s and used extensively in Desert Storm by U.S. and British army artillery forces.

16. CEP: Circular Error Probable, a circle inscribed around an aim point within which 50 percent of bombs or shells could be expected to fall, the remaining 50 percent falling outside the circle. During World War II and the Korean War, spotted artillery fire tended, on the whole, to be more accurate than unguided dumb bombs dropped from airplanes. Today, the reverse is true. In the Gulf War, for example, the average CEP for a laser-guided bomb was less than ten feet.

17. Washington, D.C.: Center for Strategic and International Studies, 1998.

18. A reference to Italian general Giulio Douhet (1869–1930), the first great air power theorist, and author of *The Command of the Air* (1921). For more on Douhet, see Col. Phillip S. Meilinger, "Giulio Douhet and the Origins of Airpower Theory," in Meilinger, ed., *The Paths of Heaven: The Evolution of Airpower Theory* (Maxwell AFB, Ala.: Air University Press, 1997), 1–40.

19. Mikoyan-Gurevich MiG-29, NATO codename Fulcrum, a Russian twin-engine supersonic jet fighter widely exported abroad.

20. AWACS: Airborne Warning and Control System, the Boeing E–3 Sentry, widely used by the Air Force and NATO for deconfliction of air war, both to improve detection, tracking, and targeting of enemy forces and to prevent "blue on blue" friendly fire.

21. Again, as happened in Afghanistan in 2001–2002.

22. Trans World Airlines Flight 800, a Boeing 747, departed John F. Kennedy International Airport on the evening of July 17, 1996, and exploded shortly thereafter off Long Island, killing all 230 passengers and crew. After examining the wreckage, the National Transportation Safety Board focused on the possibility of an arcing short from frayed wiring in the airplane's center fuel tank, subsequently issuing an airworthiness directive mandating immediate inspection of wiring in aging Boeing jetliners and other aircraft as well.

23. For example, the return of routine air defense patrols after the September 11, 2001, attacks on the World Trade Center and the Pentagon and the establishment of the new Northern Command for homeland defense under Gen. Ralph E. Eberhart, USAF.

24. The bombing of Dresden by British and American airmen on February 13–14, 1945, killed an estimated thirty-five thousand Germans. It has generated tremendous controversy, particularly the claim that Dresden was neither a legitimate target nor a necessary attack; was destroyed only to satisfy the desires of the chief of Royal Air Force Bomber Command, Air Marshal Sir Arthur Harris; and resulted in unprecedented loss of life. Actually, over time, more rigorous and dispassionate analysis has concluded that Dresden was (1) clearly a legitimate target (in fact, it had been struck before); (2) a reasonable decision at that stage of the war; (3) sanctioned for attack at the highest levels of the Allied government; and (4) that the casualties, although high, were by no means unusual by the standards of previous bombing of Third Reich targets. For further information, see Air Commodore Henry Probert, *Bomber Harris: His Life and Times: The Biography of Marshal of the Royal Air Force Sir Arthur Harris, the Wartime Chief of Bomber Command* (London: Greenhill Books, 2001), 317–21; Robin Neillands, *The Bomber*

War: Arthur Harris and the Allied Bomber Offensive, 1939–1945 (London: John Murray, 2001), 351–66; and Richard G. Davis, *Carl A. Spaatz and the Air War in Europe* (Washington, D.C.: Center for Air Force History, 1993), 556–64.

25. An allusion to the late cartoonist Walt Kelly's comic strip of the same name, whose thoughtful possum character once stated, "We have met the enemy and he is us."

26. ATACMS: Army tactical missile system, also fired from the MLRS launcher-transporter, but a larger weapon with a range of sixty miles and the ability to carry multiple submunitions.

27. Boeing (formerly McDonnell Douglas) F–15E Strike Eagle, a two-seat, supersonic, all-weather fighter and attack aircraft derived from the F–15 Eagle air-superiority fighter.

28. Boeing (formerly Rockwell) B–1B Lancer, nicknamed the Bone, a four-engine, long-range bomber with a variable-sweep wing.

29. NATO forces employed a total of 28,018 munitions during the Kosovo conflict. Of this, American forces expended 23,315 munitions during the Kosovo campaign, 6,728 (29%) of which were precision munitions, and 16,587 (71%) of which were unguided. Of these totals, the USAF expended a total of 21,120 munitions, comprising 5,285 precision munitions and 15,835 nonprecision munitions. Thus, overall, in Kosovo, the U.S. Air Force expended 91% of all American-employed munitions, including 79% of all U.S. precision munitions, and 95% of all U.S. unguided munitions. In total, American forces expended 83% of all NATO munitions. The U.S. Air Force expended fully 75% of NATO munitions employed in Kosovo.

30. For an excellent survey of the psychological dimensions of air attack, see (then) Grp. Capt. A. P. N. Lambert, RAF, *The Psychology of Air Power*, Whitehall Paper Series 1994 (London, Royal United Services Institute for Defence Studies, 1995). For the experience of the Vietnamese communists under B–52 attack, see David Chanoff and Doan Van Toai, *Portrait of the Enemy* (New York: Random House, 1986), 109, 154, 171, 185.

31. North American F–100 Super Sabre, a supersonic, single-seat (F–100D), single-engine fighter-bomber used extensively for close air support for friendly ground forces in South Vietnam. The two-seat F–100F was used as a "Fast FAC" in high-threat areas in lower North Vietnam and as an early anti-SAM "Wild Weasel" airplane. Nicknamed the "Hun," the F–100 was America's first operational supersonic jet fighter.

32. The Raytheon AGM–65 Maverick, an air-to-surface guided missile originally developed by Hughes in the early 1970s as a derivative of the Falcon air-to-air missile. An imaging-infrared (IIR) version of the missile, the AGM–65D, introduced in 1986, had much greater accuracy, and became a fearsome killer of Iraqi mechanized vehicles during the Gulf War, fired primarily from A–10 and F–16 aircraft.

33. Intended as a flying tank-killer, the A–10 was literally built around a large 30-mm cannon. This cannon, the General Dynamics GAU–8/A Avenger, can fire dense (and thus high-penetration) depleted uranium armor-piercing rounds at a rate of up to 4,200 rounds per minute over a range of several thousand meters.

34. The Pave Penny pod, a passive laser tracking system to precisely locate ground targets.

35. Air Tasking Order: "A method used to task and disseminate to components, subordinate units, and command and control agencies projected sorties, capabilities and/or forces to targets and specific missions. Normally provides specific instructions to include call signs, targets, controlling agencies, etc., as well as general instructions. Also called ATO." Department of Defense, *Department of Defense Dictionary of Military and Associated Terms*, Joint Publication 1–02 (Washington, D.C.: DoD, 12 April 2001 edition amended through 23 Jan. 2002), 23.

36. EA–6: Northrop Grumman (formerly Grumman) EA–6B Prowler, a land- and carrier-based four-seat twin-jet electronic warfare airplane flown by Navy, Marine, and Air Force crews; SEAD: suppression of enemy air defenses; HARM: Texas Instruments AGM–88 HARM (high-speed antiradiation missile), an air-launched anti-radar missile widely used by U.S. armed forces.

37. The Texas Instruments AGM–45 Shrike was a Vietnam-era antiradiation missile widely used by the first generations of anti-SAM aircraft. The HARM succeeded it in the 1980s.

38. The Lockheed Martin F–22A Raptor advanced fighter, blending stealth, supersonic cruising in military (nonafterburning) power, and advanced sensor fusion.

39. The Northrop Grumman (formerly Northrop) B–2A Spirit, a four-engine stealthy intercontinental flying wing.

40. AOR = Area of Responsibility.

41. Speaking before the National Press Club on January 12, 1950, then-Secretary of State Dean Acheson stated that the defensive perimeter of the United States ran from the Aleutians to Japan, Okinawa, and the Philippines; he pointedly excluded Korea, although he did suggest that attacks elsewhere in Asia be defended by a UN coalition. This statement, a serious misstep in the minds of many, encouraged the communists to invade South Korea later that year, particularly because the Truman administration and its Department of Defense had, at that time, no intention of defending South Korea.

42. In the summer of 1990, as Saddam Hussein contemplated the invasion of Kuwait, he apparently did not comprehend that such an invasion would trigger an American intervention due to misreading

American diplomatic intentions in the Gulf region.

43. On August 18, 1976, an American and South Korean work detail at Panmunjom was set upon by North Korean soldiers as it attempted to trim a tree blocking the view of the UN monitoring team. Two American soldiers were beaten and hacked to death; as part of the immediate American response, naval and air forces on and around the Korean peninsula were strengthened. On August 21, the tree was cut down, and Kim Il Sung subsequently expressed regret over the murders of the two Americans.

44. Effects-based targeting, although not a new idea, was considerably strengthened by the experience of the Gulf War and subsequent conflicts. In contrast to simply drawing up a list of similar things (a "target set") and then attacking items on the list one by one, effects-based targeting is rooted in so-called nodal warfare: targeting the most critical ones to ensure the most significant and meaningful impact upon an enemy's capabilities, strengths, and resources. The goal is thus not to inflict generalized rampant destruction, but focused, devastating effects on what the enemy truly holds most dear.

Chapter 8

CLOSING REMARKS

Dr. Richard P. Hallion

DR. HALLION: As we planned this session, we wanted Buzz Moseley to close this panel, but unfortunately Buzz is on call for some other issues. So I have the dubious distinction! I'm going to make a couple of closing comments on the last panel and offer a reflection on the symposium today.

I think the last panel was particularly valuable. Every single conflict is situational. What works in one particular conflict may not work necessarily well in another. I think we saw that in the comments between Chris Bowie talking about some of the very effective means that people have come to grips with the challenge of Operation Northern Watch and also General Heflebower's talking about the particular and indeed peculiar circumstances of Korea. Korea in many ways almost echoes what we saw in the Western Front in World War I, in terms of the kind of challenge you have in coming to grips with a enemy that is very much dug into the local terrain.

We also see in the presentations we had today a larger, indeed "macro," history lesson in how radically warfare has changed over the last century. In the twentieth century, we saw a change in the nature of conflict from warfare that was exclusively two-dimensional to warfare that became truly three-dimensional, where what happened above and below the surface was arguably at least of as much significance as what was happening on the surface. In many cases, it was more so. It was quite a transformation. And I'll put it another way, with Gen. Russ Dougherty's kind benevolence in this—if memory serves me right, sir, when you first joined the military, you were trained to ride with the horse cavalry, and then

Silver Wings Golden Valor: The USAF Remembers Korea

you transferred to the Army Air Forces and eventually wound up flying nuclear alert and eventually commanding the Strategic Air Command. So, if we think about it, we see the sweep of twentieth-century military affairs right there in just one person's career.

GENERAL DOUGHERTY: A point of personal privilege: my duty in that Army cavalry reconnaissance platoon at Louisville was bugler! It was command and control!

DR. HALLION: Ah, yes, it was command and control! Exactly so! Now, you know, we see this, and I think we got a sweep of some of the things going on here.

There is something that I think we need to keep in mind. Korea, however we care to cast it, was a success story. We came into Korea to help a nation that was about to be overrun, and that nation was saved. People tend to forget that, and I think they tend to forget it because Korea occurred just five years after World War II, in which we absolutely thoroughly destroyed our opponents, occupied their territory, and dispossessed the governments that we were fighting. If you take a look at the broader sweep of military history, you'll find that those kinds of total victories are the rare exceptions, not the rule. Traditionally speaking, most military conflicts are limited conflicts. The traditional limited conflict is precisely the kind of conflict that we found ourselves fighting in Korea, and this leads to my concluding comments, at least on the symposium's content. General Heflebower has said it very well—and we had an allusion to it earlier in General Ryan's and General Dougherty's remarks—and that is you have to be *extremely careful* of the signals that you send of your intentions. We paid the price for intemperate remarks by Dean Acheson in early 1950, and that price came over the next three years.

The other comment I would add is, I think, probably one of the most important lesson that come out of Korea, and it's one we forgot with regard to Vietnam, with tragic results. That lesson is *resolve*. When we settled Korea in 1953, there were an awful lot of people who said, "We will never fight a war like that again," and they wanted to forget it. Indeed, within weeks of the ending of that war, North Korea had rebuilt and reconstituted its military strength right down to the 38th parallel, but we had the resolve to stay in there and to hang tough. And we've seen that continue to the present day, where we're still hanging tough. As a result, the difference, as General Heflebower has said, is you can fly over South Korea at night and be blinded by the lights, while North Korea looks like the cold lifeless surface of another planet. We didn't have that same resolve in Vietnam. We left Vietnam in 1973 on about the same terms that we left Korea in 1953, and we cut South Vietnam adrift by a lack of resolve in 1974 and 1975, and it was overrun in six weeks. Had we done the same to South Korea in 1955, it, too, would have been overrun in about six weeks. That's the difference resolve makes. We're in a world now that is a very uncertain and fractious world. We're facing a multitude of threats. For example, think of the situation we have ensuring long-term stability in the Persian Gulf. The lesson that comes out of this is *resolve*, hanging tough for the long fight.

Closing Remarks

Wrapping this up, I think that today's symposium has been a very valuable one. We've been partnered with our good friends in Air Force Legislative Liaison. General Moseley's people did a tremendous job in helping us put this together. I'd also offer a very strong tip of the hat to the Air Force Association's board chairman, Tom McKee, and its executive director, Gen. John Shaud, both of whom were critical to getting this symposium together. We of the Air Force History and Museums Program are very fortunate to have had such energetic partners as Legislative Liaison and the AFA, and we're very grateful. Finally, of course, I wish to thank the veterans, who took the time to travel and meet with us today. Gentlemen, we—all of us who put this together, and those of us in the audience as well—salute you for all you did fifty years ago and all you are doing today.

Glossary

A & AEE	Aeroplane & Armament Experimental Establishment
AFHMP	Air Force History and Museums Program
AFSS	Air Force Security Service
AFSC	Air Force specialty code
ATACMS	Army tactical missile system
AWACS	Airborne Warning and Control System
BDA	bomb damage assessment
CALCM	conventional air-launched cruise missile
CAP	combat air patrol
CFE	Central Fighter Establishment
CONOPS	concept of operations
CSIS	Center for Strategic and International Studies
CWO	Chief Warrant Officer
DMZ	demilitarized zone
FEAF	Far East Air Forces
FEALF	Far East Air Logistics Force
FEACOM	Far East Air Materiel Command
FAC	forward air controller
GPS	Global Positioning System
GDP	gross domestic product
GCI	ground-controlled intercept
HARM	high-speed antiradiation missile
IIR	imaging-infrared
IFR	instrument flight rules
JASSM	joint air-to-surface standoff missile
JDAM	joint direct attack munition
JSOW	joint standoff weapon
J-STARS	Joint Surveillance and Targeting Radar System
MAW	Marine Air Wing
MRE	meal, ready-to-eat
MAPRW	Mediterranean Allied Photographic Reconnaissance Wing
MIA	missing in action
MLRS	multiple launch rocket system
NACA	National Advisory Committee for Aeronautics
NATO	North Atlantic Treaty Organization
OODA	observe, orient, decide, and act
PLAAF	Peoples' Liberation Army Air Force
PGM	precision-guided munition

PSP	pierced-steel planking
POW	prisoner of war
ROK	Republic of Korea
RAF	Royal Air Force
SAAS	School of Advanced Airpower Studies
SIGINT	signals intelligence
SAM	surface-to-air missile
UCAV	uninhabited combat air vehicle
VOR	vertical omnirange
VFR	visual flight rules
WCMD	wind-corrected munitions dispenser

Index

A
Acheson, Dean: 15, 109, 114, 117
Aeroplane & Armament Experimental Establishment [A & AEE]: 91
Afghanistan: 112, 113
Agan, Arthur C.: 61
Air and Space Power in the New Millennium: 101
Air University: 44
aircraft, North Korean: 11
  Il–10: 93
  Il–12: 60
  La–5: 93
  MiG–15 "Fagot": 19, 25, 28, 32, 42, 48, 57, 59, 60, 61, 90, 91, 92
  MiG–17 "Fresco": 74, 91
  MiG–19 "Farmer": 91
  MiG–9 "Fargo": 60
  MiGs [unspecified]: 30, 35, 36–38, 40–41, 45, 46, 47, 48, 50, 54, 58, 61, 70, 73, 84, 85, 87
  P–39 "Airacobras": 81, 92
  P–63 "Kingcobra": 81, 92
  Po–2: 11, 88, 91
  Yak–9: 88, 93
aircraft, other
  Bleriot monoplanes: 57
  DeHavilland Hornet: 39
  F–104 "Starfighter": 43
  Fokker D VII: 58
  L'Oiseau Blanc: 58
  Me 163 "Komet": 79, 91
  Me 262 "Schwalbe": 30, 79, 91
  MiG–29 "Fulcrum": 102, 113
  Short Sunderland: 39
  Spirit of St. Louis: 58
  Spitfire: 36, 39
  Wright Flyer: 57
aircraft, U.S.: 6
  A–1 "Skyraider": 61
  A–7 "Corsair II": 58
  A–10 "Thunderbolt II": 99, 107, 112, 114
  A–26 "Invader": 88
  AC–130 "Spectre"/"Spooky": 113
  B–1B "Lancer": 106, 114
  B–2A "Spirit": 15, 100, 108, 114
  B–17 "Flying Fortress": 65, 78, 79
  B–24 "Liberator": 79
  B–26 "Invader": 20, 66, 69, 88, 89
  B–26 "Marauder": 88
  B–29 "Superfortress": 32, 59, 69, 83, 87, 88, 89, 92, 100, 112
  B–47 "Stratojet": 60, 63
  B–52 "Stratofortress": 63, 79, 101, 106, 113, 114
  B–52G "Stratofortress": 113
  BC–1: 91
  C–5A "Galaxy": 79
  C–17 "Globemaster III": 22, 24, 91
  C–46 "Commando": 21, 80, 81, 92
  C–47 "Skytrain": 21, 66, 80, 81, 88, 92
  C–54 "Skymaster": 21, 66, 82, 88
  C–69 "Constellation": 89
  C–119 "Flying Boxcar": 21, 70, 90
  C–121 "Constellation": 68, 89
  C–130 "Hercules": 24, 101, 113
  DC–3: 88
  DC–4: 88
  E–3 "Sentry" Airborne Warning and Control System [AWACS]: 33, 48, 58, 102, 113
  E–8 Joint Surveillance and Targeting Radar System [J–STARS]: 33, 58
  EA–6B "Prowler": 108, 114
  F–4 "Phantom II": 13, 29, 31, 52, 58, 99, 112
  F–4E "Phantom II": 112
  F–5 "Tiger II": 58, 99, 112
  F–5E/F "Tiger II": 112
  F–15 "Eagle": 32, 52, 55, 56, 58, 61, 62, 114
  F–15E "Strike Eagle": 106, 114
  F–16 "Fighting Falcon": 32, 52, 55, 58, 61, 98, 99, 102, 112, 114
  F–22A "Raptor": 21–22, 32, 52, 56, 58, 108, 114
  F–51 "Mustang": 6, 20, 43, 45, 75, 77–78, 79, 80, 84, 86, 92, 93
  F–80 "Shooting Star": 6, 20, 33, 35, 43, 45, 52, 59, 60, 61, 65, 69, 70, 79, 80, 81, 82, 89, 92, 93
  F–80A "Shooting Star": 79, 89
  F–80C "Shooting Star": 79, 92
  F–82 "Twin Mustang": 69, 89

Index

F–84 "Thunderjet": 20, 31, 32, 42, 49, 61, 71, 92, 93
F–84F "Thunderstreak": 90, 93
F–84G "Thunderjet": 83, 84
F–86 "Sabre": 6, 15, 21, 28, 29, 30, 32, 33, 34, 35, 36, 37, 38, 39, 40, 41, 42, 43, 44, 45, 49, 52, 56, 57, 60, 61, 71, 72, 74, 76, 78, 87, 93
    advantages over the MiG–15: 31–32
    armament of: 60
    as the P–86: 30, 57
    comparison with MiG–15: 19
    first usage of: 19
    gunsights and radar of: 60–61
    kill ratio over MiGs: 20, 31, 44
    maximum g load of: 59
    movable tail of: 57
    qualities of: 19–20, 30–31
F–86A "Sabre": 51, 58, 71, 90
F–86E "Sabre": 51
F–86F "Sabre": 58, 60, 73
F–86H "Sabre": 60, 91
F–94B "Starfire": 91
F–100 "Super Sabre": 33, 43, 58, 107, 114
F–100A "Super Sabre": 91
F–100D "Super Sabre": 114
F–100F "Super Sabre": 114
F–101 "Voodoo": 58
F–104 "Starfighter": 58
F–105 "Thunderchief": 58
F–111 "Aardvark": 58
F–111F "Aardvark": 112
F–117A "Nighthawk": 59, 108, 112
F2H "Banshee": 57
F2H–2P "Banshee": 90, 91
F4U "Corsair": 67, 88, 93
F9F "Panther": 57, 93
F9F–5P "Panther": 89
FJ–1 "Fury": 57
FJ–2 "Fury": 57
FJ–3 "Fury": 57
FJ–4 "Fury": 57, 91
General Atomics Predator UAV: 23
Global Hawk UAV: 23
O–1 "Bird Dog": 61
P–38 "Lightning": 90
P–47 "Thunderbolt": 93
P–51 "Mustang": 39, 79
P–80 "Shooting Star": 57
P–84 "Thunderjet": 57
RB–26 "Invader": 23, 71
RB–29 "Superfortress": 23, 71
RB–45 "Tornado": 23
RC–135 "Rivet Joint": 23, 33
RF–4 "Phantom II": 63, 98
RF–4C "Phantom II": 89, 112
RF–4E "Phantom II": 112
RF–51 "Mustang": 23, 71, 90
RF–5E "Tiger II": 112
RF–80 "Shooting Star": 23, 65, 69, 70, 71, 72, 73, 74, 79, 81, 89, 90–91
RF–84F "Thunderflash": 90
RF–86 "Sabre": 23, 65, 70, 73, 74
RF–86A "Sabre": 71–72, 73, 90–91
    cameras of: 72, 90
RF–86F "Sabre": 73, 91
    cameras of: 73
SA–16 "Albatross": 61
Stearman trainer: 88
T–33 "Shooting Star": 43, 59, 80, 81, 82, 92
T–33A "Shooting Star": 92
T–6 "Mosquito": 65, 75, 76, 77, 78, 83
    contribution made by: 78
T–6 "Texan": 89, 91
TF–80C "Shooting Star": 59, 92
U–2: 23, 24, 99, 112
U–2R: 112
X–1: 31
XP–86 "Sabre" prototype: 58
XS–1: 57
Alabama: 29, 43
Aleutian Islands: 15, 114
Alexander, Joseph: 60
Allied Air Forces: 29
Allison [engine manufacturer]: 93
al-Qaeda: 113
Amell, Zane S.: 34, 58
American Fighter Aces Association: 44
Amnesty International: 104
Antung, Manchuria: 40, 41, 46, 53, 54, 91
Arms Control and Disarmament Agency: 101

Index

Army Air Forces: 62, 117
Ashiya, Japan: 80, 89
Asia: 21, 114
Atlantic Ocean: 58
atomic bomb: 14
Averin, Mikhail: 54

B

Babington-Smith, Constance: 90
Baghdad, Iraq: 106
Baker, Royal: 46
Baldwin, John: 40, 42
Balkans: 2, 21, 52, 96
Barcus, Glenn O.: 61
Bataan: 2
Battle of Britain: 2, 39, 90
Beaumont, Roland: 59
Bedcheck Charlie: 6, 11, 65, 78, 85, 91
Begert, William J.: 3
Bell [aircraft manufacturer]: 57
Belov, Ivan: 59, 60
Blesse, Frederick "Boots": 21, 44, 50, 54–55, 56, 59, 62
  author of "No Guts No Glory" publication: 55
Boeing [aerospace company]: 79, 112, 113, 114
Bogart, Humphrey: 61
bomb damage assessment [BDA]: 76
Bosnia: 13
Bowie, Chris: 96, 100, 106
Boyd, John: 55, 61–62
  influence on aircraft design: 61
Braswell, Arnold: 29, 31, 32, 42, 43, 47, 48, 53, 55, 81, 84
  on F–86 armament: 51
  on quality of enemy pilots: 47
British Broadcasting Corporation [BBC]: 41
Brokaw, Tom: 77
Brown, William E., Jr.: 29, 31, 32, 33, 41, 43, 44, 52, 53, 56
  describing typical mission: 48
  on difficulty of distinguishing F–86s and MiG–15s: 49, 50–51
  on F–86 armament: 51
  on Jabara's shootdown of Frailey: 54

Burchett, Wilfred: 58
Burning the Days: 56

C

Cage, Phil: 80
Campbell, Ben Nighthorse: 5, 10, 88
  comparing South Korea to North Korea: 10
Cantigny Center: 60
Casablanca: 61
Center for Strategic and International Studies [CSIS]: 96, 101
Central Fighter Establishment: 39–40
Ch'ongjin airfield: 92
Chaffee, John: 6
Chance Vought [aircraft manufacturer]: 88
Charles A. Lindbergh Memorial Lecture: 29
Chicago, Illinois: 48
China: 35, 38, 74, 91, 109, 110
Cho-do: 40, 53–54, 61, 73
Chongchong River: 90
"Chosin Few": 7
Chosin Reservoir: 88, 90
Chunggangjin: 60
circular error probable [CEP]: 101, 113
Clark, Lynwood E.: 54, 61, 84, 86
Clark, Mark: 61
Cleveland, Charles G. "Chick": 44
Clobber College: 40, 42, 44, 50
Cold War: 2, 9, 14, 18, 93, 103
Colorado: 5
communism: 15
  demise of: 9
concept of operations [CONOPS]: 22
Conley, Kathleen: 91
Conley, Phil: 65, 75, 79, 86, 98
  opinion of Commonwealth troops: 77
Copic, Harley: 13, 30
Curtiss [aircraft manufacturer]: 92

D

Dandong, Manchuria: 59, 91
Darien peninsula: 74
Davis, George A., Jr.: 40, 46, 54, 59
  posthumous Medal of Honor of: 40, 59, 61

123

Index

shootdown of: 54, 61
DeArmond, Michael: 33, 40, 41, 43, 46, 48, 50, 53, 54, 58
  as POW: 34–35
  on difficulty of distinguishing F–86s and MiG–15s: 49
  shootdown of: 34
Defense Act of 1947: 5
demilitarized zone [DMZ]: 8–9, 75, 99, 105, 108
Dentist radar installation: 40, 61
Department of Defense: 3, 114
Deptula, David A.: 113
Dickens, Sam: 53, 65, 70, 75, 87
Diefendorf, Allen J.: 81, 92
Dixon, Jacob: 69
Dougherty, Russ: 64–65, 68, 78, 79, 86, 87, 110, 112
Douglas [aircraft manufacturer]: 92
Douhet, Giulio: 102, 113
Dresden, Germany, bombing of: 105, 113–114

E
Eagleston, Glenn T.: 81, 92
Eastern bloc: 48
Eberhart, Ralph E.: 113
Eckman, Robert "Foots": 81, 92
Eisenhower, Dwight D.: 74
electronic warfare: 107–108
Empire Test Pilots School [ETPS]: 79
England: 36, 39, 42, 82
  queen of: 70
English Channel: 42
Europe: 46, 59, 77, 82, 93, 110
Evans, Norvin, Jr.: 92
Evidence in Camera: 71

F
Fairchild [aircraft manufacturer]: 90
Fairchild Republic [aircraft manufacturer]: 112
Far East: 69, 82, 91
Far East Air Forces [FEAF]: 25, 45, 61, 66, 73, 80, 81, 88, 89, 90
  Bomber Command: 91
Far East Air Logistics Force [FEALF]: 90

Far East Air Materiel Command [FEACOM]: 90
Farnborough, England: 79, 91
Fernandez, Pete: 21, 44, 53, 59
Fighter Mafia: 61
Fischer, Harold "Hal": 21, 35, 36, 41, 44, 46, 49, 52, 58, 70
  on difficulty of distinguishing F–86s and MiG–15s: 49
  on Jabara's shootdown of Frailey: 53
  on shootdown of George Davis: 54
Fleet Intelligence Center: 17
forward air controller [FAC]: 75, 77, 82, 83, 84, 89, 91
forward edge of the battle area [FEBA]: 75
Frailey, Richard: 53, 61
France: 68

G
Gabreski, Frances S. "Gabby": 21, 40, 46, 59
Galland, Adolf: 45, 59
Garrison, Vermont: 46, 59
Garvin, Tom: 49
General Dynamics [aerospace company]: 112, 114
GI Bill: 77
Glenn, John: 6, 21
Goddard, George W.: 90
Gouré, Dan: 96, 101
Great Britain: 39
Greatest Generation, The: 77
Green, Jesse: 82
Griffin, Lavern H.: 74
gross domestic product: 14
ground-controlled intercept [GCI]: 41
Grumman [aircraft manufacturer]: 57, 89, 114
Guam: 15
Gunga Din [poem]: 35

H
Hall, Cargill: 74
Hallion, Richard P.: 1, 13, 14, 17, 27, 29, 31, 33, 35, 39, 42, 44, 45, 46, 47, 48, 49, 52, 53, 54, 55, 64, 96, 101, 112, 116, 117

Han River: 82, 98
  bridge over: 6, 88
Handley Page, Frederick: 30
Haneda International Airport: 66, 88
Harbison, William "Paddy": 33, 35, 39, 42, 46, 47, 48, 52, 53
  on gunsights of F–86: 52
  on quality of enemy pilots: 47, 49–50
Harris, Sir Arthur: 113
Hartmann, Erich: 45
Harvard Law Review: 17
Harvard University: 17
Heartbreak Ridge: 7
Heflebower, Charles "Chuck": 88, 97, 98, 101, 105, 107, 108, 110, 111
Henebry, John P.: 68, 89
Hess, Dean: 92
History Channel: 107
Honest John: The Autobiography of Walker M. Mahurin: 58
Honolulu, Hawaii: 9
Horowitz, Jim [a.k.a. Jim Salter]: 56
Hughes [aerospace company]: 114
Hussein, Saddam: 114–115

I
I Corps: 76
Il, Nam: 28–29
Illinois: 60
Il–Sung, Kim: 15
Inchon, South Korea: 19, 56, 64, 70, 89
information warfare: 107–108
instrument flight rules [IFR]: 88
Iraq: 109
Itazuke, Japan: 69, 80

J
Jabara, Jim: 21, 44, 59, 81
  shootdown of Richard Frailey: 53–54
Jacobs, Jesse: 65, 78–79, 82, 87, 92
James, Daniel "Chappie," Jr.: 82, 92–93
Japan: 6, 15, 42, 53, 59, 64, 66, 67, 69, 114
Jenkins, Jack S.: 79
Jian, Chen: 60
John F. Kennedy International Airport: 113
Johns Hopkins University: 101
Johnson, Edward R. "Rabbit": 81, 92

Johnson, James "Jimmy" K.: 30, 46, 53
Johnson-Sachs, Anne: 3
Joint Chiefs of Staff: 61, 74
Jones, George L.: 60
Jones, Priscilla: 3
Jones, Robert T.: 57
Jordan, Michael: 44

K
Kasserine, Tunisia: 2
Kelly, Walt: 114
Khabarovsk, Soviet Union: 74, 91
Kiev War Museum: 38
Kipling, Rudyard: 58
Knight, R.: 40
Kobe, Japan: 89
Korean peninsula: 15, 32, 109
Korean War: 1, 2, 5, 8, 9, 15, 17, 21, 27, 47, 48, 52, 57, 58, 64, 65, 69, 73, 74, 79, 89, 90, 91, 97, 99, 108, 110, 111
  aces in: 44
  air superiority in: 15, 18, 19, 20, 25, 27–62, 64, 85, 98
  air war of: 1–3
  airlift during: 23
  air-to-ground operations in: 63–93
  armistice of: 18, 29, 108
  as last war fought without aerial refueling: 59–60
  as the "forgotten war": 18
  battlefield interdiction in: 64, 83, 84, 85, 93
  British involvement in: 39–40
  Chinese involvement in: 7, 9, 20, 23, 24, 28, 38, 41, 47, 48, 56, 60, 64, 70, 83, 84, 86, 93
  close air support [CAS] in: 76, 77–78, 84–85, 86, 87, 98, 101
  comparison to conflict in Kosovo: 102, 104
  comparison with current situations: 14–15
  historical significance of: 18
  June 2000 symposium on: 1–3, 27
  legacy of: 97
  lessons from: 24–25, 84–86, 87, 106, 109
  members of U.S. Congress and Senate

Index

    having served in: 6, 8
    number of U.S. casualties in: 7, 11, 18, 19
    number of U.S. missing in action from: 7, 8
    ordnance dropped during: 19
    pilot training and: 42–44
    precision-guided weapons in: 100, 112
    reconnaissance in: 23
    resemblance to Vietnam War: 7–8
    Soviet involvement in: 35, 41, 47, 48, 56, 59, 69–70
    Soviet radar in: 91
    USAF command and control in: 47–48
Korean War Memorial: 1, 78
Korean War Memorial Parade: 78
Kosovo, conflict in: 15, 18, 20, 22, 23, 24, 28, 86, 88, 105, 109
    lessons from: 104–105, 106
    ordnance expended in: 106, 114
Kuwait, invasion of: 114–115

L
Land Mine Treaty: 110
Las Vegas, Nevada: 8
Lawhon, Brooks A.: 79, 80
Lindbergh, Charles: 58
Lindsay, James D. "Douglas": 36, 45, 58
Littlefield, William "Skosh": 54, 61
Lobov, Georgy: 60
Lockheed [aircraft manufacturer]: 57, 79, 81, 89, 91, 92, 113
Lockheed Martin [aerospace company]: 112, 114
London: 39
Luftwaffe: 59
Luftwaffe Technical Office: 58

M
MacArthur, Douglas: 18, 19, 64, 68, 70, 88, 89, 110
Mach number: 57
Mach, Ernst : 57
Mahurin, Walker "Bud": 34, 46, 58, 59
Manchuria: 40, 46, 47, 48–49, 58, 59, 61, 64, 90, 91
Mannock, Edward "Mick": 37, 58
Massachusetts: 42

Mauldin, Bill: 110
McConnell, Joe: 21, 44, 59
McDonnell [aircraft manufacturer]: 90
McDonnell Douglas [aircraft manufacturer]: 89, 112, 114
McKee, Tom: 118
meals, ready-to-eat [MREs]: 24
Meilinger, Phillip S.: 113
Meyer, John C.: 55, 62
MiG Alley: 34, 37, 42, 56, 58, 60, 70, 71, 72
MiG Alley [computer game]: 39, 58
Miho, Japan: 66
Mikoyan-Gurevich [aircraft manufacturer]: 113
Milosevic, Slobodan: 102
Misawa, Japan: 69, 74, 79, 80, 82
Misawa tanks: 59, 92
Mitchum, Robert: 62
Montgomery, Sonny: 8
Moroney, Dick: 53
Morse code: 88
Moseley, Michael "Buzz": 3, 13, 14, 17, 27, 56, 63, 116, 118
Mosquito Association: 78
Mukden, Manchuria: 46
Munsan, South Korea: 89
Murray, Brian: 3

N
Nagoya, Japan: 73, 80
National Air and Space Museum: 29
National Command Authority: 64
National Press Club: 15, 114
National Reconnaissance Office: 74
National Transportation Safety Board: 113
National War College: 98
Naval Academy: 65, 74, 77
Neufeld, Jack: 3
Nevada: 32
New Zealand: 77
Nichols, Donald: 89
Norfolk, Virginia: 17
Normandy, France: 2, 107
North Africa: 79, 98, 112
North American Aviation [aircraft manufacturer]: 57, 58, 91, 114

Index

North Atlantic Treaty Organization [NATO]: 13, 18, 20, 70, 93, 113
    Chiefs of Staff Committee of the Western Union: 93
    North Atlantic Alliance: 93
    North Atlantic Council: 93
North Korea: 9–10, 28, 47, 58, 59, 60, 71, 74, 83, 84, 93, 111, 117
    current military strength of: 105–106
    infiltrators from: 7, 109
    People's Army of: 64
    rapid advance of forces of: 19
    returning remains of U.S. personnel: 8–9
    treatment of POWs by: 58
Northrop [aerospace company]: 112, 114
Northrop Grumman [aerospace company]: 96, 100, 112, 114
Nungesser, Charles: 37, 58

O

O'Donnell, Emmett "Rosie", Jr.: 75, 91
Office of Air Force History: 3, 96
Office of the Secretary of Defense: 101
Ohio: 6
Okinawa, Japan: 114
OODA Loop: 61
Operation Allied Force: 88, 96, 112
Operation Deliberate Force: 13, 96, 112
Operation Desert Storm: 100, 112, 113
Operation Northern Watch: 100, 103, 113
Osan, South Korea: 66, 74
Overton, Dolphin D., III: 53, 61
Oxford University: 100

P

Pacific Air Forces: 31
Packard, Ashley B.: 81, 92
Paengnyong-do, South Korea: 59
Panama: 46
Panmunjom, South Korea: 8, 9, 29, 99, 115
Parr, Ralph S., Jr.: 52, 60
Partridge, Earle E. "Pat": 67, 78, 88, 92
Pas de Calais, France: 107
PC Gamer magazine: 58
Pearl Harbor, Hawaii: 14
Peking, China: 60
Penn State University: 29

Pentagon: 19, 96, 113
    Checkmate division: 96
Persian Gulf War: 2, 20, 22, 28, 52, 55, 59, 96, 106, 109, 112, 114, 115
    Gulf War Air Power Survey: 96
    precision-guided weapons in: 113
Peters, F. Whitten : 1, 17
Philippine Islands: 15, 114
Poe, Bryce: 21, 63, 65, 68–69, 70, 71, 79, 85, 86
    flying both first reconnaissance sortie in Korean War and first USAF jet reconnaissance sortie: 89
Polifka, Karl L. "Pop": 71, 90
Port Arthur: 74
Pratt & Whitney [engine manufacturer]: 91
Project Ashtray: 90
Project Bout-One: 92
Project Haymaker: 91
Public Record Office: 39
Pusan, South Korea: 80
Pusan perimeter: 19, 28, 64, 66, 67, 69, 89
Pyongyang, North Korea: 9

Q

Quanbeck, Alton H.: 81, 92

R

Raines, Claude: 61
RAND Corporation: 100
Raytheon [aerospace company]: 114
Red Flag exercise: 32, 43, 62
Redmond, Lawrence K.: 90
Republic [aircraft manufacturer]: 92, 93
Republic of Korea, forces of: 80, 92, 99
Rhode Island: 6
Rice, Don: 97
Richmond, Virginia: 79
Ridgway, Matthew B.: 3, 68, 89
    on airpower in Korean War: 3, 29
Risner, Robbie: 21
Riverside, California: 39
Roanoke, Virginia: 79
Robert R. McCormick Tribune Foundation: 60
Rockwell [aerospace company]: 114
Rogge, Gene: 50, 51

Index

Royal Aeronautical Establishment: 91
Royal Air Force: 39, 42, 46, 58, 90
  All-Weather Development Squadron: 39
  Bomber Command: 113
  Fighter Command: 39
  No. 11 Group: 39
  RAF Boscombe Down: 91
  RAF Manston: 93
  rank structure of: 59
  Royal Air Force Strike Command: 39
  Transport Command: 39
Royal Army
  1st British Commonwealth Division: 77
  28th British Brigade: 77
Royal Canadian Air Force: 36, 58
Royal Danish Air Force: 70
Royal Flying Corps: 58
Royal Marines: 39
Royal Navy: 39
  HMS *Black Swan*: 69
Royal Norwegian Air Force: 70
Ryan, Michael "Mike" E.: 1, 13, 23, 27, 117
Ryukyu Islands: 15

S

Sabre Dance [painting]: 13, 30
Sakhalin Islands: 74
Salter, James [a.k.a. Jim Horowitz]: 56
San Antonio, Texas: 5
San Diego, California: 92
Savichen, Leonid: 54
Seoul, South Korea: 6, 8, 64, 67, 70, 71, 75, 78, 81, 88, 89, 92, 105
Seoul International Airport: 6
Serbia: 24
Shanghai, China: 74
Shaud, John: 3, 63, 68, 69, 70, 75, 78, 82, 86, 87, 88, 112, 118
Shenyang, China: 59
signals intelligence: 59
Sinuiju, North Korea: 34, 46, 58, 72, 83, 93
Smith, Bill: 65, 82, 87
Smith, Stanton T.: 81, 92
Snyder, Don: 104
Solomon, Gerry: 8
South Carolina: 82

South Korea: 2, 9–10, 28, 57, 105, 108, 110, 114, 117
  "Sunshine Policy" of: 9–10, 110–111
  current military situation in: 98–100
  guerrillas of: 7
  Republic of Korea [ROK] forces: 6, 10
South Vietnam: 117
Southeast Asia: 13, 29, 31, 33, 63
Soviet Union: 9, 14, 48, 74, 93, 109
  303d Air Division: 60
Soviskaya Gavon, Soviet Union: 74
Special Security Office [SSO]: 67, 89
Spragg, Brian: 40
Stalin, Joseph: 15, 48–49, 59, 60
  sending MiG–15s: 56
Stelmakh, Yevgeny: 59
Stevens, Ted: 10
Stratemeyer: 69, 88, 89, 90, 92
Stump, Bob: 8
Sugamo, Japan: 67
Suiho, North Korea: 40
Sukhaya Rechka, Soviet Union: 92
Sung, Kim Il: 110, 115
suppression of enemy air defenses [SEAD]: 108, 114
Suter, Richard M. "Moody": 55, 56, 62

T

Tachikawa, Japan: 80
Taegu, South Korea: 10, 68
Taewon, South Korea: 66, 80
Taiwan: 109–110
Taji, Iraq: 106
Taliban: 113
terrorism: 2, 104
Texas Instruments: 114
The Hunters: 56
Third Reich: 113
38th parallel: 64
Thompson, Wayne: 3, 86, 96, 97, 100, 105, 106, 112
Thyng, Harrison R.: 40, 46, 59
Time magazine: 18
Tokyo, Japan: 66
Truman, Harry S.: 89, 114
Tse-tung, Mao: 15, 28, 60
  telegram to Stalin: 56

Index

Tunner, William H.: 23, 24, 89
TWA Flight 800: 104

U

U.S. Air Force: 1, 2, 3, 5–6, 7, 9, 11, 14, 15, 18, 19, 21, 22, 24, 27, 28, 33, 35, 43, 45, 58, 60, 63, 64, 65, 66, 71, 78, 82, 87, 88, 89, 90, 93, 100, 108, 112, 114
  1st Fighter Group: 39, 42
  3d Air Division: 93
  3d Bombardment Group: 89
  4th Fighter Group: 33, 35, 40, 42
  4th Fighter Wing: 33–34, 40, 41, 44
  4th Fighter-Interceptor Wing: 29, 30, 31, 33, 39, 45, 46, 47, 53, 54, 56, 59, 60, 62, 72, 73, 81, 87, 92, 93
  Fifth Air Force: 15, 20, 28, 59, 61, 73, 78, 83, 88, 92
  Fifth Air Force Advanced: 65, 81
  Seventh Air Force: 98
  7th Fighter-Bomber Squadron: 79, 80
  8th Fighter-Bomber Group: 33, 35
  8th Fighter-Bomber Squadron: 79, 81, 92
  8th Fighter-Bomber Wing: 80, 93
  8th Tactical Reconnaissance Squadron: 69, 71, 89
  9th Fighter-Bomber Squadron: 79, 80, 81, 92
  12th Tactical Reconnaissance Squadron: 68, 71
  Thirteenth Air Force: 15
  Fifteenth Air Force: 91
  15th Tactical Reconnaissance Squadron: 71, 72, 73
  16th Fighter-Interceptor Squadron: 61
  18th Fighter Wing: 93
  19th Bomb Group: 88, 112
  20th Fighter-Bomber Group: 82, 93
  Twentieth Air Force: 15
  27th Fighter-Escort Wing: 83, 92, 93
  39th Fighter-Interceptor Squadron: 58, 59
  45th Tactical Reconnaissance Squadron: 71
  49th Fighter-Bomber Wing: 31, 49, 65, 79, 81, 82, 84, 86, 92, 93
  51st Fighter Interceptor Group: 35, 41, 45, 47, 49, 59, 60, 93
  67th Tactical Reconnaissance Wing: 71, 90
  82d Tactical Reconnaissance Squadron: 69
  315th Air Division: 89
  334th Fighter-Interceptor Squadro: 29, 59, 61, 92
  335th Fighter-Interceptor Squadron: 30, 33, 34, 56, 58, 59, 60
  336th Fighter-Interceptor Squadron: 59
  355th Squadron: 42
  452d Bombardment Wing: 88
  1503rd Air Transport Wing: 88
  6147th Tactical Air Control Squadron [Mosquitos]: 75, 76–77, 78
    contributions of: 78
  Air Force Academy: 5, 98
  Air Force Air Armament Center: 101
  Air Force Air Proving Ground: 60
  Air Force Association: 1, 3, 63, 118
  Air Force History and Museums Program: 1, 3, 27, 118
  Air Force History Support Office: 96
  Air Force Legislative Liaison: 1, 3, 27, 118
  Air Force Magazine: 31–32
  Air Force Security Service: 59
  Air Force Space Command: 5
  Air Staff: 61, 100
  Air Training Command: 63
  Air University: 113
  Alaskan Air Command: 61
  Beale Air Force Base: 24
  Bergstrom Air Force Base: 81, 92
  Bolling Air Force Base: 96
  Chinhae Air Base [K–10]: 58
  Combat Cargo: 89
    contribution of: 89
  Craig Air Force Base: 29, 43
  Edwards Air Force Base: 59
  Eglin Air Force Base: 101
  Hickam Air Force Base: 9
  Itami Air Base: 80
  Johnson Air Base: 77
  Joint Operations Center: 81
  K–16 Air Base: 6

Index

K–55 Air Base: 74
Kimpo Air Base [K–14]: 34, 40, 41, 47, 58, 61, 66, 71, 73, 78
Komaki Air Base: 73, 80
Kunsan Air Base [K–8]: 58
Lackland Ai Force Base: 5
Langley Air Force Bases: 79
Luke Air Force Base: 43
March Air Force Base: 40, 42, 74
Maxwell Air Force Base: 44, 113
Nellis Air Force Base: 8, 32, 42, 43, 47, 51, 56
North American Air Defense: 92
Northern Command: 113
Pohang Air Base [K–3]: 67
Pyongtaek Air Base [K–6]: 75
Secretary of: 17, 65, 96
Shaw Field: 82
Strategic Air Command: 60, 62, 65, 82, 83, 91, 93, 117
Supreme Headquarters Allied Powers Europe: 63
Suwon Air Base [K–13]: 58
Tactical Air Command: 62
Taegu Air Base [K–2]: 65, 67, 80, 81, 82, 92
Williams Air Force Base: 33, 42, 43
U.S. Army: 6, 21, 35, 66, 76, 77, 78, 83, 89, 98, 106, 107
   1st Cavalry Division: 6, 68
   2d Infantry Division: 98
   Eighth Army: 20, 28, 64, 78, 89
   24th Infantry Division: 66
   25th Infantry Division: 65, 83, 84
   64th Artillery Battalion: 83
   187th Regimental Combat Team: 82
   Army Air Forces: 14
      Mediterranean Allied Photographic Reconnaissance Wing: 90
   operations with Air Force: 76, 83
   Special Forces: 113
U.S. Army Air Force: 57
U.S. Marine Corps: 2, 6, 21, 22, 42, 60, 61, 70, 83–84, 87, 88, 90, 93, 98, 114
   1st Marine Air Wing: 93
   1st Marine Division: 76
U.S. Naval Institute: 60

U.S. Navy: 2, 17, 21, 27, 35, 42, 57, 60, 69, 70, 87, 88, 89, 90, 93, 114
   Carrier Air Group 11: 88
   USS *Helena*: 69, 89
Udet, Ernst: 37, 58
Ugryumov, Konstantin: 38
uninhabited combat air vehicles [UCAVs]: 11
United Kingdom: 39, 41
United Nations: 2, 3, 18, 20, 28, 29, 57–58, 59, 64, 114
   Far East Command: 89
   United Nations Command: 89
United States: 2, 9, 14, 15, 18, 24, 39, 52, 59, 61, 69, 72, 90, 111, 114
United States Military Academy at West Point: 29, 31, 33, 53, 56, 63, 64, 65, 74, 81, 104
University Club: 66
unmanned aerial vehicle [UAV]: 97, 98
Ural mountains: 74

V

Vandenberg, Hoyt: 90
vertical omnirange [VOR]: 88
Veteran Affairs Committee: 8
Viet Cong: 106
Vietnam War: 2, 18, 21, 35, 43, 52, 55, 61, 68–69, 90, 92, 96, 98, 107, 108, 114, 117
   area bombing in: 106
   number of U.S. missing in action from: 8
   precision-guided weapons in: 100
   treatment of U.S. POWs during: 58
Virginia: 6
Virginia Polytechnic Institute: 79
Virginia Tech: 79
visual flight rules [VFR]: 88
Vladivostok, Soviet Union: 74, 81, 91

W

Wagner, Robert: 62
Walker, Walton H. "Bulldog": 20, 28, 78, 89
Warner, John: 6
Warsaw Pact: 59
Washabaugh, Walter: 3

Index

Washing Machine Charlie: 11
Washington, D.C.: 3, 39, 56
Watson, Billy B.: 92
weapons
  AGM–45 Shrike: 108, 114
  AGM–65 Maverick: 107, 114
  AGM–86C conventional air-launched
      cruise missile [CALCM]: 22, 113
  AGM–88 high-speed antiradiation missile
      [HARM]: 108, 114
  Army Tactical Missile System
      [ATACMS]: 106, 114
  GAU–8/A Avenger cannon: 114
  joint air-to-surface standoff missile
      [JASSM]: 22
  joint direct attack munition [JDAM]: 22,
      100, 113
  joint standoff weapon [JSOW]: 22
  multiple launch rocket system [MLRS]:
      101, 106, 113, 114
  surface-to-air missile [SAM]: 22, 97, 106,
      108, 114
  VB–3 Razon: 112
  wind-corrected munitions dispenser
      [WCMD]: 22–23
Weathersby, Kathryn: 60
West Bridge: 67
West Raynham, U.K.: 39
Wolk, Herman: 3
Wonsan: 68
World Trade Center: 113
World War I: 37, 57, 58, 68, 70, 71
World War II: 2, 6, 7, 11, 14, 15, 18, 19, 21,
    24, 30, 32, 34, 35, 36, 39, 40, 41,
    46, 47, 48, 55, 57, 59, 62, 65, 68,
    71, 74, 75, 76, 77, 78, 79, 83, 84,
    88, 89, 90, 91, 93, 98, 102, 105

Y

Y'Blood, Tom: 3
Yalu River: 28, 36, 38, 39, 40, 46, 53, 58,
    61, 64, 73, 81, 84, 85, 104, 109
Yeager, Chuck: 31
Yellow Sea: 40, 59
Yokota, Japan: 69
Y-Service: 40, 47, 59

www.ingramcontent.com/pod-product-compliance
Lightning Source LLC
Chambersburg PA
CBHW081324040426
42453CB00013B/2291